BELFAST

THE EMERGING CITY 1850–1914

BELFAST

THE EMERGING CITY 1850–1914

EDITOR
OLWEN PURDUE

IRISH ACADEMIC PRESS
DUBLIN • PORTLAND, OR

First published in 2013 by Irish Academic Press

8 Chapel Lane
Sallins
Co. Kildare

920 NE 58th Avenue, Suite 300
Portland, Oregon,
97213-3786 USA

British Library Cataloguing in Publication Data
Belfast : the emerging city, 1850-1914.
1. Belfast (Northern Ireland)--History--19th century.
2. Belfast (Northern Ireland)--History--20th century.
3. Belfast (Northern Ireland)--Social conditions--19th century.
4. Belfast (Northern Ireland)--Social conditions--20th century.
I. Purdue, Olwen.
941.6'7081-dc23

978-0-7165-3145-6 (cloth)
978-0-7165-3167-8 (paper)
978-0-7165-3209-5 (e-book)

Typeset by www.sinedesign.net

Contents

Acknowledgments

The editor would like to thank the following people without whom this volume would not have been possible.

Ministerial Advisory Group (MAG) Ulster-Scots Academy.

The Belfast Harbour Commissioners for their generosity in allowing us to reproduce a selection of their very fine collection of paintings of Belfast, one of which has been used for the front cover of the volume. A particular word of thanks to Tom O'Connor for the interest he has shown in this book. Thanks also to Bryan Rutledge for allowing us to reproduce his photographs of these paintings.

Belfast City Council for permission to reproduce the John Luke mural of the granting of Belfast's charter in 1613 from Belfast City Hall.

The Irish Linen Centre and Lisburn Museum for permission to reproduce the painting of the Robinson & Cleaver's building.

The Naughton Gallery at Queen's University Belfast for their permission to reproduce their watercolour of the Lanyon Building.

The Rector and members of the Redemptorist Community, Clonard Monastery and the Diocese of Down and Connor for their kind permission to reproduce their images of Clonard past and present.

The Deputy Keeper of the Public Record Office of Northern Ireland for permitting access to and reproduction of a range of photographs.

Lisa Hyde and the staff at Irish Academic Press for their patience, professionalism and continuing enthusiasm for this project.

This Project is supported by the
Ministerial Advisory Group
(MAG) Ulster-Scots Academy

Department of
Culture, Arts and Leisure
www.dcalni.gov.uk

List of Contributors

Éadaoin Agnew is a lecturer in English Literature at Kingston University, London. She completed her PhD and MA at Queen's University. Her research interests include nineteenth-century travel writing, popular Victorian literature and nineteenth-century women's representations of nature. She has published articles on Lady Hariot Dufferin, Vicereine of India (1884–1888) and continues to work on Lady Dufferin's letters and photographs from India.

Edwin James Aiken is a lecturer in human geography at the University of Bristol. His interests revolve around historical geography, particularly in the nineteenth century, and the history of geographical ideas.

Ruth Bowman Bayles holds a BSSc in Social Anthropology, an MA in Irish Studies and a PhD in History of Science, all from Queen's University Belfast. Her PhD concentrated on the Belfast Natural History Society and the place of science in a rapidly industrialising nineteenth-century city.

Sean Connolly is Professor of Irish History at Queen's University Belfast, where he has taught since 1996. The main focus of his research has been on different aspects of popular and elite politics, religion and culture between the late seventeenth and the nineteenth centuries. His books include *Priests and People in Pre-Famine Ireland 1780–1845* (1982), *Religion, Law and Power: The Making of Protestant Ireland* (1992), *Contested Island: Ireland 1460*–1630 (2007) and *Divided Kingdom: Ireland 1630–1800* (2008).

Lesley E. E. Donaldson graduated in December 2009 with an MSSc in Irish Migration Studies from Queen's University Belfast in association with the Centre for Migration Studies at Omagh. Her research interests include industrial migration and civic improvement in nineteenth- and early twentieth-century Belfast.

Pamela Emerson is a final year PhD student at thc University of Ulster at Coleraine. Her particular interest is nineteenth-century social history. Her current research is on book-lending facilities in Ulster with particular reference to the type of reading material available and who was using these facilities. Pamela previously worked in museums and education.

Patrick Fitzgerald is Lecturer and Development Officer of the Mellon Centre for Migration Studies. He is joint author with Brian Lambkin of *Migration in Irish History, 1607–2007* (Palgrave Macmillan, 2008).

Paul Harron is a communications professional with a special interest in the built environment. He holds a PhD (QUB) on Young & Mackenzie Architects, is a former architecture specialist at the Arts Council of NI and was a senior architecture and design editor at Laurence King Publishing, editor at Phaidon Press and Publishing Manager at Appletree Press. He is an Honorary Member of the RSUA, a Member of the Historic Buildings Council, is a past lay judge for the RIBA Awards, and sits on the boards of Arts Care, Hearth Housing Association and the committee of the UAHS. He is arts columnist for the *Ulster Tatler* and writes regularly for a range of publications, including *Perspective* and the *Irish Arts Review*.

Liam Kennedy is Professor Emeritus of Economic History, Institute of Irish Studies, Queen's University Belfast. His interests include rural economy, price history and demographic history.

Brian Lambkin is Director of the Mellon Centre for Migration Studies at the Ulster-American Folk Park, Omagh and past Chairman of the Association of European Migration Institutions. He is joint author with

Patrick Fitzgerald of *Migration in Irish History, 1607-2007* (Palgrave Macmillan, 2008).

Matteo Manfredini is researcher in Anthropology, Department of Genetics and Anthropology Evolution, University of Parma. His interests include demographic history and biodemography.

Caroline M. McGee is a doctoral candidate in the School of Histories and Humanities, Trinity College Dublin where she is researching church building projects by the Irish Catholic Church between 1850 and 1932. She holds a first-class honours degree in History of Art and Architecture from Trinity College Dublin and has worked on a number of collaborative digital humanities research projects.

Glenn Patterson is an author and a lecturer in Creative Writing in the Seamus Heaney Centre for Creative Writing, Queen's University Belfast. He is author of eight novels and a memoir, *Once Upon a Time on a Hill: Love in Troubled Times*. He has written plays for Radio 3 and Radio 4 and is co-writer of *Good Vibrations* (BBC Film). His most recent novel, *The Mill for Grinding Old People Young* (Faber) was the inaugural 'One City One Book' selection for Belfast.

Lucia Pozzi is Professor of Demography in the Department of Economics and Business, University of Sassari, Italy. Her research interests include historical demography and the history of medicine.

Olwen Purdue is a lecturer in Irish Social and Economic History at Queen's University Belfast. Her research has focused on various aspects of social class and power in nineteenth- and twentieth-century Ulster. She is the author of *The Big House in the North of Ireland: Land, Power and Social Elites 1870–1960* (2009). Her current research project examines poverty, welfare and public health in Belfast from the end of the Great Famine through to the introduction of the Welfare State.

Stephen A. Royle read geography at St. John's College Cambridge and took a PhD at Leicester. Appointed as a lecturer in Geography in Queen's University Belfast in 1976, he remains there as Professor of Island Geography. Books include *North America; A Geography of Islands*; *Enduring City: Belfast in the Twentieth Century*; *The Company's Island*; *Doing Development Differently: Regional Development on the Atlantic Periphery*; *Company, Crown and Colony and Portrait of an Industrial City: 'Clanging Belfast', 1750–1914*. Royle is Treasurer of the International Small Island Studies Association; Deputy Editor of Island Studies Journal; Chair of the Royal Geographical Society NI Region and past-President of the Ulster Society for Irish Historical Studies and the Geographical Society of Ireland. He is a Member of the Royal Irish Academy.

Johanne Devlin Trew is lecturer in the School of Criminology, Politics & Social Policy, University of Ulster, Jordanstown (Belfast). Previously she held teaching and research posts in Irish history at the University of Ulster, Magee and Queen's University Belfast, in folklore at Memorial University of Newfoundland, and in Irish studies at Concordia University, Montreal. She is the author of *Leaving the North: Migration, Conflict and Society, Northern Ireland, 1921–2011* (Liverpool, 2013) and *Place, Culture and Community: The Irish Heritage of the Ottawa Valley* (Newcastle, 2009).

List of Figures and Tables

List of Plates

Plate section 1

1. View of Belfast, 1859, Hugh Frazer (1813-1861). Collection of the Belfast Harbour Commissioners (all of which are reproduced by kind permission of Belfast Harbour Commissioners; images courtesy of Bryan F. Rutledge B.A). Frazer was Professor of Painting of the Royal Hibernian Academy and first President of the Belfast Association of Artists.

2. Trade card for Marcus Ward & Co. Established in Belfast in the 1830s, Marcus Ward & Co. became one of the country's fine printers and stationers, using colour lithography to produce striking greetings cards, book illustrations and illuminated addresses. The company gained further international acclaim as the producers of the famous Vere Foster copy books.

3. Bird's Eye Map of Belfast in 1890.

4. White Linen Hall, Belfast, Joseph William Carey (1859 – 1937). Ulster Museum. Opened in 1783 to much acclaim, this building reflected the increasing importance of the linen trade in Belfast. The City Hall now occupies the site where it once stood.

5&6 Samples of linen seals, guarantees of the quality of Irish linen. Mulholland's Mill in York Street was the largest and most iconic linen mill in Belfast

7. The Long Bridge, Belfast, J.W. Carey. Belfast Harbour Commissioners. Carey trained as an illustrator with Marcus Ward where he worked until 1899. Following this he set up his own firm specialising in specialised in high quality illuminated addresses and book plates. He was also a founding member of Belfast Ramblers Sketching Club.

8. Royal Chambers, Royal Avenue

9. Robinson & Cleaver building. Detail from Chichester Street showing the first-floor balcony

10. Robinson and Cleaver's Royal Irish Linen Warehouse and department store, Belfast, 1888, Marcus Ward and Company. Reproduced courtesy of the Irish Linen Centre & Lisburn Museum Collection.

11. Belfast Royal Academy, photograph by W. Lawrence c.1890-1900. Public Record Office of Northern Ireland, T/2418/1/64.

12. Belfast City Hall, photograph by W. Lawrence, c. 1910. Public Record Office of Northern Ireland, T/2418/1/69

13 & 14. Further examples of illustrative material produced by Marcus Ward.

15. Queen's College, Belfast, Original proposal for Queen's College by Sir Charles Lanyon (1813-89). Reproduced courtesy of Queen's University Belfast. Lanyon was architect of some of the principal buildings in Belfast, including the Crumlin Road Gaol and Courthouse (1843-50) and the Custom House (1854-7).

Plate section 2

FOREWORD

Alf McCreary

One of the most challenging commissions I have received in recent years was to write the history of Belfast Harbour. When the Harbour Commissioners gave me permission to consult their extensive archive, I was aware that a great deal of hard work lay ahead. However, I was not prepared for the shock of finding a hidden treasure of material locked away in a strong-room behind a ladies' toilet on the first floor of the historic and elegant Harbour Board Office in Corporation Square. The strong-room had been built by the Commissioners in 1917, but contained material dating back for many decades, including the original document signed by the members of the Belfast Ballast Board which had been established in 1785.

This research became, like all such work of inquiry, a modern-day adventure story as I pieced together the history of the Commissioners, who had not only opened up the mudlocked harbour to a much greater range of shipping but also had helped to change the skyline of Belfast. They included Edward Harland and Gustav Wolff of shipbuilding fame, the celebrated architect Sir Charles Lanyon, and Thomas Sinclair who built Sinclair Seamen's Presbyterian Church beside the Harbour Office in memory of his late brother. The Corry family of shipbuilders and merchants had also contributed significantly to the completion of the former Presbyterian Church in Elmwood Avenue, as well as the construction of Corry Crescent near Queen's University, better-known today as Upper Crescent.

By the time my own work was completed I had come to realise the inter-connectedness of so much of the history of Belfast, and that so much of the defining nature of the city's culture and history was no mere coincidence, but much more a matter of cause and effect. I also came to admire greatly the vision and ingenuity of those who turned their vision for the city into a reality, though often at the cost of poor labour relations, back-breaking work and ruthlessness in carrying out a project. The exercise reminded me that historical research should not be confined to the dry dust of libraries full of old books slowly ageing, but that it should also approach with freshness the vivid humanity and the triumphs and tragedies which made such progress possible.

It was therefore with particular interest that I read the essays contained in this volume, each of which makes an important contribution to our understanding and appreciation of the past, and of the history of those generations of men and women whose collective contribution helped to shape the distinctive culture and infrastructure of this city and province as we know it today. My own experience in writing about the Harbour made me realise the complexities and subtleties of the city, and the need for a constant revision of its origins and development within the society in the north of Ireland. This significant collection of essays provides new insights, and collectively represents an important addition to the growing body of research which is being carried out on the social, economic and cultural history of this fascinating city. The collection is both authoritative and accessible and contains much of interest not only for the academic specialist, but also for the general reader who wants to know more about Belfast and who also wants to appreciate and to understand it better.

Alf McCreary MBE

Introduction

Olwen Purdue

On 27 April 1613 Belfast's first charter was granted by James I, thus establishing the town's Corporation, permitting the opening of markets and granting it parliamentary representation. In this ceremony the town of Belfast might be said to have been born. Three centuries later, as the nineteenth century gave way to the twentieth, she came of age. Granted city status in 1888, Belfast was emerging as Ireland's largest and most dynamic urban centre and as a key player in the British industrial landscape. The rapid expansion of the linen industry, the growth of the port, the development of the shipbuilding industry and of related heavy and light engineering contributed to an explosion in population. As Thomas Sinclair, Ulster Liberal and leading businessman, stressed in the 1890s, Belfast was a success story:

> ... her population had quadrupled in fifty years, her wages rates were higher than anywhere in Ireland ... as to customs revenues she ranked as the third port in the United Kingdom ... she had the largest weaving factory, the largest shipping output, the largest tobacco factory and the largest ropeworks in the world.[1]

This phenomenal growth had significant implications for the character of the city, for the experience of living in and visiting it and for its relationship with its rural hinterland, with other industrial cities and with trading partners around the globe. Yet despite the fascinating social and economic developments of these years they have received limited scholarly attention, much of the research and writing on Belfast in past decades having tended to focus more narrowly on the theme of sectarian politics and conflict in the city.

Thankfully that is now changing, and recent years have seen a growth of research into many aspects of the social, economic and cultural history of Belfast. In 2010 a conference, organized jointly by Queen's University Belfast and the University of Northumbria, brought together scholars from a range of disciplines working on various research projects relating to the development of Belfast. This book represents a small selection of the papers presented at that conference as well as a number of additional chapters, all of which have their focus on the period between the Great Famine and the First World War. Some of the contributors are established scholars, well known for their important contribution to Irish studies; others are emerging scholars who represent fresh voices in the field. All of the contributions present new and exciting ways of looking at the city's development, exploring many aspects of this important time in its history and highlighting the relationships that existed between civic responsibility, economic activity, demography, class, religion, learning, culture and the built and natural environment.

The city is a complex and multi-faceted thing; therefore it is impossible to provide a comprehensive survey of its character and the nature of its development in a single volume. This book does not attempt to do that; there are many important aspects of Belfast at this point in its history that have not been included – poverty and welfare, philanthropy, crime, labour and leisure to mention but a few. Rather, through a series of snapshots of Belfast's social, cultural and physical landscapes, this volume seeks to provide a flavour of some aspects of the life of the city from the time of its great economic and physical growth in the 1870s through to the beginning of the First World War, the same period of prosperity and cultural and scientific advances experienced in France as *La Belle Époque*.

It is not by chance that the book opens with an exploration of the rapid growth of the linen industry and its significance for the city of Belfast. As W.A. Maguire argues elsewhere, Belfast was *Linenopolis* before she was a great port and centre of shipbuilding and engineering; it was the remarkable success of the linen trade that provided the impetus for the improvement of the port facilities and led to the growth of shipbuilding and related industries.[2] As Edwin Aiken and Stephen Royle demonstrate in the opening chapter of this volume, it was largely the resolve shown by Belfast's industrialists in overcoming the significant difficulties presented by the city's remote geographical position that led to its development as a world leader in terms of linen export, a central player in an international trade network of luxury goods.

Following on from this industrial and commercial success came a flourishing of architectural and cultural activity in some ways parallel to, yet in other ways very different from that experienced in British industrializing cities of the same era. As the contributions by S.J. Connolly and Paul Harron both clearly demonstrate, this period saw a remarkable transformation of Belfast's built environment, particularly in the civic and commercial heart of the city. The expansion of the linen industry brought wealth and status to the city's bourgeois elite, encouraging its members to invest huge sums in building premises that would adequately reflect the success and importance of their businesses. Thus offices, department stores and even warehouses were built and refashioned in the heavy, ornate and lavish style so characteristic of the urban architecture of the late-Victorian period.[3] As Harron points out, the building of impressive department stores such as Robinson & Cleaver's- and Anderson & McAuley's was not just about displaying the commercial significance of the city's mercantile class; it was also a direct response to the increased spending power of this wealthy elite and their desire to engage in conspicuous consumption of luxury goods, to experience something of the great department stores of London or *grands magazins* of Paris. The city's political elite in the form of the Corporation also engaged in what might be termed cosmetic surgery as entire streets were transformed in order to improve at least the outward appearance of the city. As Connolly argues, however, this outward demonstration of prosperity and civic pride, most clearly manifest in the building of the City Hall in 1906, deflected attention from the singular failure of that same bourgeois elite to make much-needed improvements to living conditions in the city, particularly in terms of the provision of a clean water supply and adequate sanitation for the rapidly growing population. The essay goes on to evaluate the role of this urban elite in responding to the challenges they faced in the context of the obvious manifestations of civic pride that helped transform similarly expanding industrial cities on the other side of the Irish Sea.

The impact of the city's emerging middle-class elites was not just evident in built architecture and civic governance, but also in the cultural pursuits and 'improving' activity in which many of its members engaged. One theme that binds many of the essays in this volume together is the pattern of networks that made up the fabric of the city and also that connected it to the world beyond. Pamela Emerson's chapter on the growth of reading clubs and that by Ruth Bowman Bayles on the establishment of the Belfast Natural History and Philosophical Society each provides valuable insight into some of the social and intellectual networks that were emerging in the city at this time. In their exploration of middle-class associational culture and the pursuit of learning, these essays provide a fascinating insight into the ways in which the city's middle and professional classes formed informal spheres of influence.

The emphasis, as might be expected, was on personal and intellectual improvement while also enjoying the pleasure of meeting together with like-minded people. There was also, however, a desire to improve the city and the experience of all those living in it, most notably through the provision of affordable access to the newly-built museum and the botanic gardens. It is interesting to note the identity of those involved in these clubs and societies – often the same people, or closely related to those, who were involved in the town's commercial and professional spheres of influence as well as in many other forms of cultural and philanthropic activity, civic improvement or local governance. There is much more work to be done on the wide range of clubs and societies that existed at every social level in order to develop our understanding of the way in which associational culture was developing in Belfast at this time in its history.

The networks that made up the fabric of Belfast's social and economic activity, however, reached much further than the physical boundaries of the city. As is shown in the opening chapter, the port of Belfast was an important part of a global trading network that extended from the USA and the West Indies to Australia and Japan. It was also at the centre of a network of migration patterns. People flocked to the city in search of work, they travelled through it as they sought to make a new life for themselves in a different place and they occasionally returned to it after having spent part of their life elsewhere. The chapter by Patrick Fitzgerald, Brian Lambkin and Johanne Devlin Trew explores these movements to and from and within the city. This is the only chapter in the book to step outside the chronological boundaries of the Great Famine and the First World War, thus facilitating a broader exploration of the complex themes of leaving, travelling, arriving and the way in which Belfast has been at the heart of and affected by this movement over centuries.

One form of migration, which Belfast experienced extensively in the second half of the nineteenth century, was the constant flood of people moving into the city in search of work. The city's two shipyards – Harland and Wolff and Workman, Clarke & Co. – attracted significant numbers of men, particularly skilled labourers for whom the production of world-class shipping provided ample opportunity for employment. In this respect, Belfast was similar to other shipbuilding cities such as Glasgow and Barrow-in-Furness; however, as Lesley Donaldson argues, the thriving linen industry meant that Belfast had the added attraction of offering employment for other members of the family as well. The possibility of multiple wages in a household ensured that Belfast's labouring classes had the potential to enjoy a better standard of living than might be experienced in other shipbuilding cities across the Irish Sea, thus adding extra incentive for people to migrate to Belfast. Such was the economic success of the Belfast region that the population of the city had multiplied ten fold between 1821 and 1914. The chapter by Liam Kennedy, Lucia Pozzi and Matteo Manfredini explores the impact that the industrialization of the city had on its demographic character. On census night, 2 April 1911, every household in Belfast completed a census form, containing detailed information on occupations, religion, birthplaces, marital status, family size and fertility. Drawing on this resource, these authors present a fascinating snapshot of marriage, fertility, occupation and religion in the city in 1911, comparing this with established patterns for the rest of Ireland and exploring the ways in which Belfast was beginning to develop its own very distinctive character.

One thing that these census returns make very clear is the fact that large numbers of Ulster Catholics moved to the city during the period covered by this volume. As Caroline McGee's chapter on the building of the Church of the Most Holy Redeemer at Clonard highlights, the rapid increase in Belfast's Catholic population caused by this influx of migrant workers, particularly to the north and west of the city where most of the linen mills were situated, placed extreme pressure on those churches responsible for serving these areas. The fact that the expansion of Belfast's population coincided with the expansion of the Catholic Church in Ireland brought not only a surge of church building projects within the city but also the inevitable tensions between individuals and congregations over matters such as the architectural style, size and position of some of these buildings. McGee's work on the origins and building of Clonard Church provides a fascinating insight into the internal politics associated with religious architecture and into the important place that Clonard has had in the hearts and lives of the people of west Belfast. It also comes at an opportune moment: at the time of writing, Clonard Church has just reopened after a major four-year refurbishment project which has successfully restored this beautiful building to its former glory.

Finally, despite its phenomenal growth, its economic successes and what Harron describes as its 'big city feel', Belfast was always the most rural of cities. For generations of writers who have travelled to the town, later city, the first impression was often that of the hills and the sea and the fact that the countryside is never far away. As Éadaoin Agnew suggests in her chapter on travel writers and their experiences of Victorian Belfast, many visitors were attracted to it both by the romantic wildness of its setting and by the fact that, compared to the rest of the country, Belfast appeared relatively civilized and comfortingly familiar. The sense of its rural surroundings is never far away in any depiction of the city, whether on canvas or in prose. Over the centuries, artists have frequently depicted Belfast as viewed from an idyllic rural location, while the distinctive outline of Cave Hill features in many – Jonathan Fisher's eighteenth-century 'View from Belvoir House, Belfast', Andrew

Nicholl's view of Belfast from Newtownbreda Churchyard or J.W. Carey's view of from the Castlereagh Hills are but a few examples. Cave Hill also provides the backdrop to John Luke's depiction of Sir Arthur Chichester receiving the Royal Charter in 1613 that graces the interior of Belfast City Hall. As Agnew points out, many travellers to Belfast chose Cave Hill as the best vantage point from which to view the city while, for its inhabitants, the hills offered an easy escape from urban life. Michael McLaverty Monaghan-born but Belfast bred, captures this experience of the city in his 1939 novel, *Call My Brother Back:*

> At the top of the mountain, they lay in the heather and gazed at Belfast spread out in the flat hollow below them, its lean mill chimneys stretched above the haze of smoke. Rows of red-bricked houses radiated on all sides and above them rose blocks of factories with many of their windows catching the sunlight. They saw their own street and could make out the splash of whitewash on the wall that Alec had daubed there as a mark for his pigeons; it was all very far away like a street seen through the wrong end of a telescope.[4]

For Glenn Patterson, the latest in a long line of renowned Belfast writers, the hills around Belfast are central to his most recent novel, *The Mill for Grinding Old People Young*, the writing of which he explores in his fresh and engaging contribution to this volume. A church is built in the gently rolling Castlereagh hills to the south and a man meets a girl on an ill-fated walk in the more rugged Belfast hills to the north and west of the city. The sea features as another important element in the novel, appropriately given its central importance to the story of Belfast: as Patterson argues, the story of the passing of the 1831 Port of Belfast Act could well serve 'as a kind of foundation myth for the modern city of Belfast'. In using this as his starting point, Patterson explains how he came to construct the novel that captures the essence of the town at this pivotal time in its history.

So, too, in Burgess' painting, 'View of Queen's Bridge, Harbour and Timber Pond, Belfast', which graces the front of this volume, are represented the various elements that gave the city its very particular character. Dominating the skyline above the town is the unmistakable outline of Cave Hill. Below that, the spires and towers of the town's civic and religious life mingle with the host of ships' masts that indicate not only Belfast's significance as a hub on international trade but also the comings and goings of individuals and families for whom Belfast might have been the first stage in an onward journey or the final stage in a homecoming. In the foreground, people are going about their daily lives, some engaged in the hard graft of labour that was the experience of living and working in the city, others, with the fruits of agriculture labour, serving as a reminder that the countryside was never that far away. Finally, and most prominent of all, the sea that carried Belfast's goods, and its peoples, to the far reaches of the earth and that made the city the success story it was.

1

Markets and Messages: Linenopolis Meets the World

Edwin James Aiken
Stephen A. Royle

In the United Kingdom the Victorian era was, above all else, one of immense energy and creativity. Perhaps this is displayed most clearly in any consideration of the nineteenth century's industrial history when 'long-standing local industries collapsed in the face of competition from major capitalist concerns'.[1] This was the age of the industrialising city, when in addition to meeting local and regional demands, some conurbations and industrial districts developed said major capitalist concerns to produce significant trade in export goods, often associated with the era's increasingly global outlook given colonial expansion and other commercial development.

Belfast was a prime example. The town's early industrial districts were characterized by water-powered cotton mills and, as the geographer Emrys Jones pointed out, later developments in other sectors such as linen and engineering consolidated what he recognized as this 'industrial belt'.[2] This was then joined by that prime example of an export industry, shipbuilding, which with the foundation of a small number of significant firms, principally Harland and Wolff and Workman Clarke, occupied mostly reclaimed land in the harbour area. The range of industries in Belfast was great: Benn's 1823 history in addition to textiles mentions rope, paper, iron (casting and engine manufacture), glass, salt, vitriol, brewing, soap, candles, hats, leather, flour, starch, wood, glue, bricks and lime.[3] The *Irish Historic Towns Atlas* fascicle for Belfast between 1840 and 1900 lists 2,078 entries under 'Manufacturing' in 70 different categories.[4] Many of these, especially in engineering, chemicals and rope-making, contributed to the shipbuilding and textile export industries. Others were for the local market, but some were important export industries in their own right as with aerated water, led by Cantrell and Cochrane.

Despite this range, and despite the global significance of its shipbuilding, Belfast became known as 'Linenopolis'. The vice-president of the Linen Merchants' Association stated in 1899 that: 'We have other industries in our midst, some of which are so vast as to enable us to launch in our harbour the largest vessel in the world [RMS *Oceanic*] – (applause) – [but] we must look upon the linen trade as our staple industry in this province.'[5]

The Belfast linen industry of the nineteenth century thus demands attention: as an enterprise it was conducted on a vast and comprehensive scale, with single weaving factories employing more than 4,000 workers,[6] and having more than 1,000 power looms, and single spinning mills boasting more than 60,000 spindles.[7] The sheer scale of the premises matched in every way the importance of the 'staple industry' to the local economy: the York Street Mill was claimed as both the largest spinning mill and weaving factory in the world.[8] In 1894 alone Belfast mills spun 644,000,000 miles of yarn.[9] In the same year linen was estimated to employ more than 100,000 persons in Ireland, paying them total annual wages of £2,750,000, and estimated to be investing capital sums of between £13,000,000 and £15,000,000.[10]

This chapter considers how the Belfast linen industry reached such proportions in spite of a relatively unfavourable geographical situation. The industry didn't struggle with the local growing of flax – the Irish climate was well-suited to that – nor with obtaining capital and labour, despite the unhealthy working conditions some of its operatives had to endure.[11] There was also a usually steady demand for its high-quality finished products until the Great War, although there were some slumps as in the 1870s; rather the struggle was in communicating with those purchasers who were often at enormous distances and in getting the linen to them quickly and reliably.

BELFAST AND ITS LINEN INDUSTRY

By the early nineteenth century linen manufacture had already been a local industry in the north-east of Ireland for centuries, principally as a domestic enterprise in rural areas, with Belfast being an important place of trade for the finished products with its Brown and White Linen Halls for unbleached and bleached cloth respectively.[12] Linen was, however, briefly eclipsed by cotton from the close of the eighteenth century. Cotton manufacture required much the same skills as linen work and gave workers similar conditions of employment, but crucially it offered much higher wages than linen was able to at this time. Unlike linen, cotton production became an urban activity in both home and factory and this activity dominated Belfast until the linen industry enjoyed an almost accidental rise to prominence. It has been regularly argued that the destruction, by fire, of the Mulholland brothers' York Street cotton-spinning mill in 1828 dealt the cotton industry in Belfast a heavy blow, thereby opening the way for linen.[13] The Mulhollands had already opened an experimental flax-spinning facility in Wine Tavern Street in

1827 and took the opportunity to rebuild York Street as a linen mill.[14] Other manufacturers transferred too. Belfast's cotton did continue to run alongside linen, but struggled to achieve much until the very end of the nineteenth century. It never again attained the levels of productivity and profit it had achieved a hundred years earlier, not least because the industry suffered heavily after the relaxation in 1827 of import duties on items including cheaper cotton from places like Manchester.[15]

By 1830 textile processing had reached such technical sophistication that Belfast's first steam-powered mill was opened.[16] Economies of scale and the friction of distance involved in importing the necessary coal to run steam engines meant that the most successful mills and factories in industrial areas were now those with easy access to a source of coal: Belfast's geographical location as a major port in a sheltered sea lough would facilitate the delivery of coal and assist its growing dominance in linen manufacture.

But how did the linen industry become such a dominant feature of Belfast's economy? Local demand was generally insignificant and always variable, so overseas markets were required: linen was an export product. Belfast's linen merchants were fully aware of the need to expand their market to the world and did so with a remarkable vigour. By 1914 linen trading partners for Belfast merchants were found in places as diverse as the USA, France, Australia, Spain, Greece, Romania, Russia, Haiti, Brazil, Cuba, Japan, the West Indies, Brazil and Mexico.[17] The remainder of this chapter looks at the dealings that the influential Linen Merchants' Association (LMA) had with the wider world and the issues of getting the linen to that world. Without the linen merchants the flax spinners' and linen weavers' products would never have been sold: the LMA was the key link in getting Belfast's linen produce to the point of sale, and it took its responsibility seriously.

The LMA was established in April 1872 to represent the interests of the linen merchants, mainly of Belfast as a whole, enabling them to respond quickly and effectively to developments that affected the sales sector of the industry. In practice, however, the LMA gave itself a much wider remit than matters impinging directly or obviously upon the linen trade and the Annual Reports it produced yield much to a careful reading. The Association had concerns about all manner of economic, social and political issues, many of them far from the shores of Belfast, emphasizing for us the international nature of the industry. Issues that occupied the LMA's time can be seen in a brief thematic appraisal of the content of the Association's annual reports. These reports were produced each year from 1873 until after the Great War.

MARKETS

The LMA Annual Reports are rich with detail concerning overseas contacts. Throughout the nineteenth century the USA was by far the largest consumer of Belfast linen, at times consuming roughly half the annual output,[18] and as early as January 1875 the customs tariff on the entry of linen to America was a matter of interest to the LMA.[19] Given the extent of what was therefore at stake, it is not surprising that this interest was zealously maintained. The USA's linen utilisation was followed closely in Belfast: between 1873 and 1914 America is mentioned with more frequency and at greater length than any other single place. The LMA devoted careful hours to the examination of American import duties, watched the development of the USA's domestic linen production capabilities carefully and was even so diplomatic as to send the wife of the American President William McKinley, and the American people more generally a message of condolence at the time of the president's assassination in September 1901.

At the Annual Meeting of the LMA in 1880 the American economy was subjected to particular analysis, the LMA arguing optimistically:

> That the revival of trade in the United States, upon the duration of which the prosperity of our manufacturers and merchants so depends, is not a passing spasm, but a lasting movement, can scarcely be doubted by those who have considered the subject, for it is the result of three agencies which have long been at work. The strict economy practised by all classes in the United States for five years – the painful process of reducing the paper currency and bringing it to a specie basis – above all, the succession of abundant harvests which that country has enjoyed – have all combined to prepare it for prosperity, and to form a solid foundation for a structure of sound commercial enterprize, of which the late outburst of activity may be regarded as only the beginning.'[20]

No immediate improvement had been apparent, however, and the LMA President's own in-depth analysis still showed hopes of great gains in American sales, noting matters as specific as that the USA was now in a position where it needed to lay thousands of miles of new railway tracks – a definite boon to employment and spending powers. The linen industry, it was pointed out, had only to wait for the trickle-down effect: 'If the people of these islands have not yet felt the improvement as it has been experienced in America, we must remember that it was some time after the crisis of 1873 before its full effect was realized here, and that the flow of prosperity will also take some time in reaching these shores; but it is certain to come sooner or later.'[21]

Trade indeed improved soon enough and the problem then became not so much lack of sales to the USA, but the import tariffs that were imposed on the linen. President Cleveland's speech at the opening of the US Congress in 1887 was read carefully and the content was welcomed: a likely reduction in import tariffs, falling short of an absolute free market that the LMA naturally hoped for; nevertheless, members were reminded, 'It must not be forgotten that the Protectionist Policy has powerful adherents even among the Democratic party.'[22] Despite this good news, a later financial crisis in the USA was being felt in Ireland by 1893, and it meant increasing customs tariffs on linen and therefore drastically reduced sales.[23]

By 1904 the American linen market was once more in good condition, and Belfast's staple trade was able to rejoice in increasing prosperity:

> The demand in the United States for dress linens during the past year was abnormal, and [the LMA President] was glad to say the prospects for the coming year were equally good. Very large quantities of these goods had been shipped, and still had to be shipped, for the coming season. Fashion out there was still running upon white linens and cambrics for blouses. This had for Belfast been a very important matter. Looms which would otherwise have been idle, owing to the lack of demand for bleached fronting linens, had been kept going upon dress goods, and it had meant employment to workers, many of whom would otherwise have been idle.'[24]

This boom was remarkable in its longevity, and was still strongly marked in 1909 as demand for Irish linen in the USA rose sharply. This was warmly welcomed by the LMA: 'This year the demands of the United States importers have been almost insatiable, and the year's totals show an increase of 26.1 per cent over their largest previous takings'.[25] Within a year, however, the boom was over and sales dropped enormously.[26]

While it was the most important market, America was not the only overseas consumer of Belfast linen products. The LMA closely followed political affairs in Haiti, the West Indies, Brazil, Argentina and France, Cuba, Venezuela, Columbia, Japan and Australia, noting carefully the bearing that every new development might have on the imports of linen.[27] The analyses were often exhaustive in their minuteness, accounting for sales variations in many ways:

> ... in the case of those old and valued customers for Irish linens, the West Indies and South American Republics, it was not difficult to understand the decrease in demand. The principal products of those countries were sugar and coffee, and unfortunately the price of those articles was at present so very low ... there is at present 800,000 tons of sugar in Cuba for which no market can be found, and to this must be attributed the almost total collapse of this once favourite market for Irish linens.[28]

Given the strength of Belfast linen's international links, it seems appropriate that, in 1897, the members of the LMA were able to rejoice as Mr Lowenthal, a former President of the LMA, was appointed by the Brazilian government as Vice-Consul for the northern region of Ireland, further evidence of the international nature of the linen industry in Belfast itself.[29]

Such international acclaim for a product did, however, have its drawbacks, and the LMA was forced to complain to the Foreign Office in 1907 about large quantities of inferior goods being fraudulently stamped as Irish Linen in Egypt and the Sudan.[30]

MAIL

The frequency, reliability and cost of the mail was a constant source of concern to the members of the LMA, and from 1881 onwards the mail, its collection or delivery, was mentioned at almost every meeting of the LMA. The LMA was greatly impressed by the 'prompt attention of our local Post-Master and the Directors of the Railways and Carrying Companies in furthering the wishes of the [LMA's] Council when practicable', noting that 'measures have been sanctioned for hastening the delivery of the day mail letters by extra carriers in Belfast'.[31] Thus enthused, the Council of the LMA conducted an investigation into the mail's operation between Belfast and Dublin; as Dublin was the main port for transatlantic freight their interest was understandable. The Council of the LMA found itself unsatisfied with mail arrangements and 'suggested to the Post-Office authorities the advisability of establishing a receiving office in the neighbourhood of the Great Northern Railway Terminus [where most LMA firms had their offices], to expedite the delivery of the box-holders' letters in that locality'. Finding still further grounds for investigation the Council reported that 'As the mail trains between Dublin and Belfast are represented to be the "fastest in Ireland, and the speed considerably greater than could be legally required, and as no appreciable acceleration of the trains is practicable", it may not be uninteresting to mention the relative speed of the fastest trains in England and Ireland...'[32] Attached to the report is a table displaying the speeds of various mail trains and showing that the Belfast to Dublin train was undoubtedly slow: with admirable political tact the LMA left the figures to speak for themselves.

By 1882 the LMA was demanding a new and larger Post Office for Belfast and the Town Council obligingly laid aside a plot on the new Royal Avenue. The LMA was the chief instigator of the new building and argued that 'The erection of a Post-Office worthy of this populous and flourishing town would be a great convenience, and would tend to accelerate the delivery of the mails.'[33] The new Post Office was well into the planning stage by January of 1883 and among the new services the Post Office was to offer was a Parcels Post, which the LMA saw as 'of great advantage to the business community'.[34] Nevertheless, in the meantime the letter post was still causing grave complaints and at its January 1883 meeting the President of the LMA addressed members rousingly and at length on this provocative issue:

> And I think this meeting will approve of the demand made on behalf of Belfast in the report of the Council [of the LMA] that we should not rest satisfied until we had the London letters of the previous day delivered in Belfast at ten a.m. (Applause.) This does not seem to be an extravagant demand, and is one, I believe, quite possible with the means at the command of the authorities. It is only a question of expense, and public money might be more profitably spent in this way than in many of the schemes promulgated for the regeneration of Ireland. (Hear).[35]

The new Post Office building was begun by January 1884 and the LMA was soon submitting amendments to the plans to the Postmaster General.[36] The Parcels Post had already got under way 'with much benefit to the Linen Trade for Samples and Small Packages.' The report found optimistic developments as the 'extension of the service to Foreign Parcels is under consideration by the Postal Authorities'.[37]

The Foreign and Colonial Parcel Post eventually came into operation in 1885 and was warmly welcomed by the LMA as it was generally considered a great boon to the industry, allowing the reliable and relatively speedy conveyance of linen samples around the globe.[38]

However, it was not until 1893 that rumours began to circulate of the Penny Postage system for letters being extended to the whole British Empire.[39] A large-scale campaign, including vigorous representations by members of the LMA, sought to sway the government,[40] and in 1896 the Association was able to report that:

> Imperial Penny Postage has been one of the principal reforms advocated by the Linen Merchants' Association. All parties have united in demanding it. There is now Universal Halfpenny Postage for all printed matter under two ounces in weight, and it is extraordinary that there cannot be penny postage for letters half-an-ounce in weight. No one pretends that it is on the ground of expense, because the cost of introducing it is the tenth of the price of a war-ship, and a few years ago a guarantee was given [to] the British Government against loss for the first three years.[41]

Nevertheless, the Post Office both nationally and locally was not always disposed to meet the requirements of the LMA's members by providing such services and at the same meeting the President of the LMA pointed out that they 'all knew to what extent red tape existed in the Post Office, and that it was almost impossible to get an improvement effected if any prominent official there had the slightest desire that it should not take place'.[42]

By the end of the century, postal services in Belfast were giving a much more satisfactory service, with new deliveries and later collection times allowing the LMA members to reply to more letters by return of post. However, the LMA continued to campaign for more effective postal services well into the twentieth century.

A reliable postal service was crucial to the firms that comprised the LMA. In an era when mail was the main means of communication the linen merchants were almost wholly dependent on the service to keep in touch with their customers at all distances, to send samples and orders and receive their empty linen containers back. The vexation caused to the members of the LMA when the last train for Belfast left Dublin a few minutes before the delayed transatlantic freight vessel arrived from New York was severe, and perhaps understandable, adding as it did days to the time taken to respond to orders in a linen market where prices could change markedly in a short period of time. A reliable mail service meant a much more stable and secure linen industry.

TELEPHONES

Belfast's telephone network was heavily utilized by the members of the LMA from the date of the connection of the first line. Indeed, before a Belfast system was even established the LMA was keen to explore the possibilities of telephonic communication as an aid to business. In 1880 the LMA President was able to report to the Association on the activities of the inner Council of the Association over the previous year: 'The Council has been in communication with the Edison Telephone Company regarding the establishing of a branch in Belfast, which would be very desirable. The great pressure upon the Company's resources, and the domestic demand for telephones have prevented the completion of the company's arrangements in Belfast.'[43] Nevertheless, the LMA was an efficient lobbying group, and the President was able to draw public attention to the relative state of advancement of communication networks in Ireland and America. Such familiarity with the North American continent's arrangements can only be presumed possible due to the close trade links and frequent visits of linen importers and exporters that necessarily occurred in both directions:

> Many cities in the United States not so large as Belfast have their telephonic exchange, with which most of the merchants have their offices connected ... they may thus be in instant communication with almost all those in the town and vicinity with whom they have business or private relations.[44]

As one powerful and influential member among a group of lobbyists, the LMA was successful, even if not in the direction expected, and by the next year the President of the LMA was welcoming the fact that:

> Early ... in 1880 the "Scottish Telephonic Exchange" opened a Branch in Belfast, and immediately inaugurated a system of intercommunication, and as appears from their last list of subscribers, have secured as members a large number of our leading Manufacturers, Merchants, Bankers, Railway and Shipping Companies, whose lines already form quite a net-work of wires over the town.[45]

In 1885 the LMA was looking forward to the extension of the telephone network to several other important towns in rural Ireland, and perhaps even as far as Dublin, welcoming also the prospect of a new system of sending telegrams by telephone.[46] The range of the LMA's interests and the enthusiastic and encompassing manner in which they were prosecuted is indicated by the way in which they followed up the telephone question from this point onwards. The opening of public call offices in Whitehouse, Hollywood, Newtownards and Lisburn was duly noted in 1886,[47] and in 1887 the LMA was comparing the numbers of telephone subscribers in Belfast (419) with those in Glasgow (1,202), Bradford (545), Birmingham (469), Leeds (461), Edinburgh (363),

Nottingham (308), Dewsbury (123), Huddersfield (81) and Wakefield (17). The predominance of textile towns in the list demonstrates just how the LMA was thinking in considering the provision of technological advantages to its competitors. Evidently the LMA thought it worthwhile carrying out and reporting research of this nature, considering that such matters had an effect on business. We can also note the relative size of Belfast's telephonically-active population and thereby see the significance of the town's importance to not just the Irish economy, but is prominent place in the British economy as a whole.

After sustained campaigning, by 1891 the annual cost of a telephone subscription in Belfast was reduced to £10 per annum. Once more the sheer breadth of the LMA's reach and its hunger for connections outside of Belfast is notable, as its members followed in minute detail the spread of the telephone wires. They greeted with enthusiasm the news that 'The Dublin Trunk Line is now being energetically proceeded with, and in the course of a few months Belfast subscribers will be able to speak to Dublin friends at a fixed charge per conversation. The connection between Banbridge, Newry and Dundalk with the General Telephone System seems to be within measurable distance'.[48] However, this gain was offset by the report of a loss: the original hope that telegrams could be sent and delivered through the telephone network was disappointed. The immense cost of the infrastructure for this refinement meant that it could not be extended to Belfast.[49] On the other hand, by 1892 the mood of the LMA was jubilant as the President was able to report that:

> The hope held out this time last year of Telephonic communication with Dublin and intervening towns is now on the eve of being realised. After many difficulties the National Telephone Company and the Telephone Company of Ireland have at length been able, telephonically, to join

> hands, and within a few weeks Belfast merchants will be able to speak to their friends in the Irish metropolis. It is understood that the voice is conveyed with a distinctness hitherto unattained in this country, the reason for this being that extraordinary precautions have been taken to make the wires electrically perfect.[50]

This leap forward in technical provision to the linen merchants was not bettered until 1894, when still further increases in the abilities of telephone engineers and even greater profits on the part of the telephone companies meant that cables could be laid connecting Ireland and Great Britain. Belfast was the closest major town to a part of Great Britain and so was the first to benefit from this new link: 'In April, Telephonic communication was opened between Belfast and Glasgow, being the first of several Trunk Lines contemplated as regards Ireland and Scotland. Merchants in Belfast can now speak with correspondents in Edinburgh, Glasgow, Dundee and other towns in Scotland.' The report enthused further about the project: 'This arrangement is only preliminary to opening up a complete Telephonic Trunk System to connect all the large towns in the United Kingdom.' The boon did not end there, as in contrast to previous shortcomings, 'Telephonic subscribers in Belfast can now arrange to have their telegrams transmitted and received by telephone'.[51] The predominance of Scottish textile towns on the list shows once more the competitive spirit of the Belfast merchants. Unfortunately, while the new facility to telephone Glasgow was now available, the President of the LMA noted that almost no use was made of the service due to prohibitive costs.[52]

The influence of the LMA in determining the direction of Belfast's communication networks is evidenced in the roles that its members were invited to play in the milestones of the development of the infrastructure. The Annual Report for 1896 records that 'Great progress was made with the Telephonic communication during 1895. The State Telephones connecting the principal large Towns were formally opened in the month of June, and by the courtesy of the Post Office officials in Belfast, the President and Secretary of the Linen Merchants' Association were present on this interesting occasion.' The report noted, however, the more practical business opportunities now presented, recording that 'It is now possible for subscribers to the Belfast Telephone Exchange to speak direct from their offices to London, Liverpool, Manchester, Leeds, Bristol, Dublin, Edinburgh, Glasgow and other large towns on the payment of fixed rates.'[53] Unsurprisingly, this increasing utility of the telephone meant that 'The number of local telephones at Belfast and neighbourhood has been largely increased during the past year.' The LMA was, however, quick to note the cost of telephoning, and to argue that 'a reduction in the Trunk Wire charges would still further tend to augment the use of the Telephonic System.'[54]

The telephonic communications system now began to expand much more rapidly and evenly throughout Belfast's rapidly growing area and in 1898 the LMA registered this massive urban growth in its own way, reporting that:

> During the past year almost 200 lines have been added to the National Telephone Company's exchange in Belfast, bringing the total number for the city alone up to at least 1,150 thereby adding 220 miles to the length of wire, and making the total number of miles over 2,000 ... The City Council has granted permission to the Company to place the wires underground ... These works will, of course, entail an enormous expenditure; but it is hoped that the service will be improved sufficiently to compensate for this.[55]

The business benefits that these works and the building of a new and larger telephone exchange on Upper Queen Street would bring was not lost on the LMA, whose members were keen to speed any such developments on their way, the Annual Report for 1899 noting that 'It is hoped that, by the close of this year, all the subscribers in Belfast will be actually working on the new system, and the efficiency of the Service should thereby be materially enhanced'.[56] Such efficient operating was no doubt a necessary concern on such a speedily expanding network: in 1899 the LMA reported that 'The number of connections to the National Telephone Company's Belfast Exchange System has been increased during the year by 213, making a total of 1,688. The mileage of wires has been increased by 473 miles, bringing the total up to 2,479 miles'.[57]

Inevitably, the price of telephoning was set to rise, and the rise in cost brought a bitter response from the LMA, whose calculations of the new system of charging introduced in 1899 showed that 'Any of the present subscribers who may have an average of over five calls *per deim* [*sic*], would, under the new proposals, actually pay more *per annum* than under the old rating.' In response, the LMA was quick to demand the opening of the telephone market to competition, reminding members that:

> Another point to which public attention should be directed, in view of the monopoly which the National Telephone Company holds, is the want of intercommunication between provincial towns within a radius of say 100 miles from Belfast ... When any remonstrances on this defect are addressed to the National Telephone Company, the blame is thrown by them on the Post Office, who hold, or presumably hold, command of the trunk lines. On the

> other hand, when the Post Office are approached on this point, they reply that the Telephone Company will not give the necessary guarantees etc., which they may require.

The report concludes on the matter, bitterly noting that due to this evasion of responsibility by all involved:

> ...the commercial interests involved naturally 'fall between two stools', and accordingly suffer. Your Council [of the LMA] are of the opinion that it is a national disgrace that the public should be placed in such a ridiculous position. We have one of the most modern appliances of science before us; but, by a display of red tape on one side, and by a monopoly on the other, we are prevented from availing ourselves of its manifest advantages.[58]

The LMA's deep interest in telephones can only be understood in terms of the geographical isolation of their location from their customer base. The members of the LMA knew exactly where its market was, and in an industry where records bear witness to the importance of even weekly fluctuations in prices,[59] the members of the LMA knew the value of keeping in the most regular possible communication with their clients.

EXHIBITING

The nineteenth century has often been noted as the era of the exhibition and the spectacle: the second half of the century teemed with grand displays of progress and productivity initiated by the Great Exhibition in London in 1851. Typically self-confident, the LMA argued that Belfast linen had played a key role in the Great Exhibition's inception as it was at the time in 1849 that Queen Victoria and Prince Albert 'viewed an exhibition representing the Linen Industry in its various processes, in the Old Linen Hall ... and expressed much interest in the display; it is said to have suggested to the Prince Consort the idea of holding the first International Exhibition, in 1851, where the Ulster Linen Trade was very strongly represented by numerous exhibits'.[60] Whether this was an overstatement or not, the linen trade of Belfast was very much part of the display phenomenon. Belfast's linen manufacturers and merchants attended exhibitions internationally, and frequently won prizes for their wares. Almost from its inception the LMA was concerned with exhibiting overseas.

In January 1876 the Association was actively encouraging its members to publicize their wares at the International Centennial Exhibition to be held in Philadelphia in 1876.[61] More properly called the International Exhibition of Arts, Manufactures, and Products of the Soil and Mine, it ran from 10 May to 10 November 1876 in Philadelphia's Fairmount Park. More than 30,000 firms exhibited, about a third of which were American concerns. Almost ten million people visited the fair in total.[62] This provided unparalleled exposure for Irish linen products in the country that was already their largest customer.

In 1878 Irish linen products were on display at the Paris Exhibition and the LMA was able to note proudly that 'At the Paris Exhibition the Staple Trade had its representatives in several Members of our Association, all of whom gained prizes.' The meeting moved immediately to discuss invitations to further exhibitions in Sydney, Australia and, closer to home, in York.[63] Similarly, in 1887 the LMA was pleased that at the Royal Jubilee Exhibition of British Products to be held in Manchester, Irish flax products would be given a large space. A committee was appointed to oversee the 'Ulster Linen Trade Exhibit'.[64] By the next annual meeting the LMA was able to report on the exhibition:

> The Royal Jubilee Exhibition of British products held in Manchester last year was a great success. The committee appointed to superintend the Ulster Linen Trade Exhibit, under the auspices of this Association, deserve great praise for the manner in which their duties were discharged. The Exhibits, which were supplied by firms connected with the staple trade, represented the various processes through which Flax passes from the seed to the ready-made articles for clothing and household use.[65]

So effective had the committee apparently been that the same members were appointed to take charge of the linen exhibit at the Exhibition of Industry, Science and Art in Glasgow in May of 1888.

The LMA firms' attendance at the Paris Exhibition of 1889 was considered 'an unprecedented success', with the York Street Flax-Spinning Company representing Belfast linen interests. This meant that, at the same meeting, the 'World's Fair' to be held in the USA 1892 was eagerly anticipated.[66] Further details later emerged that it was 'expected to be on a very extensive scale',[67] eventually leading to 'several firms connected with this Association purpose exhibiting'.[68] In the event, six LMA firms attended, all of which won prizes for the quality of their goods.[69]

Given so much success at international exhibitions, it was hardly surprising that the LMA members were optimistic about the success of one closer to home. With eagerness the LMA report for 1895 pointed out that:

> ...the Belfast Art and Industrial Exhibition will be opened in the Linen Hall grounds about the end of March, and it is fully expected will prove a great success. The Committee,

> of whom the Right Hon. the Lord Mayor of Belfast is Chairman, have received numerous applications for space. The additional Buildings, covering nearly three acres, for the reception of exhibits in the Central Square, are rapidly progressing'.[70]

When Edward VII visited Belfast in 1903 the linen trade also took the opportunity to present an Address to the king, and to point out that the Address was:

> …not the only means used to show how much those engaged in the Linen Trade of Ulster appreciated His Majesty's visit to the North, a very happy conception found fitting expression, in a tangible and prominent addition to the street decoration, a handsome and graceful Arch was erected in Wellington Place. This was carried out by a joint committee representing all branches of the Industry, and the entire outlay was met by voluntary subscriptions.[71]

This success behind them the linen merchants then discussed a forthcoming exhibition in St Louis, USA and a further one in Dublin.

Where no international exhibitions were being organized the LMA was keen to attend local displays, and closer to home the linen industry engaged in public spectacle with vigour. When the Belfast Industrial Development Association wanted a parade through the city streets of local produce, 'the Linen Merchants' Association, being appealed to, responded at once, and made a good display'.[72] Where no other body was organizing any opportunities for linen display the LMA was not slow to create its own. On the evening of 27 March 1904 the LMA held a Linen Ball in Belfast's Ulster Hall and the ladies in attendance wore linen. Indeed,

> It was a matter of general comment at the Ball in question, in fact the representatives of the cross channel fashion journals admitted, that never before had anything been seen so attractive in linen as the costumes worn upon that occasion. Whether the Ball was responsible for the active demand which followed, or not, the fact remains that the consumption of linen dress material, both in the United Kingdom and in the States was probably never before equalled, and it is anticipated that the coming season will be even better.[73]

The political importance of linen, or of those in the linen industry, was also apparent. Mr Otto Jaffe, Lord Mayor of Belfast in 1904 and a leading figure in linen production, gave a Linen Garden Party at which:

> The ladies appeared, almost without exception, in garments made from linen, and it was a matter of surprise and pleasure to even those who knew the possibilities of linen as a dress fabric to see how many beautiful dresses were there displayed. It was, indeed, one of the most brilliant social functions of the year.[74]

Such attention to catching public notice means that it is not surprising that Irish linen was to become the first industry in Britain to advertize corporately, and spend generous sums on doing so.[75] Belfast linen was keen to display itself to the largest possible audiences and almost all of these exhibitions were on an international stage, often as distant as America or Australia, or at the metropole of the British Empire: all of them reached enormous audiences. Belfast's linen industry was strongly export-based and needed such exposure to maximize profits.

CONCLUSION

The evidence presented in this chapter indicates how Belfast's linen merchants were part of a network of trade that encircled the globe in the nineteenth century's international web of exchange. That most international of eras provided Belfast linen with the customers whose purchasing power was vital to what was, essentially, an industry producing luxury goods. Without its worldwide markets Belfast's linen industry would never have been able to operate on anything but the most modest footing.

Two years before its reorganization in 1916 the LMA's president was perceptively commenting that 'We find ourselves in the middle of a World Wide convulsion, which is certain not only to alter the Map of the World, but also to considerably change the channels and currents of commercial enterprise.'[76] Notwithstanding the unpredicted and ambiguous results the Great War would have for linen, after the conflict the linen industry was never to recover the heights it had attained in the nineteenth century: cotton was always going to be more readily available, cheaper and more versatile. As Armstrong noted long ago, the nature of the product itself was in part to blame for the undoing of one of Belfast's chief industries: 'Even the greatest virtue of linen – its durability – was against it in its competition with cotton and other fabrics.'[77]

2

Belfast: The Rise and Fall of a Civic Culture?

S.J. Connolly[1]

I

The spectacular rise of Victorian Belfast, from a town of 53,000 inhabitants in 1831 to a city of 349,000 by 1901, took place during what is now widely seen as a golden age in the history of the British city. Municipal reform transferred power from oligarchic corporations and territorial magnates to a new class of wealthy entrepreneurs. Confronted by the problems created by unprecedented urban growth, and empowered by the still limited scope of the central state, this urban elite embarked on a massive programme of reorganization and investment. Their efforts reshaped town centres, created giant networks for the distribution of water and power, the transport of goods and people and the disposal of waste, and brought into being a whole new corpus of municipal public architecture. The Europe of the middle ages and the early modern period had its palaces and cathedrals. In Victorian Britain the appearance in every major centre of town halls, museums, libraries and concert halls, in classical or gothic style, provided similar testimony to a collective vision of community and social progress.[2]

This is a story familiar to anyone interested in urban history. For Irish historians, however, it remains a narrative firmly located on the other side of the Irish Sea. It is true that the second half of the nineteenth century saw a significant increase in the proportion of Irish men and women categorized as living in urban areas: from one in seven in 1841 to almost one in three by 1901. Yet compared to England and Wales, where three quarters of the inhabitants now lived in towns and cities, Ireland at the start of the twentieth century remained a rural society. The rising proportion of town dwellers, moreover, had come about not through urban growth but through a fall in overall numbers: between 1851 and 1901 most Irish towns actually lost inhabitants. Hence it is hardly surprising that urban development has been relatively slow to establish itself as a field of research for Irish historians, and that the work that has appeared has focused primarily on themes of economic decline, physical decay and social deprivation.[3]

In the context of this divergence of national historiographies, the case of Belfast presents particular problems. Its rapid growth, and the scale of its industrial achievement, would seem to locate it firmly within the British rather than the Irish narrative. By 1911, after all, it was the United Kingdom's eighth largest urban centre. The architectural record, equally, provides apparent evidence of the same thriving culture of civic pride and self-confidence that has so impressed historians of Birmingham, Leeds and elsewhere. Yet no historian of the city has been tempted to follow Tristram Hunt or Simon Gunn in charting the building of an urban Jerusalem on the banks of the Lagan. In place of parallels between Belfast and its British counterparts, historians have focused instead on issues arising from its Irish context; as a Protestant and unionist city menaced by a predominantly Catholic and nationalist hinterland. The emphasis has thus been on recurrent outbreaks of sectarian violence, on the domination of political life by a narrow

Protestant elite and on the negative impact of this political and sectarian exclusiveness on municipal administration and civic culture.[4]

To say this is not to overlook the attempts that have been made to construct a more rounded appraisal of public life in nineteenth-century Belfast. As long ago as 1956, A.T.Q. Stewart, in a pioneering study, comprehensively disposed of the idea that Protestant liberalism simply disappeared after 1798. Subsequent work has confirmed his argument that support for political reform, and a degree of religious liberalism, remained significant for several decades after the union. Where pressure for change did lose some of its urgency over time, moreover, the reason was at least partly that many of the aims of the radicals of the 1790s had, by the 1840s or 1850s, been achieved.[5] More recently John Bew has offered an ambitious reassessment of the town's political culture, arguing that Protestants in Belfast and its hinterland saw incorporation into the United Kingdom not just as a protection against Catholic nationalism but as an opportunity to pursue progressive social goals and to take part in the affairs of a larger political world.[6] Bew's analysis, however, focuses on a small selection of mainly fairly cerebral individuals, whose links to the civic life of Belfast were in some cases distinctly tenuous. Even with less tendentious accounts, moreover, there remains a problem of balance. It is important to acknowledge the continued existence of a liberal and reformist element in Belfast Protestant politics. But it is also important to recognize its limitations. The Belfast Liberal party was Presbyterian led, but for electoral purposes it depended heavily, throughout its existence, on Catholic votes. Even with this backing it remained close to a permanent party of opposition. Against this background, it is all too easy for the legitimate attempt to do justice to the diversity of Protestant political attitudes to degenerate into an obsessive hunt for good deeds in a naughty world. In the case of later manifestations of Protestant radicalism – the Independent Orange

Order, and the brief rise of Labour in the years before the First World War – that danger becomes even greater.[7]

What all this implies is that any real appraisal of the civic culture of Victorian Belfast must look beyond the dwindling ranks of post-union radicalism and liberalism to their opponents in the governing elite. How are we to characterize the circle of mainly wealthy figures, drawn primarily from the commercial and manufacturing world, who from the 1840s onwards had charge of the town's affairs? Did they share to any significant degree in the positive vision of the potential of urban living, and the strong sense of civic pride, that elsewhere provided the impetus for the achievements of the Victorian city? And how did their attempts to respond to the massive environmental challenges created by unprecedented urban and industrial expansion compare with those of their counterparts in other regions of the United Kingdom?

II

In Belfast as elsewhere municipal reform during 1835–41 transferred power from an aristocratic patron and the clique that surrounded him to a more broadly based representative body. Up to the end of the eighteenth century the management of the town had been in the hands of a corporation: a self-perpetuating body comprizing a sovereign and twelve burgesses, all in practice nominees of the earl (from 1791 marquis) of Donegall. From 1800 responsibility for street cleaning and lighting, and other aspects of the infrastructure of the expanding town, passed to an elected Police Board. The new municipal authority, however, was a two-tiered structure, in which the executive body, the Police Committee, was subordinate to the direction of the Police Commissioners, thirteen of whose twenty-five members were the sovereign and burgesses, while the remaining twelve were elected on a narrow franchise, and subject to a high property qualification.[8]

Meanwhile, the Corporation itself remained in effect the property of the Donegall family. The post of sovereign, bringing an income of £500 a year, passed back and forth between the second marquis's father-in-law Edward May, his son (and hence Donegall's brother-in-law) Edward junior, and Thomas Verner, who was married to another of May senior's daughters. An enquiry in 1835 into the workings of Irish municipal corporations also noted a range of unlawful or illegal fees extorted by the borough's legal officers, as well as compiling a catalogue of sums, amounting in all to over £3,000, appropriated by Donegall, the Mays and others from corporation funds intended for the relief of the poor.[9] Control of the corporation further allowed the marquis to control the return of members to Belfast's one remaining parliamentary seat, which in turn allowed him both to assert his claim to much of the patronage associated with the town and to present himself as its rightful spokesman to parliament and government alike.[10]

The control thus exercised over the affairs of Belfast by Donegall and the clique surrounding him depended on inherited wealth and position, protected by a legal and political system that gave priority to corporate and proprietorial rights. The political values that informed their management of the town were those of the same traditional and hierarchical political and social order. They consistently opposed movements for political reform, just as they had earlier rejected the radicalism of the United Irishmen. At the same time they showed no disposition, in the period after the rebellion, to engage in displays of loyalist triumphalism. Instead the public celebrations sponsored both by the Donegall family and by the municipal authorities sought to promote a consensual British patriotism, focusing on royal birthdays and anniversaries, and on the war against revolutionary France. The centre for much civic activity of this kind was a Nelson club set up after the battle of Trafalgar, while one of the most elaborate public demonstrations staged during the period was in celebration of the triumphal return of a local hero, Major General Charles Stewart, second son of the marquis of Londonderry and half-brother to the Foreign Secretary, Viscount Castlereagh, from service in Spain and Portugal.[11] A second major theme, alongside loyalty to throne and constitution, was social hierarchy. In 1818, for example, the whole town was illuminated to celebrate the coming of age of Donegall's eldest son. Specially commissioned transparencies depicted the young earl alongside emblems representing agriculture and commerce, as well as Sir Arthur Chichester, founder of the dynasty, while a motto displayed at the White Linen Hall offered the deferential message that 'one resident landlord is worth a hundred parliamentary representatives'.[12]

Perhaps the most striking expression of the outlook of the pre-reform political elite, and of the political culture it sought to promulgate, was the elaborate ceremonial that marked the accession of a new king, George IV, in 1820. A printed document, prepared by the sovereign, set out in detail the composition of the procession that was to make its way through the centre of the town, stopping at four points – the Donegall Arms in High Street, the White Linen Hall, the Exchange and the Parade – while the town clerk read the proclamation acknowledging the new monarch. At its head came the superintendent of the recently established town police, followed by his constables, the town crier, the sergeant at mace and other lesser corporation officials, as well as the band of the garrison. Next came Donegall, mounted on horseback in tribute to his status as 'lord of the castle'. He was followed by the sovereign and burgesses, the magistrates, the clergy of different denominations, the members of the police board and then – pointedly placed before the members of the less prestigious police committee – the staff and students from the Academical Institution. Behind these again came other inhabitants of the town, separately classified as 'professional and other gentlemen', 'merchants', and then 'tradesmen &c &c'. The whole document was a late but elaborate expression of the traditional notion of the urban population as a stratified corporate community.[13]

III

These details are important because they serve to highlight the contrast between the interests that dominated Belfast's affairs in the first decades of the nineteenth century and the very different urban elite that took control from the 1840s onwards. Parliamentary reform in 1832 put an end to Donegall's control of the parliamentary constituency, giving Belfast two members returned by an electorate of approximately 2,000. Municipal reform, enacted in 1840 and taking effect two years later, replaced the self-perpetuating corporation with an elected mayor and council. In the new industrial towns of Great Britain, reform of this kind most commonly ushered in a generation or more of Liberal and Radical political dominance. In Belfast, by contrast, a Conservative party, managed by the formidable John Bates, enjoyed victory in all but a handful of parliamentary contests, as well as retaining a complete monopoly of seats on the councils elected from 1842 onwards. Yet this apparently anomalous outcome should not be allowed to conceal the extent to which municipal government in Victorian Belfast was the product of new political structures and circumstances. Belfast may not have aligned itself with the self-defined forces of progress. But the body of urban notables that managed the town's affairs from the 1840s onwards was nevertheless very different, in social composition and in outlook, from the Donegall interest it replaced.

To appreciate the importance of not being misled by superficial political labels, it is only necessary to look at the outcome of the election that followed the reform act of 1832. In the conventional narrative this Conservative electoral success marks the beginning of the long domination of the town's politics by the forces of reaction. The impression is reinforced by the appearance as one of the two successful Conservative candidates of one of Donegall's sons, Lord Arthur Chichester. But appearances are deceptive. In the two years before the passage of the reform act the Donegalls had gone out of their way to advertize their willingness to accept reform gracefully. Against this background, the selection of Lord Arthur for the party's first electoral outing was a shrewd one, representing the adoption of a familiar figure and a symbol of continuity, rather than a concession to proprietorial authority. The other candidate, meanwhile, was James Emerson Tennent, a leading supporter of parliamentary reform who had been won over only after the town's Liberal party had failed to make him one of its candidates. There is no denying that the campaign in support of these two figureheads was in some respects an unsavoury one. *The Northern Whig* complained of pubs paid to keep open house in Sandy Row, while Orange bands regaled supporters with party tunes. Later, after the results were declared, the provocative chairing of the successful candidates close to the Catholic stronghold of Hercules Street degenerated into a riot in which four men were killed.[14] But the Conservative choice of Chichester and Emerson Tennent must also be contrasted with the decision of the Liberals, carried away by victory on the Reform Bill, to put forward two candidates standing on a platform of further radical change, including tithe reform, the secret ballot and the introduction of triennial parliaments. Seen in this light, the Conservative victory can be understood less as the triumph of sectarianism and reaction than as a successful capture of the centre ground.

The contrast between the traditional Toryism of the Donegall circle and the outlook of the emerging new urban elite is also evident in the rhetoric of the Belfast Conservative Society, founded almost immediately after the 1832 election to provide the basis of a permanent political organization. In January 1836 some 800 guests assembled for a public dinner to celebrate the Society's third anniversary. The mood, following further electoral victories in 1835 and 1836, was celebratory. But the speeches nevertheless continued the tone of studied moderation set in 1832. The Belfast Society, Emerson Tennent insisted, was 'not to be supposed ... a mere faction in the state'. Instead, he claimed, it was their Liberal opponents who had sought to establish a monopoly of the representation. In response a broad coalition of men of good will – 'men who, some years ago, would have been found, in all probability, on different sides, or, more likely still, connected with no party whatsoever' – had come together to frustrate the designs of an extremist minority. John Bates, speaking at the fourth anniversary celebrations a year later, took up the same theme. 'Here the honest Tory and the true Whig have united together as Conservatives; the episcopalian, Presbyterian, and Methodist as churchmen, rally and defend those principles and that faith which they in common hold.' Both men also made clear their acceptance of the new political order introduced by the Reform Act. The people of Belfast, Bates asserted, had secured their liberties through two victories: first by obtaining the elective franchise and then by defeating the attempt of the Liberals 'to succeed to Lord Donegall's power of nomination in the borough'. This was Conservatism, but it was the pragmatic, forward-looking Conservatism of Sir Robert Peel, rather than the traditional Toryism of the old Belfast corporation. And indeed Emerson Tennent appealed directly to the inspiration of Peel recalling for his audience a speech to the merchants of London, advising them that they should no longer look to the prerogative of the crown, or the votes of the House of Lords, to protect their interests. Instead, Peel had argued and Emerson repeated, they must adapt to the requirements of the new political system: 'it was henceforth at the registries and the hustings that the battle for the constitution was to be fought'.[15]

The pious disclaimer of a stake in party politics, from men at the head of a political machine of unmatched efficiency and ruthlessness, can be dismissed out of hand. The appeal to a forward looking and constructive Conservatism, on the other hand, has undoubted substance. After a brief struggle, the new council secured the transfer to itself, in January 1844, of the powers and assets of the Police Commissioners. Between the following year and 1850 it secured the passage of four separate improvement acts authorizing it to borrow money for a range of new projects. By 1857 it had raised and spent a total of over £270,000 (roughly ten times that year's income from rates and other sources). The most important scheme was Belfast's first major exercise in urban planning: the construction of a broad new thoroughfare, eventually to be named Victoria Street, to enable traffic crossing from County Down by the newly built Queen's Bridge to by-pass the town centre. The project was not the immediate commercial success envisaged: early construction revealed expensive problems with subsidence, and it proved difficult to lure shoppers away from established localities. However, there was general agreement that the new street replaced an unsavoury slum, and in time it became the site of Belfast's show-piece town hall, as well as of some of its major commercial premises.[16] A second major area of expenditure was the purchase of land between the town and the River Lagan for the erection of new market buildings. These became the site for the sale of cattle, removed from the inner city market at Smithfield, as well as for the pork market that had regularly taken over Waring Street in the very heart of the town, and the horse fair formerly held in York Street.[17]

These early investments in urban improvement were subsequently to become the cause of controversy when a suit in chancery led to a finding that the council had exceeded its powers. However, there was no suggestion of personal profiteering. (The one exception was a claim that Bates had benefited from excessive fees in his dual role of town clerk and town solicitor. However, this charge was rejected by a commission of enquiry in 1859.) Instead the council's main offence was to have exceeded the borrowing powers provided in the Improvement Acts. It had also abandoned plans to municipalize the gas works, in response to a much improved price for supply offered by the owners, and had instead spent the money on street improvements, an action ruled illegal by the lord chancellor but judged legitimate by the commission of enquiry. The fairest verdict was probably that of William Tracy, as long-serving resident magistrate a well-informed outsider, who believed that the councillors had erred 'in a moment of ambition. They wanted to make Belfast a great city before its time; and they condensed into some seven years the taxation that should have been spread over three times that period'.[18]

In assessing the spirit behind these early improvement projects it is important to note that the work carried out, while involving heavy capital expenditure, was at least partly self-financing. By 1857 the council was paying interest of £9,000 a year on its borrowings, but was also receiving an income of £5,200 from tolls levied on those trading in the new market premises.[19] Expenditure on Victoria Street was also intended to be recouped, over time, by the granting of building leases along both sides of the new thoroughfare. Improvements that did not yield an income were less attractive. A frequently quoted example is the refusal of the council to contribute to the public baths and wash-house opened in 1847 by a voluntary society. Here, however, Belfast was not alone. Parliament had indeed recently passed legislation empowering councils to invest in these vital amenities. But it appears to have been generally assumed that they should, once established, become self-financing, and neither Glasgow nor Liverpool made significantly better provision.[20] Belfast council, moreover, was not wholly indifferent to social improvement. The Act of 1847 laid down minimum standards for new houses, including the mandatory provision of a piped water supply and a yard with space for an ash pit and privy. In consequence, it was later pointed out, practically all of the houses built in Belfast in the 1850s and 1860s were still in use a century later.[21]

IV

The improvements undertaken by the town council in the late 1840s came at a significant time. The widespread rebuilding that had taken place under the control of the first marquis of Donegall between the 1760s and the 1790s had created an elegant, if still compact-town whose most prestigious street, what became Donegall Place, was proclaimed as Belfast's Grosvenor Square or St James's.[22] Further building in the 1820s and 1830s, on the other hand, increased the size of the town without adding to its aesthetic appeal. Henry Inglis, visiting in 1834, complained of 'unbroken lines of buildings, uniform in height, and unrelieved by the least architectural ornament'.[23] By the early 1840s the newspapers had begun to carry regular expressions of dismay at Belfast's undistinguished appearance. In particular they complained of the lack of large-scale public buildings and of substantial constructions in stone.[24] Already by the end of the decade, however, the council's projects in the markets area and Victoria Street took their place alongside several other notable contributions, completed or in progress, to the urban landscape: the new railway terminus at York Street, reconstructed in 1848 with the frontage of a Tuscan palazzo; its counterpart on the New Dublin Road, finished in the same year; the Queen's College, completed in 1849; and those classic institutions of the Victorian city, the courthouse (1846) and gaol (1850), strategically located on the Crumlin Road so as to dominate the skyline of the unruly working-class district that had helped call them into existence.

The impulse to give physical expression to Belfast's new sense of its own importance continued into the following decades. During the 1850s, the town acquired two more of the impressive public buildings whose absence had earlier been lamented: the Harbour Office in 1854 and the Custom House in 1857. The Town Hall followed in 1872. Meanwhile the expansion of the commercial centre during the 1850s and 1860s, redeveloping peripheral areas or swallowing up formerly residential addresses like Donegall Place and Donegall Square, provided an opportunity for the town's business elite to make their contribution. Buildings like the Ulster Bank in Waring Street (1857–60) or the McCausland Brothers' great warehouse on Victoria Street (1867–8) were major architectural statements as well as functional premises. Even a site of primary production, such as Jennymount Mill off the Antrim Road (1856–64), was given the elegant external lines of an Italian palazzo, a common architectural choice selected as recalling a previous great age of urban civilization.

Buildings such as Jennymount and the Custom House were only the most visible and enduring evidence of the new confidence and assertiveness that now characterized the civic culture of the town. The visit of Queen Victoria in August 1849, itself a landmark in the growth of Belfast's self-awareness, inspired the town council to equip itself with an elaborate corporate uniform – scarlet gowns trimmed with ermine, worn over blue dress coats with velvet collars and buttons bearing the town's crest.[25] In 1874, just after the opening of the new Town Hall, the mayor acquired a new chain of office. From about the same time, in a further expression of corporate self-awareness, the council began to commission portraits of each holder of the office, eventually extending the series back to the 1860s.[26] Meanwhile the opening in 1862 of the Ulster Hall, funded by public subscription, gave Belfast a first-class venue for classical music – the art form of choice of the Victorian bourgeoisie, to whom it offered opportunities for sociability and display in an environment untouched by the moral hazards of the theatre and informally but firmly restricted to the circle of the reasonably affluent.[27] There were also landmark publications. James Adair Pilson's *History of the Rise and Progress of Belfast* (1846) offered only a sketchy narrative chronicle, but combined it with a detailed topographical account of the modern town and an enthusiastic description of its economic achievements. The first volume of George Benn's history, in 1877, was by contrast a meticulously researched compendium of information. There were of course those who preferred to argue that Belfast had no significant history: such a claim served both to link the town's very existence to the act of union, and to avoid the embarrassing events of the 1790s. But for those who wanted to give their town an identity in time, Benn had now provided the materials.[28] Meanwhile David Patterson, a lecturer at the Institute for the Deaf and Dumb, provided another insight into a changing urban culture when he published a handbook designed to instruct Belfast's inhabitants in the non-standard words, pronunciations and grammatical constructions they were to avoid now that their town had become a place of consequence in the world.[29]

By the middle of the nineteenth century, then, municipal affairs in Belfast were in the hands of a self-assured, forward-looking elite with the confidence and vision to undertake large-scale schemes of urban development, both public and private. In this respect its development seems closely to mirror that of the other thriving industrial and commercial towns of Victorian Britain. But there was another side to the town's public life. Recent political histories emphasize that it was not until the 1880s that politics in Belfast came to be rigidly divided between Catholic nationalism and Protestant unionism. It would be convenient, on this basis, to divide the town's history into two phases: the first characterized by communal harmony and a flourishing civic culture and the second by deepening sectarian rancour and a narrowing of political vision. But no such distinction is in fact possible. The town council of the 1840s and 1850s, however progressive its vision of urban development, was already a narrowly exclusive body. The primary purpose of John Bates's notorious machine politics was to ensure that neither Catholics nor Protestant Liberals played any part in the management of the town. At this point the politics of the Belfast elite wholly diverged from the pragmatic, Peelite Conservatism suggested by some of its rhetoric. In doing so, they gave to Belfast municipal politics an element of bitterness, and a denial of the legitimacy of opposition, that set it quite apart from the public life of other urban centres. The corrosive effect on local politics can be seen in the determined way in which Liberals pursued the issues raised by the chancery suit, despite the damage to the town's reputation, and the paralysing effect on municipal business over several years.[30]

The determination of Belfast Conservatives to maintain their hold on power can be attributed to the deeper ideological divisions that existed in Ireland, as compared to Great Britain, and the resulting sense of playing for the highest political stakes. But some of the evidence seems to point less to political self-defence than to a petty and spiteful sectarianism. In 1844 the town's mayor, John Clarke, attended the opening of Belfast's third Catholic church, St Malachy's, and made the ceremonial gesture of assisting in taking up the collection. The same had been done, by the marquis of Donegall and other prominent members of the Protestant establishment, at the opening in 1815 of St Patrick's church at the top of Donegall Street. Thirty years later, however, against the background of the repeal movement, Clarke's gesture was no longer acceptable. According to his own account, he was denied the expected vote of thanks at the end of his term of office, and was not re-elected to the town council thereafter. In 1858 Bernard Hughes, a Liberal of impeccable moderation and one of the town's most substantial businessmen, described the difficulties he had encountered in placing his son in an apprenticeship in the town. 'Roman Catholics will not be taken in as apprentices; I went to several myself, and offered a fee of £500 with my own son, and they would show me a list of applications – perhaps twenty or thirty – as an excuse; and whenever a month or two would pass, I would find one or two taken, that were not on the list; they would say it was a case they could not avoid.'[31]

Already by the mid-nineteenth century, then, the rhetoric of civic pride and the iconography of a prosperous, harmonious urban community served to mask what were in fact deep political and religious divisions. The sharpness of the contrast between image and reality sets Belfast apart from the British towns and cities it sought to emulate. But it would be naïve to draw too absolute a distinction. Belfast differed from other centres in the presence within its boundaries of a large ethnic minority, along with a majority threatened with engulfment in an island dominated by that same ethnic and religious group. At the same time it had no monopoly, among the towns of the United Kingdom, on either prejudice or exclusion. Bernard Hughes's problems, as part of Belfast's small Catholic middle class, may not have differed all that much from those encountered by many Jewish businessmen in major Victorian cities. In other respects, too, evidence from elsewhere makes clear that a civic pride capable of inspiring real achievement in the development and management of growing cities could perfectly well exist side by side with quite vicious internal conflict. In towns across the United Kingdom, the ambitious reshaping of urban centres coincided with the development of new and intrusive forms of policing designed to control a disruptive, potentially menacing, plebeian culture.[32] In Paris, likewise, Baron Haussmann's redevelopment gave Europe a new standard of urban planning. But some at least of his broad, straight boulevards were also intended to provide a suitable terrain, if needed, for the use of cavalry and volley fire against any further outbreaks of revolt among the city's working classes.[33]

V

There are suggestions that the trauma of the chancery suit, threatening individuals with personal bankruptcy and casting a shadow of impropriety over much of the work of the preceding decade, led Belfast town council temporarily to reduce the scope of its activities.[34] By the last quarter of the century, however, it was once again willing to initiate large-scale projects. The most dramatic was the construction during 1880–1 of Royal Avenue, a spacious boulevard of shops and offices resembling Birmingham's show-piece Corporation Street. There were also other street widening projects, at North Street, Bridge Street and elsewhere. Meanwhile the council, like its counterparts in English and Scotland, had substantially expanded the scale of municipal trading. It took over the town's gasworks in 1874 at a cost of £386,000, and by 1891 had spent a further £300,000 on increasing capacity. In 1892, largely as a result of this investment, the city's debt stood at £985,544 against total income in that year of £575,000.[35] In 1897–8, however, the council went on to spend a further £100,000 on a first electricity generating station. Its purchase in 1904 of the street tramway network cost a further £364,000, as well as requiring a doubling of generating capacity to permit electric to replace horse-drawn vehicles.[36] The completion in 1906 of the elaborate new City Hall, at a cost of over £360,000, was thus only the latest, if by far the most dramatic, in a succession of ambitious investments in urban improvement.[37]

The civic elite of late Victorian and Edwardian Belfast, then, clearly did not lack energy or boldness. Yet assessments of their performance in managing the affairs of what was now a major industrial city have been uniformly unfavourable. A number of accounts contrast the impressive external appearance of the city, in particular the expensive grandeur of the City Hall, with the poverty that existed in working-class districts.[38] Others have pointed to the consequences for civic culture of a changing political climate. By this time the Home Rule movement had established itself as a formidable and threatening force. From 1897, following the Belfast Corporation Act, Nationalist representatives appeared on the city council of Belfast itself. Distrust of the British government's Irish policy added further to the climate of insecurity, reflected in the coarsening of public political rhetoric and in the more violent character of sectarian affrays. At the same time sectarian conflict within the working class helped to prevent the development of an effective, combative labour movement, thus removing what elsewhere operated as a powerful spur to urban improvement. Instead the city's elite was free to neglect its social responsibilities, at both corporate and municipal level. Against this background, it is argued, Belfast fell steadily behind comparable centres in terms of effective and progressive urban government.[39]

How are these criticisms to be assessed? The first point is that any judgement must rest on realistic standards of comparison. It is undoubtedly true that in urban planning external grandeur took precedence over considerations of public welfare. The construction of Royal Avenue, for example, involved the demolition of some 550 houses, with no attempt to provide alternative accommodation for those displaced. Indeed questioning before a Royal Commission in 1885 extracted from the borough surveyor an admission that the rebuilding, partly justified as the clearance of an overcrowded and unsanitary district, had proceeded under a local act of parliament, rather than already available national legislation, precisely in order to avoid incurring any responsibility for rehousing.[40] Yet Belfast was not alone: only a few years earlier Birmingham Corporation had used a variety of devices to avoid rehousing the 18,000 persons displaced in the construction of Corporation Street.[41] In the same way the rise of municipal trading, sometimes called 'gas and water socialism', is often taken as an index of progressive urban management. Yet there was also an important financial calculation. At a time when only the more affluent paid rates, the municipalization of gas and tram services, run as profit making concerns, helped to transfer part of the financial burden from middle-class householders to the much wider section of the population that used, and paid for, these amenities.[42] Any appraisal of the successes and failures of Belfast, in other words, must take account of what was everywhere a complex interaction between civic pride, commerce, and considerations of the public good.

Turning to specific issues, the picture that emerges is of a municipal authority that over time steadily widened the range of amenities it provided, but showed little energy or enthusiasm in doing so. Public baths, denied support in the 1850s, began to make their appearance over twenty years later: at Peter's Hill in 1879, followed by Ormeau Avenue (1888), Templemore Avenue (1893) and the Falls Road (1896). In the same way, Belfast did not get its first public park, at Ormeau, until 1871, two decades or more after the need for such an amenity had begun to be seriously agitated. But thereafter progress was rapid. The Falls Park opened in 1876, followed by Alexandra Park (1885), Woodvale Park (1888), Dunville Park (1892), and Victoria Park (1906), as well as the transfer to municipal ownership of Botanic Gardens in 1895.[43] The passage of new legislation in 1877 encouraged discussion of a public library. But it was only after a vigorous public campaign that the impressive building on Royal Avenue finally opened in 1888. Meanwhile the council, along with the city's leading industrialists, ignored calls for improved technical education, despite evidence that the Ulster linen industry was beginning to fall behind competitors in design and finish.

The eventual establishment in 1901 of the Belfast Technical College came about only as a result of pressure and inducements from the newly established Department of Agriculture and Technical Instruction.[44]

Another, potentially more important, area in which local government in Belfast is frequently held to have failed to keep pace with achievements elsewhere is in housing. Here there was no attempt to make public provision of any kind until a first small slum clearance scheme launched in 1917. On the contrary, as the case of Royal Avenue made clear, there were strenuous efforts to avoid any such commitment. However, this evasion of responsibility must be seen in context. Although the first council housing in Great Britain was erected as early as 1867, the scale of provision remained small: local authorities built less than 5 per cent of the houses erected between 1890 and 1914.[45] Moreover, Belfast, unlike Dublin or the main Scottish cities, had no tenements; even poorer families generally lived in single-occupancy units. The late growth of the town meant that the quality of its housing stock was relatively good, and the easy availability of building land kept prices low. Indeed, affordable, good quality housing was recognized as one of the major attractions of Belfast for skilled workers recruited from Scotland or England.[46] Public housing might well have made a difference to the most poorly paid workers (though only if rents were fixed at a sufficiently low level). Suggestions that the failure to provide it was due to the self-interested opposition of councillors themselves involved in property development may well be correct. But the problem the city failed to address was not, by contemporary standards, particularly pressing.

Where the charge of serious failings in urban governance becomes more compelling is in relation to public health. Irish legislation in this area lagged significantly behind the rest of the United Kingdom. However, an act of 1848 gave councils discretionary power to appoint a medical officer of health; Dublin got round to doing so in 1864.

Belfast, by contrast, waited until the Public Health Acts of 1874 and 1878 had forced it to take on the responsibilities of an urban sanitary authority. Its first such officer, Samuel Browne, was a former mayor of the town, now seventy-one years old. A later appointee, in 1906, was likewise a Conservative member of the council. *The British Medical Journal*, in 1896, pointed out that Belfast spent only £15,000 per annum on public health, where Glasgow, with twice the population, spent £100,000.[47] Lack of care was also evident in the chaotic organization of services, with no attempt to coordinate the work of the separate bodies responsible for sewers, the collection of refuse and the enforcement of building standards.[48]

Water was also a problem. The domestic supply, drawn from a miscellaneous collection of springs and rivers added to piecemeal across the nineteenth century, was of poor quality and liable to constant interruptions. Work to bring a clean, reliable supply from the Mournes was completed only in 1901 – forty-two years after Glasgow began to receive its water, across roughly the same distance, from Lough Katrine. The problems in this case were not the direct responsibility of the council, since supply was managed by a separate body of elected Water Commissioners. As early as 1859, however, an enquiry into municipal affairs had advised that the council should take over all responsibility for water supply, on the grounds that the borrowing powers of the Commissioners were inadequate and that the council would be better placed to secure any necessary parliamentary legislation. The point was reiterated by an enquiry into the town's public health record in 1908, suggesting that the council's failure over several decades to take charge of such a vital resource constituted a significant omission.[49]

Sanitation and waste disposal, meanwhile, was the council's direct responsibility, and represented its greatest failure. The Blackstaff river had been recognized as a dangerous nuisance as early as the 1840s. Despite recurrent protests, however, it continued for a further four decades to flow as an open stream, converted by the hot water discharged from factories along its banks into an unsavoury warm soup of human waste and industrial effluent. It was eventually culverted over in 1887, but this was a cosmetic solution, ignoring a warning from the borough engineer, James Montgomery, that what was really required was a proper system of sewers.[50] The inadequacy of the sewers also impeded the adoption of the water closet. In the 1890s about two fifths of all houses were still served by a privy or ashpit that had regularly to be cleaned out; more than a quarter of these, moreover, had no rear access, so that the waste had to be carried through the dwelling for disposal. As early as 1866–7 Montgomery, in collaboration with the celebrated Sir Joseph Bazalgette, drew up comprehensive plans for a system of sewers. Yet it was not until 1893 that a main drainage scheme was completed. Even then an inadequate wooden pipe for discharging waste into the Lough allowed what proved to be a lethal level of pollution, until it was replaced by a better constructed outlet in 1913.[51]

In the area of public health and sanitation, then, the record of municipal administration in late Victorian and Edwardian Belfast presents an unattractive picture of parsimony and, in the appointment of medical officers, clientelism. The social cost of these failings, however, appears to have been less than might have been expected. Enquiries by the council in 1896 and by the Irish executive twelve years later discovered that Belfast suffered abnormally high levels of two specific forms of mortality: respiratory diseases, linked to conditions in the textile mills, and typhoid, linked to the consumption of shellfish polluted by sewage in Belfast Lough. But the overall death rate, though higher than in Leeds, Sheffield, Bristol or Birmingham, was about the same as in Manchester and Liverpool. Rates of infant mortality, meanwhile, were lower than in all but one of these British comparators.[52] All this, of course, meant only that the inhabitants of Belfast were lucky. A favourable environment – better than average levels of employment opportunities and relatively good housing stock – compensated for the complacency and negligence of the civic elite. But the verdict is less damning than it would be if the ratepayers' pennies had been saved at the cost of a conspicuous level of excess mortality.

It is also necessary to place this aspect of Belfast's performance in a realistic comparative context. British cities too had their 'dirty parties', resisting the mounting evidence of the links between poor sanitation, pollution and disease in the interests of keeping rates down and allowing industry to flourish unchecked. In many cases, it has been pointed out, real efforts to provide for the effective treatment and disposal of sewage came about only when the town concerned faced the threat of costly litigation from other communities or from private interests affected by their effluent.[53] Belfast, likewise, was only one of many centres in which illusory hopes that the conversion of sewage into fertiliser could make waste disposal a source of profit rather than expense further helped to delay progress towards effective disposal systems.[54] It is also important to recognize that a sewer system for Belfast presented particular technical challenges. The town's location on flat, reclaimed land below or only slightly above sea level meant that there was no natural flow to carry waste away, while the river estuary was tidal to a point well beyond the town centre. The long delays in tackling these problems make clear that Belfast's urban administration fell well short of the best standards seen elsewhere in the United Kingdom. How far it fell below the average is less clear.

VI

What then emerges from a survey of civic culture in nineteenth-century Belfast? Three central points suggest themselves. The first merely confirms what is evident to anyone who walks into the city centre and looks around: Belfast was profoundly affected by the same spirit of assertive civic pride, and confidence in the potential of urban living, that shaped the great cities of provincial England, Scotland and Wales. Secondly, there is the need to look more closely at the conservatism that dominated the politics of the town and city. Its sectarian exclusiveness is beyond question: there was no golden age of communal harmony. But, in the mid-nineteenth century at least, the impression is of a flexible and dynamic conservatism, capable of inspiring large-scale development projects.

What, finally, became of this civic culture as the nineteenth century turned into the twentieth? Here assessment is more complicated. The governing elite of late Victorian and Edwardian Belfast had clearly not lost its desire to give visible expression to the city's rising status. Nor had it lost the capacity to plan and execute large-scale projects. On the other hand its record in providing the public amenities required by a modern city, and in dealing with the environmental problems associated with a large industrial population, was mediocre; in the key area of public health and sanitation it was positively poor. To some extent this combination of external magnificence and hidden, parsimonious neglect can be seen as evidence of a civic culture undermined by bitter sectarian political divisions and the narrow, defensive outlook of a local elite under siege. From another perspective, however, it may be that Belfast was no more than an extreme example of the contradictory blend of commerce and vision, self-interest and idealism, that everywhere lay behind the spectacular achievements of the Victorian city.

3

Big Vision City: The Physical Transformation of Belfast by Provincial Architects, 1870–1910

Paul Harron

A passing glance at central Belfast today – despite the many assaults on its fabric for all sorts of reasons over the past seventy years – reveals that it was largely the creation of the Victorian and Edwardian eras. Certainly the 'big city' feel of its urban core, where commercial, civic and ecclesiastical buildings are large and flamboyant, is almost entirely the product of the period 1850–1910. This chapter examines aspects of the architectural transformation of Belfast the provincial town to Belfast the industrialized, showy metropolis it became, a city in the mould of British counterparts like Manchester, Glasgow or Bradford (albeit more the size of the last of these). The physical form of the city was largely the result of the work of local architectural practices, which grew up to satisfy the need to design the buildings required, not only to simply accommodate its expanding businesses and workforce (across the social spectrum) but also to do so with vigour and style, advertizing economic success and civic progress at home and abroad.

The particular focus of this chapter is on the work of arguably the busiest architectural and civil engineering practice of all in Belfast from the late 1870s to 1910: Young & Mackenzie.[1] Examples of this firm's output demonstrate that in the building of this large-scale city, architects and clients alike sought to create a vision of a place that engaged the citizen in new participatory ways: both actual physical engagement with the built environment and civic life as well as mental engagement with notions of a new, thriving and up-to-date Belfast. The centre of Belfast, built on its improbable, sleechy foundations, was physically transformed during this period with an energy, rapidity and sense of belief that it *was* somewhere. Its central thoroughfares sprouted new warehouses, department stores, shops and offices. By the turn of the twentieth century, the Presbyterian Church in Ireland was erecting an enormous assembly hall complex and the Church of Ireland had begun the process of building a massive cathedral, while the city corporation, which had built a Town Hall in 1871, quickly replaced it with the architectural and symbolic centrepiece of the city, Belfast City Hall, to the design of Alfred Brumwell Thomas (1896–1906). In 1909, looking back over the previous fifty years, the *Irish Builder* noted that in the second half of the nineteenth century 'In Belfast a new city arose … 1859 to 1889 were extremely busy times for architects. Some did a vast amount of work – to an extent almost incredible in a small and poor country'.[2]

THE PRE-1870 CONTEXT

In 1847 the *Belfast News Letter* stated:

> It has been a reproach to Belfast, almost since its first emergence into the status of a great provincial town, that its public buildings have been of an ordinary and mean appearance, totally unworthy of the rank which the borough has attained – that of the very first commercial port in Ireland.[3]

As is well known, the growth of Belfast as a centre of industry in the 1840s led to developments at the harbour-side and docks and to the establishment of the railways. The development of the linen industry made a huge impact on the growth, wealth and appearance of the town.[4] The town had, however, few resident architects and civil engineers. Thomas Jackson was the most prominent architect while the county surveyor for Antrim, Charles Lanyon, was the foremost architect-civil engineer.[5]

In 1840, Robert Young, an artistic yet practically minded son of a successful Belfast wool merchant, who had been educated at Belfast Academy, recognized that a career in civil engineering and architecture could be a sensible one and went to the University of Glasgow to receive a grounding in higher level mathematics as a useful foundation for this course of action. In his later memoirs he declared that he had been shocked at the physical shape of Belfast compared to Glasgow in the 1840s. He recalled that he felt 'pain and humiliation, thinking of the poor shabby mean brick and plaster of my native town' and he remembered that, on his return to Belfast as he disembarked the boat, he thought 'what an awfully shabby second rate place compared to Glasgow … I never quite got over it'.[6]

Returning to Belfast, Young served his indentures with Charles Lanyon. His training at the time brought him into contact with Thomas Turner (son of ironmaster Richard Turner) and William Henry Lynn, who was later to become Lanyon's business partner and also a very notable contributor to Belfast's architecture. Under Lanyon, and particularly following the Belfast Improvement Act of 1845, Belfast began to change its outward appearance as a city of visibly increasing stature. Edifices such as the Crumlin Road Gaol of 1843–5, built on a Panoptican plan on the design of which Young worked,[7] Queen's College by Lanyon of 1846–9, and the County Courthouse opposite the Gaol of 1848–50 (which Young & Mackenzie would later remodel significantly in 1905) were all added to the city.

Further grandly scaled public buildings were erected in the town in the 1850s, notable among them Lanyon & Lynn's heavily rusticated Custom House, a Renaissance Revival palazzo in Glasgow freestone (1854–7) and several banks including the Ulster Bank in Waring Street (1857-60) by James Hamilton of Glasgow, with its exuberant entablature (now The Merchant Hotel). Nonetheless, the *Irish Builder* provided 'an architect's thoughts on Belfast' in 1859 that lamented Belfast's continuingly underwhelming overall architectural impression, with a predominance of brick-and-plaster porticoes, stating that 'one of the prominent wants of Belfast is good building stone' and that there was a need for 'better architectural taste'.[8]

In the 1860s, the development of a more prepossessing Belfast gained greater momentum, the architect William J. Barre – designer of the Ulster Hall (1859–62), the Albert Memorial Clock (1865–9) and the former Provincial Bank on Royal Avenue (now Tesco) (1864–9), for example – adding considerably to the city's fabric, along with solid work by Thomas Jackson & Son, William Hastings and Lanyon, Lynn & Lanyon (Charles Lanyon and W.H. Lynn having been joined by Lanyon's son John). By the 1860s, Robert Young had left Lanyon's office fully qualified and well experienced, had spent time working on railway engineering designs for William Dargan and had set up his own architectural practice. Based in Belfast by 1854, he was then one of ten architects and seventeen civil engineers and land surveyors in the town according to the *Belfast Street Directory*. He built up a steady stream of work across Ulster including surveyorship work in the towns of Lurgan and Magherafelt, the design of the City Factory, Derry, of 1863 and, in Belfast, a large warehouse on Donegall Place for Riddell & Co in 1860.[9] Young took on an apprentice in the 1860s: John Mackenzie, the son of the Presbyterian minister of Malone, bringing him into business partnership quickly thereafter.

By 1868 the *Belfast Street Directory* listed as many as twenty-nine architects including Young.[10] Several of these firms were now busy garnering big commissions: in addition to Lanyon, Lynn & Lanyon; Thomas Jackson; William Hastings; and W.J. Barre's successors, Sherry & Hughes (Barre having died in 1867), firms such as Thomas Turner; Anthony Jackson and Boyd & Batt were producing works of some scale. Anthony Jackson, for example, was by the end of the decade designing a new Town Hall in Victoria Street, while Hastings' warehouses in Donegall Street and Lytle's and McCauseland's adjacent warehouses in Victoria Street (now Malmaison Hotel), with vigorous decorative carvings, were good examples of the kinds of visually striking town centre warehouses with stone-faced principal elevations required and increasingly supplied during the period. Lanyon, Lynn & Lanyon's Richardson Sons & Owden's red sandstone warehouse in Donegall Square North (1867–9) (now Marks & Spencer) – a Florentine Gothic Revival four-storey (on basement with attic) set piece – marked probably the finest building of its type around this date. It won the praise of Oscar Wilde, no less, for its beauty of design.[11]

TRANSFORMATIONS: BUILDINGS OF PARTICULAR NOTE, 1870–1900

Almost by way of an answer to Lanyon, Lynn & Lanyon's fine Richardson Sons & Owden's, Young & Mackenzie designed a handsome Venetian-palazzo-like stone warehouse block of 1878 and 1882 for William M. Kirk & Partners at 15 Donegall Square West. The building (demolished to make way for the Northern Bank headquarters in 1970 along with the adjacent former Northern Bank also by Young & Mackenzie of 1903) was initially built as a warehouse with an office block section facing Donegall Square added four years later. The fully completed building had a rusticated ground floor and arcaded top floor with a fretted and balustraded parapet.[12] In its combination of pinnacles and sculptural adornment, especially around the main doorway, it was deliberately lively. The *Irish Builder* described in detail the sculptural treatment of the entrance (by sculptor Alexander Stevens), designed to reflect the firm's status as exporters of finished linen worldwide: a flax plant was carved on the pilasters either side of the door, with heads placed between folds of linen in the caps representing different nationalities and life-size heads representing the five continents.[13]

These Italianate palazzo-like warehouses in Belfast – of which Richardson Sons & Owden's and William M. Kirk & Partners were but two of many examples – echoed those in other British industrialized cities. As Girouard remarked in the context of nineteenth-century Manchester:

> ... warehouses dominated the centre ... Drapers and shopkeepers flocked to them from all over the country, and engravings of them on the firm's bill-heads became a guarantee of success and reliability for overseas buyers ... Victorian merchants and manufacturers were always

> intrigued and flattered by comparisons between themselves and the merchants of the Renaissance. The palazzo style caught on, and became popular all over the country.[14]

Belfast was, therefore, following Victorian British commercial architectural fashion.

Elsewhere during the 1870s, architectural firms were making their mark in the town with buildings of greater architectural pretension where opportunities arose, such as in the case of institutional buildings. Notably, Young & Mackenzie designed the new prestigious-looking Belfast Academy (later Belfast Royal Academy) at Cliftonville in 1878–80. They did so in prized stone for this venerable institution (established in 1785, originally as a Presbyterian educational foundation). Young & Mackenzie was here using the Presbyterian connections of its two principals – now also joined in the latter part of the decade by Robert Young's son Robert Magill Youngs' (who was to become a major chronicler of Belfast)[15] – and the Young's own direct involvement with Belfast Academy as past pupils and through active involvement in the school's governance.

The new school is a Late Gothic Revival and Scots Baronial edifice with an almost symmetrical principal façade, built of uncoursed Scrabo stone. A drawing of the new building was published in *The Architect* in 1879,[16] while the *Irish Builder* gave a detailed description of it in 1880,[17] noting its 'striking' large square tower, details and mouldings, and the spacious dimensions of the entrance hall 'abundantly supplied with light from large mullioned staircase windows'. It was a building meant to impress.

In its presentation it both immediately invited comparisons with Lanyon's Queen's College and placed itself within collegiate architectural traditions in general, while differentiating itself by adding a specific

Scottish Baronial twist in corner stair turrets with conical roofs and corbelled tourelles to the tower. The Scottish Baronial elements echoed those used by Lanyon, Lynn & Lanyon at Belfast Castle at nearby Cave Hill (completed in 1870). These Scottish details also made neat allusion to the Academy's Presbyterian foundations – the faith having been transported from Scotland. Probably partly because of the decision to build in expensive stone,[18] the actual scale of Belfast Academy is rather smaller than it seems. Through its massing, and extensive use of buttressing between bays and splayed buttresses to the projecting gable walls, which accentuate height and width, it has the appearance of being bigger than it actually is. In all, the Academy, with its strong exterior presence, was a building of real importance to the firm and to Belfast's townscape.

From the 1880s Belfast Corporation was intent on developing Royal Avenue, a continuation of Donegall Place, as 'a splendid business thoroughfare'. The *Irish Builder* reported in 1882 that the Corporation was leasing sites, demanding high rents and requiring compliance with strict conditions, at speed:

> … an enormous addition will be made to the appearance of the city; for according to the conditions under which the ground is let all buildings must be completed within twelve months, and must not be less than four storeys in height. The cornice upon the fourth storey must be at an elevation of 50ft from the ground, and the shop front must be at least 15ft in height, the civic authorities evidently intending that the new street shall form one of the finest business thoroughfares in the kingdom.[19]

A number of architects from Belfast, Dublin and England designed large commercial premises on the new avenue, with a considerable use of stone in evidence or at least stone dressings to brick buildings or using fancy terracotta – as at the Gresham Life Office by William Gilliland (1887). Notable contributions were the Reform Club by Maxwell and Tule of Manchester (1883–5), the former Northern Bank by John Lanyon (1883–5) and the Central Library by W.H. Lynn (1883–8). Young & Mackenzie received two sizeable commissions for shops and offices: the Royal Chambers (1882)[20] and Spencer House (1884).[21] The Royal Chambers turns the corner of Rosemary Street with rather stage-set-like abruptness, the run of window layers curving round the corner and stopping against a pilaster mid-air, while Spencer House turns the corner into Lower Garfield Street more emphatically. The Royal Chambers were built for Sir Robert J. McConnell, auctioneer, valuer and estate agent (later Lord Mayor in 1900) to provide him with business premises as well as lettable shop space. This was occupied initially by woollen merchant Mr John Reilly, who relocated from the Bank Buildings to have the distinction of being the first shop in the Avenue, and one that had 'one of the longest woollen counters in Ireland'.[22] The entrance to the Royal Chambers originally had a prominent clock over the main entrance for practical purposes and as distinctive street furniture.

Both the Royal Chambers and Spencer House are built of brick and stucco in a loosely Italianate style and – following the Corporation's orders – are four storeys high with lively roof lines denoted by dormer windows, each given different treatment; with a conical corner turret on Spencer House originally with a weather-cock on top. Spencer House, which has lively zoomorphic carved panels at first-floor level, was built for J.C. Mayrs & Co. cabinet makers. The buildings are not in themselves exceptional, but, as Larmour has said, they 'gain by the coherence of the whole'.[23] In all, the newly built Royal Avenue would have clearly signalled that Belfast was a thriving commercial success, home to a variety of flourishing new business premises and visually appealing in its variegation to those perambulating its length, resident or visitor.

Young & Mackenzie designed many other retail premises in and around the central streets of Belfast; however, it was in 1888 – the year Belfast received its Royal Charter as a city – that the firm received its largest and created undoubtedly one of Belfast's most impressive commercial commissions, Robinson & Cleaver's, originally the Royal Irish Linen Warehouse, on a prime site on the corner of Donegall Square North and Donegall Place. It is a six-storey giant of white Scrabo sandstone on the upper floors and imported polished red Scottish granite on the ground floor and the window colonettes. Three ogival copper domes enliven the roof line, which includes the name of Robinson & Cleaver carved into the balustrade. It was building as advertisement and was designed to speak of commercial and industrial success on national and international scales, of Belfast as 'Linenopolis'.

Robinson & Cleaver's, which replaced two three-storey houses, was two storeys higher than Richardson Sons & Owden's and looked down magisterially on the two-storey White Linen Hall in the centre of Donegall Square for the decade before the City Hall was built. The *Irish Builder* remarked that it 'dwarfed' Richardson Sons & Owden's and 'makes the venerable Linen Hall close by look like a mere shed'. It went on to say, 'it is evident that the first idea of Messrs. Young and Mackenzie has been to give all the dignity consistent with strength and utility, there is still to be seen at every hand an amount of refined delicacy of detail that points suggestively to a new era in the annals of the architectural history of Belfast'.[24]

The massive scale – originally 128ft to Donegall Square, 78ft to Donegall Place – also dwarfed its neighbouring buildings in Donegall

Place. It caused considerable practical engineering difficulties in erection, requiring deep piling (500 piles, 40 to 45ft long with heavy timber courses filled in with concrete).[25] The enormity of it must have thrilled the Belfast Corporation. Robinson & Cleaver's, with its tallest ogee dome and circular tower turning corner with confidence, and with impressive flag standards on the roof and plate glass display windows all along street level, set a new tone for the newly declared city and its commercial core.

It is designed in an Italianate style with Mannerist flourishes: here was another, but vaster, hybrid palazzo transplanted to burgeoning Belfast. The loose and eclectic architectural style is, and was described at the time of erection as, quintessentially 'Victorian', making architectural references beyond Ireland, not least in its use of Venetian windows on the first floor. The building also incorporates lavish sculptural decoration (by sculptor Harry Hems) which is consciously internationalized. As well as cherubs and swags of fruit, there are fifty sculpted heads of the firm's patrons and notables, including Queen Victoria, the Prince and Princess of Wales, the Maharajah of Cooch Behar, the Crown Prince and Princess of Germany and George Washington as well as symbolic depictions of Australia, Greenland, India and Canada (modelled on Lady Dufferin) and a Highland chief.

The clients, Edward Robinson and John Cleaver, had founded Robinson & Cleaver's in 1870 selling Irish linen and tweed, and had created such a success of the business that by 1887 one third of all parcels leaving Belfast came from the company.[26] The firm had originally been established in Castle Place, moving to High Street in 1879.[27] Its lavish new headquarters and retail emporium cost £50,000, for which the *Northern Whig* was moved to say, 'and Belfast is greatly indebted to them for having raised in its midst one of the most superb commercial buildings of the century'.[28]

While clearly business premises, newspaper accounts make clear that the building also incorporated distinctly wider civic and public functions within the design. A clock on the corner turret with two six-feet diameter dial faces and Westminster chimes served the time-keeping of the populace below, like that which had been erected at the Royal Chambers. In addition, a unique view from the corner tower 150ft up, and a first floor verandah on Chichester Street, gave an emphasis to the building of one that was *for* the citizens of Belfast. The *Northern Whig* considered that the tower viewing point would be:

> … no doubt largely used by strangers, who disinclined for the long climb of Cave Hill, are still naturally anxious to see Belfast from the most elevated and accessible point … the lift, that has been placed on the premises by the American Elevator Company of Queen Victoria Street, London, will render ready access to this elevated point so that it will be one requiring absolutely no exertion whatever to attain.[29]

Of the verandah, it was noted that, 'A pleasing feature on the Chichester Street side is the recessing of the building above the ground floor. This will afford a delightful promenade in summer time, and is readily gained from any part of the showrooms on the first floor'.[30]

Internally, the eight-floor building must have felt like a modern mirage to citizens. Lit by electric arc and incandescent lights, and with pumps in the basement driving a hydraulic lift; a hive of activity in the strongroom and the receiving, packing and dispatching departments. The ground and first floors formed the main salesrooms, dominated by an impressive focal staircase of white Sicilian marble (which was the work of Messrs. Robinson & Son, statuaries, York Street, Belfast).[31] These floors were 'provided with every convenience, including a ladies' parlour and suitably appointed fitting rooms, one of which can be instantaneously darkened for judging colours by artificial light'.[32] The second floor, reached by a staircase of Australian jarrah wood, housed sample rooms, postal, despatch and shipping departments and offices, while the third floor was occupied by linen and damask looms and jacquard machines. The upper floors were workrooms for shirt- and collar-making, hemming and dressing, with a dining-room and kitchen on the top floor. The enormity of the building project was an evident source of superlative statistical pride:

> The materials used in the construction of the building comprise 400,000 bricks; 30,000 cubic feet of sandstone; 29,000 cubic feet of timber; 360 tons of iron; 6,000 cubic feet of concrete; 4,300 square feet of polished granite; 11,500 square feet of polished plate glass; 25 ½ miles of electric wire; 30,000 square feet of polished teak and mahogany; and about 3,000 square feet of mirrors.[33]

Robinson & Cleaver's was designed to amaze both outside and in, but also apparently to be enjoyed by the public. While it was not wholly given over to being a 'department store' it was made up of several shopping departments: boots and shoes; travelling requisites; fancy stationery; perfumery and toiletries as well as its damask, linen, shirts and hosiery. Through its design it intended to engage with customers, particularly women, in open and inviting ways. Its two retail floors spoke of consumer seduction over and above mere supply in the tradition pioneered in Paris (Boucicauts' Bon Marche, 1852; Le Printemps in 1865) and introduced in London at Bon Marche, Brixton in 1877. The 'refreshment salon' was described as 'a very novel feature ... where ladies and gentlemen can obtain tea, coffee and light refreshments, and for the supply of bread, pastry and cakes required therein, a bakery on the most approved principles has been established on one of the top floors'.[34]

The year after it opened it was expanded again from three to four bay sections by a further bay-wide section in the same style on Donegall Place, Robinson & Cleaver having acquired the premises of neighbouring William Gibson, the jeweller.[35] A large watercolour of Donegall Place and Royal Avenue produced by Marcus Ward & Co., showing the newly enlarged store, was subsequently included in Robinson & Cleaver's exhibition case at the Paris Exhibition in 1889 (see Plate 10). The *Northern Whig* noted that the *Daily Telegraph*, in reporting on the British Section, commented that:

> Ireland will also demonstrate to the world that her industries are not so insignificant as generally supposed, and are well worth the encouragement of those who have the interest of the Empire at heart. To Messrs. Robinson & Cleaver, of Belfast, has been assigned a large space in a prominent position in the Industrial Gallery, fronting one of the main avenues leading to the Belgian Court. Here, under glass, they will show some hundreds of samples of linen...[36]

The inclusion of the watercolour of the building in the show indicates the significant part that building played in the business's as well as the city's advertising: the architecture of Robinson & Cleaver's sent out a confident and exuberant 'message' of Belfast's commercial success and progress.

With the experience of building the giant, internationally marketed Robinson & Cleaver's, Young & Mackenzie was well place to produce designs for another sizeable retail commission in 1895: Anderson &

McAuley's new five-storey, stone-faced department store was completed by 1899. Situated on the corner of Donegall Place and Castle Street, it was adjacent at the rear (at Castle Street and Fountain Street) to another, less showy, five-storey shop and furniture warehouse for David Mitchell (1896), also designed by the firm.

Like Robinson & Cleaver's, Anderson & McAuley's turned a corner, this time with a single large clock face at the top but no tower (one was planned but not executed;[37] a large bell in an open frame was placed behind the clock). The new Anderson & McAuley's in beige sandstone transported from Scotland replaced the company's original modest two-storey stuccoed premises on the same site and was by contrast massive.[38] Anderson & McAuley was in a fortunate position in being able to expand its business and build upwards on its existing site.

Anderson & McAuley's shares several strong similarities with Robinson & Cleaver's, and both were complex builds. The inclusion of a basement for all the services required deep piling, and wells were bored beneath for the building's water supply; the addition of a further, later bay to adjoin the adjacent property was also a complicated process. In the case of Anderson & McAuley's, an addition of a fourth bay to Donegall Place in 1912 connected it immediately with its neighbour, Lindsay Brothers, a classical stucco warehouse of 1879 designed by Robert Watt. In the same way as Robinson & Cleaver's 'trumped' its neighbour, Richardson Sons & Owden's, Anderson & McAuley's raised the roof level up from Lindsay Brothers by a tall extra storey, something that was further emphasized by channelling of the stonework at this level.[39]

The newspaper accounts of the newly unveiled department store were nostalgic about the radical physical transformation of this part of the city and about what had been on the site in preceding generations.[40] The *Northern Whig* also, as with earlier observations made about

Robinson & Cleaver's, commented on the civic contribution that the building made to the city and the streetscape at another major road junction:

> From the main roof an extensive birds-eye view of the entire city can be obtained, and access has been arranged by means of the electric elevator. At the angle of the parapet facing Castle Place a large clock will be erected by Messrs. William Gibson & Co., Limited, encased in a specially designed copper-gilt case, above which will be placed a full-toned bell, weighing 6 cwt. This will form a conspicuous feature from Royal Avenue and High Street.[41]

Externally, the style is eclectic: classical detailing, with repetitive tall, thin, round-headed windows, and the impression of the building is grand, enlivened by architectural sculpture by Thompson of the firm of Winter & Thompson,[42] particularly on the first-floor frieze, and further enlivened in the shallow canting of the four bays to Donegall Place, relieving the flatness of the façade – a new introduction to Donegall Place by the architects. While less flamboyant than Robinson & Cleaver's, it is a building of visual variety: full-height pilasters are treated differently on each floor; there are twenty-nine portrait heads and some mythological ones as first floor keystones; arabesques over the first-floor and on the parapet; miniature pediments over heavy keystones and panels of roses below the cornice. The name of the firm is also – as at Robinson & Cleaver's – incorporated into the stone parapet plinth, here within a panel.

The style and sculptural detail of the exterior of both Young & Mackenzie's major shop buildings in Belfast resonate with Briggs' description of the Victorians' predilection for 'imposing buildings':

> The [Victorians] liked a diversity or a blending of styles … they took immense pains to educate people in taste or to use one of their favourite verbs, to 'elevate' taste. They liked 'imposing' buildings with 'pretensions'. They loved symbolism. They were seldom afraid of exuberance. Individuality and status-seeking were both expressed in their villas: their banks and shops became more and more ornate and decorated as the century went by.[43]

Internally, the store shared another feature that had enjoyed praise at Robinson & Cleaver's: a grand staircase from the ground to first floor in Sicilian marble, sculpted by Purdy & Millard, with large newels on which were Cupids holding electric lamps. Marble featured substantially in the interior decoration, including a large mirror with a carved female head on the first landing.

The *Northern Whig* noted that 'ample provision for abundant light and air … has been made the special feature of the internal treatment of the shop'.[44] The building was more completely a department store than Robinson & Cleaver's, with the accommodation comprising the various retail departments, such as millinery on the second floor, and offices elsewhere; like Robinson & Cleaver's the upper floor had a dining room and kitchens. The internal layout lent itself well to the serving of customers. Much was made in the newspaper accounts of the store about the modernity of the fittings: the lift, the electric lights, the prismatic lights to the basement, the steel structure for the large ground-floor windows, for example; all at a high cost, which was evidently a point of pride. If the stylistic references were drawing from the past, the function of the building and the commodious nature of the fit-out were nonetheless assertively of the present and looking to the future.

Young & Mackenzie's warehouses in Queen Street and College Street for Swanston & Bones in 1890, while not extraordinary in themselves, are also illustrative of the radical changes taking place in central Belfast during this period. They drew press attention, which indicated the extent to which citizens felt that the architectural changes to the city were both exciting and alarming in their scale, the *Northern Whig* stating:

> Perhaps one of the most gratifying duties of the Press is that of recording progress … and when to the record of progress is added the improvement and ornamentation of our streets the pleasure of the duty is greatly enhanced. Such is the feeling created when viewing the handsome block of warehouses now approaching completion in Queen Street. To some minds, however, this steady advance in our street architecture may have its sad side. Old landmarks are rapidly disappearing … the scene so altered, its quiet and suburban character changed to the noise and bustle of business … Some of our most active citizens, still in the thick of battle, have lived in the substantial three-story houses which were removed to make room for the buildings we at present notice. But it is, perhaps, the departed cottage and garden which occupied the corner of College and Queen Streets that will be best remembered … The new buildings which have sprung upon the site form a pleasing and striking feature, with an imposing frontage of 150 feet to Queen Street and 80 feet to College Street, and form five distinct warehouses…[45]

The building was by now quite typical of Young & Mackenzie design for central Belfast,[46] the firm having designed a large number of warehouse and factory buildings such as the Grattan & Co. Aerated Water Manufactory in Great Victoria Street (1883); Murray & Sons Tobacco Factory on Callender Street (1888) and Murphy & Stevenson's redbrick warehouse on Ormeau Avenue and Linenhall Street (1890). Swanston & Bones is four storeys high, of predominantly red brick but enlivened through the use of brick pilasters; a facing of Ashley glebe quarry stone on the entire ground level; sandstone dressings around the numerous windows (rhythmically positioned in pairs); moulded brick string courses and a marked cornice and parapet with a small triangular pediment marking a gateway opening at ground level. William Swanston developed the whole site, but gave his own business, Swanston & Bones, a firm of linen collar- and cuff-makers, occupation of the most prominent corner site. The entrance at the corner is finely handled, with a richly sculpted circular headed doorway surrounded by polished granite colonettes with foliate capitals. A semi-circular tower on the corner, topped with a circular turret with a steeply pitched conical roof rising to a height of 75 feet was, as the *Belfast News Letter* reported, originally covered in green slates and surmounted with a weather vane; these have since gone.[47]

The sculptural detail of the doorway is notable for both its quality and its subtle wit (unfortunately records do not reveal the sculptor's identity). The head on the keystone depicts Sir Arthur Chichester, a central figure to the history of Belfast's development, wearing a deep ruffle of the seventeenth century, which neatly alludes to the collar- and cuff-making purpose of the business. Amidst sculpted foliage, including national emblems of a rose, shamrock, thistle and oak, there are also carved shields bearing the coats of arms of Belfast and Ulster. Citizens who took notice of these things would presumably have read such visual referencing, if even only subconsciously, as consolidation of the idea that Belfast was a place with a history and with a strong identity and proud industrial place within Ireland and Britain.

Warehouses in Belfast continued to occupy the firm during the 1890s (although many have since been demolished). A warehouse for Messrs. Watson & Valentine & Co. in Amelia Street of 1893[48] leaves behind a remnant of its existence with a sandstone doorcase with keystone of a female head wearing a cap. A plain but notably wide five-storey, red-brick warehouse block was designed for McBride & Williams in 1891[49] adjoining the Murphy & Stevenson warehouse on Ormeau Avenue designed by the firm the previous year (both still extant and in use). It is not in itself a landmark building but it has a definite presence on the street. Such warehouses were, like the shops in Royal Avenue, radically changing the cityscape.

A further example of this big, dominant warehouse look can be found in Young & Mackenzie's Fulton's Warehouse on Howard Street and Great Victoria Street of 1901, a five-storey building on the grounds of the old House of Correction, which combined retail accommodation for six shops at ground-floor level with extensive warehouse space above.[50] Built of red brick with Aspatria sandstone dressings and pilasters of red polished granite from Finland, it extends 120ft to Howard Street and 100ft to Great Victoria Street. While relatively conservative architecturally, its scale and mix of materials gives it street presence too.

In 1902, a six-storey, fourteen-bay, red-brick warehouse on a rusticated sandstone base was designed for the linen and handkerchief manufacturers Murphy & Stevenson (with whom the firm had built a solid working relationship elsewhere), on Linenhall Street.[51] It is a robust building with a bold doorway and with turrets, a scalloped roof line and an interesting doorway flanked by rusticated pilasters carrying a bold cornice. Above this is a pierced parapet with blockings, terminated in obelisks. A female head indicative of the linen industry forms the keystone, contrasting with two boldly modelled lions' heads at the level of the caps of the pilasters. Once again, the architects were integrating both stone and decorative detailing with reference to industry, layered with mythology.

LANDMARKS OF THE TURN OF THE CENTURY

By the turn of the twentieth century, the image of Belfast had, then, been radically altered. It was now an urban environment with a large-scale city centre. However, from the late 1890s to the first years of the 1900s, there were several architectural commissions that cemented the city's 'big city look': Belfast City Hall; the Scottish Provident Insurance Buildings; Bank Buildings (by W.H. Lynn); the Ocean Accident Guarantee Corporation Buildings; the former Municipal Technical Institute (by Samuel Stevenson – who had trained under and worked at Young & Mackenzie); the Presbyterian Assembly Buildings; St Anne's Church of Ireland Cathedral (by Thomas Drew, initially, 1898–1904) and the Scottish Temperance Buildings (by Henry Seaver – who had also trained and worked at Young & Mackenzie). The Scottish Provident Buildings, Ocean Buildings and Presbyterian Assembly Buildings were all designed by Young & Mackenzie. The firm chose to treat these big commissions in contrasting architectural styles, demonstrating a catholicity of architectural tastes and proving that building on a large scale was a speciality. Brett commented, no doubt with some of these buildings specifically in mind, that 'no city can have a formal centre more variegated than Belfast'.[52]

Scottish Provident in Baroque style on Donegall Square West and Wellington Place of 1899–1902 was a huge project, built in two distinct stages. The first, which housed Scottish Provident's own insurance business, turned the corner and abutted a turreted Y.M.C.A. on Wellington Place of 1895 (a big scheme of 1896 also by Young & Mackenzie, now demolished). The second, which was built as rentable office and shop space, expanded along over half of the west side of the

Square, with an octagonal turret and fishscale copper cupola at the far end to match the one at the Wellington Place corner, and a gently bowed central section with a strong pedimented attic storey above. The whole edifice, which provides an exceptional civic presence, is faced in a cream-coloured Giffnock sandstone, with rusticated granite pilasters between the shop fronts, rustication on the first floor, and ten giant order semi-fluted attached Corinthian columns on plinths supporting a dentilled cornice and balustraded parapet, with a central pediment originally topped with a statue (since removed).

Architectural sculpture in stone and copper abounds, carried out by Purdy & Millard. Carved keystones depicting trading continents and countries were laden with the symbolism of Empire. There were also cupid-like sculptures atop the cupolas, which have not survived *in situ*. The building was to be a favoured location for many architectural practices in the twentieth century, including Young & Mackenzie itself, whose offices on the top attic floor afforded superb views across the Square to the City Hall and their own edifices of Robinson & Cleaver's and the Ocean Buildings.[53]

Ocean Buildings at the corner of Donegall Square East and Chichester Street (1899–1902) is, by marked contrast, a fantastical, spikey Perpendicular Gothic five-storey building in red Ballochmoyle sandstone, rearing up on an iron frame through five storeys, with an attic storey and a prominent corner tower. In its corner site, choice of distinctive coloured material, size and its wealth of sculptural adornment (by James Edgar Winter), it is also of special significance to the cityscape. It even bears some comparison with historicist American skyscrapers with Late Gothic detailing at roof level (predating the rather similar, famous Woolworth Building of 1913 by C. Gilbert in New York City), although, while big for Belfast, the Ocean Buildings could not, of course, be considered a 'skyscraper' in the American sense. The *Irish*

Builder noted, however, that the Ocean Buildings were at the time 'the highest [buildings] in Belfast'.[54] In addition to the appropriate aquatic sculptural references of mermaids and lighthouses (the Corporation's trademark) at the main doorway, an oriel window above is held up, as it were, by carved heads of Edward VII, Queen Victoria and Queen Alexandra, adding the embodiment of empire to the building's symbolism – as elsewhere.

As has been alluded to already, Young & Mackenzie was a firm with strong Presbyterian connections, something that undoubtedly played a major part in its success as a thriving business. It received numerous commissions from Presbyterian congregations and institutions (such as Belfast [Royal] Academy already described) and via Presbyterian patrons. Among its Belfast churches were big ones such as Fitzroy Presbyterian at University Road (1874), Townsend Street (1878), Windsor, Lisburn Road (1887) and Malone at Balmoral Avenue (1899); institutional work with a strong flavour of Presbyterian connections at work included the design of the Belfast Ladies' Collegiate School at Lower Crescent (1874) established by Mrs Byers (later Victoria College, now the Crescent Arts Centre). However, the commission that marked the apex of the firm's connection with Presbyterianism was that of the denomination's new Assembly Buildings at Fisherwick Place and Howard Street, begun in 1901 and completed in 1905. In what can only be described as highly dubious circumstances, the firm was awarded the job for the design of these after an abortive competition of 1899. (Robert Young established the terms of the competition with a set budget of £30,000, which was wholly inadequate to create the accommodation and building of architectural presence required. In the end, the winning competition entry – by a young Rupert Savage of London – was set aside and the Church appointed Young & Mackenzie to design the buildings. The firm then went on to prove that cost limit of £30,000 was impossible by spending over £70,000 on the building).

For all of that, the Assembly Buildings form one of the principal buildings of Edwardian Belfast – while somewhat dated in appearance for 1906, and of mixed success architecturally, it is a striking ensemble. It is unlikely that the motivation to embark upon the project was not also partially influenced by the contemporaneous building of St Anne's Cathedral in Donegall Street. Presbyterians may well have wanted to assert in their headquarters that the city belonged as much, if not more, to them. Presbyterians had no need for a cathedral, of course; rather, the function of the complex was (and is) to provide an administrative headquarters for the Church together with spacious accommodation for meetings of the General Assembly. The requirement for such a large building in central Belfast reflected the supremacy of Presbyterians as the largest single religious group in Belfast and Counties Antrim and Down, and their position of economic and social dominance.[55]

The site was central, and situated conveniently close to Great Victoria Street railway station (opened in 1846) for out-of-town Assembly delegates.[56] The significance of the physical location and appearance of the new Assembly Buildings was not underplayed by contemporary promoters of the project, who wrote in 1905:

> On the site of the old historic church of Fisherwick Place – right in the line of advance westward, which the centre of Belfast is making – stands a building which not only fulfils every requirement for which it is intended, but adds very much to the beauty and architecture of the city.[57]

The accommodation was impressive, comprising a reading room and news room on the ground floor, as well as six lettable offices, with the second and third storeys mainly devoted to rooms for use by the Young

Men's Association such as reading rooms, classrooms for 'moral and intellectual improvement', a large gymnasium and (quaintly) 'other facilities for innocent amusement'.[58] A minor hall, accessible from Howard Street, accommodated 500 people and was available for let to the public as well as for prayer and missionary meetings. On Fisherwick Place, a boardroom and offices for the various societies and associations of the Church were accommodated.

The main entrance on Fisherwick Place led to a central hall useful as an inner lobby for house divisions and intervals during Assembly business. Off this, doors led to the main D-shaped, two-tiered assembly hall, a fine space as originally conceived arranged around a platform with galleries suspended behind a running arcade of Tudor arches on thin octagonal stone columns. In all there was seating for 2,300 people. In an internal reconfiguration of the building in 1990 the hall was reduced by a storey, thereby reducing some of its architectural impact.

The building was built of uncoursed Scrabo sandstone and is in predominantly Late Gothic style, with a liveliness to its roof line. The most prominent feature is its 170ft corner tower topped by a copper crown-spire (manufactured by Ewart & Son of London). There can be little doubt that the crown-spire was a deliberate attempt to create an easily understood identifier of the connection between Scotland and Ulster Presbyterians – the crown-spire most commonly associated with Scotland and, most famously, the High Kirk of St Giles in Edinburgh. Further overtly Scottish visual referencing on the building's exterior is found in the Scottish Baronial tourelles which frame the formal centrepiece of the Howard Street elevation.

The 'Scottishness' of the Assembly Buildings could also be considered to form a deliberate counterpoint to the perceived 'Englishness' of the City Hall, which has been described as 'a quintessential example of the cult of Wren, asserting Englishness in Northern Ireland',[59] and described as the 'Wrenaissance's … apogee … the grandest municipal building in the British Isles' by Curl.[60] If English influences were being utilized to consolidate visual and symbolic links with the Union politically at the City Hall, then specifically Scottish links were visually asserted at the Presbyterian Assembly Buildings to the west.

The physical form and visual appearance of the Assembly Buildings also performed a quasi-civic function in the Belfast streetscape beyond its religious and administrative purposes. The Assembly Buildings had a declared 'public' dimension in that much of the ground floor was intended for rented offices and warehouses – the plainer block adjacent to the minor hall on Howard Street and Upper Queen Street – and, as described, the minor hall was to be available for public meetings from the outset. The complex, rather than appearing to be a free-standing structure, forms a streetscape in and of itself and links visually with its neighbouring buildings on both Howard Street and Fisherwick Place. Rather than being set back from the thoroughfares in the way most churches would be, even by a little, it hugs the street pattern; in this it also utilizes the maximum site space available. The placing of the distinctive tower on the corner was a dominant architectural statement both at street level and on the city's 1905 skyline. The tower would have been visually read in relation to the neighbouring Grand Opera House on Great Victoria Street (Frank Matcham, 1894–5) with its lively onion-shaped ventilator domes, and the contemporaneous Municipal Technical Institute at College Square East (Samuel Stevenson, 1900–07), a big Baroque Revival building with corner cupolas; as well as the dome and cupolas of City Hall and those at the Scottish Provident and Robinson & Cleaver buildings. The Assembly Buildings provide a lively roof line on both streets, with castellated parapets, pitched gables, corbelled tourelles with candle-snuffer roofs, crocketted spires and finials, and, similarly on both streets, a varied rhythm across the façades. In this contribution to the streetscape the building functions in a similar way to other examples of monumental British Victorian 'civic Gothic' architecture, bearing some comparison to – in form if not style – Manchester Town Hall (Alfred Waterhouse, 1868–76) and even – albeit on a smaller scale – St Pancras Station (Sir George Gilbert Scott, 1868–74) or the Royal Courts of Justice (G.E. Street, 1874–82) in London.

CONCLUSION

Young & Mackenzie's lively and sizeable buildings of the period 1870–1910, along with those designed by other, mostly Belfast-based, architects, provide evidence in themselves that the city's patrons, from industrialists and retailers to the educational and religious institutions, were intent on creating an urban environment that was big, that advertised the patron's credentials and that impacted directly upon people within the city. Often this was an inviting experience, allowing people to explore new places and sometimes their wider contexts, as well as to do business or worship or learn in them. Sometimes it was to enjoy their external decoration and the variety of the appearance of new streetscapes. Even more clearly, the impact upon citizens was felt in the provision of a lasting impression that the city itself was ambitious, self-assured and now a place of some wealth.

As Young & Mackenzie's work typifies, the city was also capable of producing the designers and civil engineers it needed to make the metropolitan experience a reality – these were powerhouses of provincial architecture. Robert Young, Young & Mackenzie's founding principal (who was uniquely honoured as an architect by being made an Irish privy councillor in 1906), may very well have felt like master of much of what he surveyed from the top floor of the firm's offices in the Scottish Provident Buildings at the end of the first decade of the twentieth century. The mortification he had felt in the 1840s concerning Belfast's 'mean' appearance had been largely remedied by the creation of a big vision city, very significantly by his own practice.

4

Reading Shakespeare at 22 University Square

Pamela Emerson

Book clubs, literary societies and lending libraries have been in operation in Belfast since at least 1788. The Belfast Reading Society, more familiar to us as the Linen Hall Library, is soon to celebrate the 225th anniversary of its foundation. But other reading societies and book clubs familiar to the citizens of nineteenth-century Belfast have long since vanished and their existence has gone largely unrecorded. Ronnie Adams, long regarded as the seminal researcher on reading and popular culture, has claimed that 'Reading Societies were rare in the latter part of the century'.[1] His research suggests that the informal clubs and small businesses that lent books were adversely affected by the introduction of the Public Library system that gave free access to books thus negating the need for small-scale private enterprises. Yet surviving records suggest that there were over fifty nineteenth-century examples of such clubs in Belfast. From reading the local newspapers, the residents of the town would have been familiar with Aitcheson's Select Library, Belfast Athenaeum, the Coal Exchange News Room, the Gas Office

Private Subscription Library, the Commercial News Room, the United Church of England and Ireland Young Men's Society Reading Rooms, St Thomas' Literary Society on the Lisburn Road, Balmoral Reading Society and numerous circulating libraries run by the booksellers of the town. Belfast Reading Club, or as it was informally referred to in rule one of the minute book, 'Our Reading Club', appears to have been formed in 1889.[2] This particular late nineteenth-century book club has not been investigated nor has it been mentioned in previous research on book clubs in Ulster. This chapter on Belfast Reading Club hopes to redress the balance in order that this club will, for the first time, receive recognition as a fascinating part of the history of Belfast.

This chapter makes use of the extant minute book of the Belfast Reading Club, which is currently in the archives of the Public Record Office of Northern Ireland.[3] No other records relating to this club have been found in other archives so the minute book is a unique record of this book club. The first page of the minute book, a hardback notebook, records the eleven rules and regulations of the organization. The subsequent pages contain information about the date and location of the meeting, the members and visitors present, the texts read and occasionally other information relating to future meetings or the election of new members. The records in this handwritten document begin with the formation of the club in 1889 and continue through to 5 February 1901 when the minutes stop without any explanation or conclusion. This chapter explores each of the rules in turn and links these to the people and activities of the club. A prosopographic approach has been adopted to reveal the social context and networks as well as learn more about those who were attracted to reading, book clubs and related activities. Other information contained in the minutes, such as the texts read and the attendance patterns, is analysed in order to understand what type of literature the group was interested in reading and whether the members showed commitment to this chosen leisure activity.

Many of the names involved in the Belfast Reading Club will be familiar to anyone interested in the history of nineteenth-century Belfast as the members were part of the professional, social, political and religious fabric of the developing city. Extensive use has been made of contemporary street directories, newspaper articles and the 1901 and 1911 census information to discover more about the people involved, where they lived, their occupations, interests and backgrounds, how the members were related or how they knew each other and how the club's membership changed over the thirteen years it was in existence. The reason for the title 'Reading Shakespeare at 22 University Square' will become apparent as the chapter progresses.

RULES ONE AND TWO

While the first rule simply reported the name of the organization, the second rule concerned the entry procedures of the Belfast Reading Club:

> The club shall consist of 12 original members, and shall not be extended, except in the event of the death or resignation of a member; when a new member may be proposed & seconded by two members and balloted for. One black bean to exclude.

In order to join the Belfast Reading Club a prospective member had to be proposed and seconded by current members. This follows the pattern of many clubs during the nineteenth century and enabled the organizers to keep numbers manageable and the membership select. Any prospective member had to be approved and be of good standing in order to be accepted. This in itself was not unusual as most book clubs had formal rules and regulations regarding the membership requirements, the conduct of members and the organizational procedures.

The membership of twelve was maintained throughout the existence of the reading club, although there were many changes in the personalities involved. Analysis of the minute book shows that there were thirty-three members between 1889 and 1901, of which fourteen were male and nineteen female. Only four of the original members remained as members for the full twelve years recorded. Although 134 meetings were held during this time some of the minutes in 1889, 1890 and 1893 do not list the attendees so the following statistics are based on the 111 records when the names are given. The most dedicated members were Miss A. Ferguson who attended ninety-six of these meetings, her sister Miss Mary Ferguson who attended ninety and their brother Mr Godfrey Ferguson, architect of the Northern Bank, who attended ninety-three.[4] The fourth long-term member was Mr John Bristow, a solicitor, who attended seventy-seven meetings. When he joined the Belfast Reading Club he would have been 23 years old.[5] Other members had varied attendance patterns, ranging from Miss Bristow, probably a daughter of Canon Bristow, who only attended on one occasion during her one year of membership to fifty attendances by Miss B.H. Lanyon over ten years of membership.

Mention was made about some nominations and resignations, although the majority of the members appeared and disappeared without any introduction or farewell being recorded. Based on their attendance status in the minutes the average attendance was twenty-nine meetings, and most of the members joined for less than five years so there was not a long term commitment. For example, Mr Cooper, Miss Cuming and Miss Davidson were only members from 1890 to 1891, while Mr and Mrs Adam Duffin and Miss Gibson were all members for five consecutive years. Only ten members had membership lasting between six and eleven years. Two of the original members do not appear as having attended any meetings. Mr Pooler was listed as an original member but he must have resigned prior to the names being recorded at the nineteenth meeting of the club on 3 March 1890. Mrs Parker was also included as an original member and again she is not mentioned in the proceedings as a member, but a Mrs Parker was listed as a guest on two occasions in 1891. Mr R. Parker LLD was a guest on 3 February 1891 and was presumably her husband. He was probably Henry R. Parker LLD, headmaster of Methodist College.[6]

RULE THREE

Rule three stated the specific purpose of the club and defined its objective: 'The object of the Club shall be to read in parts the writings of British authors'. The minutes show that of the 134 meetings held, fifty-four were based on the works of William Shakespeare. At another two meetings they considered the parts of Shakespeare's heroines and the female characters and on another evening they read some of his sonnets. The members read twenty-one out of the thirty-eight plays that Shakespeare wrote. Of the titles read, nine were comedies, six were historical and another six were tragedies.[7] Many of titles were read more than once and others were only read in part. *The Merchant of Venice* featured on five occasions, while *A Midsummer Night's Dream* and *Henry V* were each recorded four times. As well as the more popular Shakespearean works they also read *Cymbeline* and *Coriolanus*. It appears that they enjoyed reading the comedies best as they featured on twenty-two occasions, with tragedies read at eighteen meetings and historically themed plays on fourteen occasions.

Seventy-seven evenings were devoted to the readings of works by other authors, Goldsmith and Sheridan being the most popular. Sheridan's *The Rivals* was read on five occasions and Goldsmith's

She Stoops to Conquer on three evenings. Other titles read included Goldsmith's *Good Natured Man*; Sheridan's *The Critic*, *The Duenna* and *School for Scandal*; Longfellow's *Evangeline*; Bulwer Lytton's *The Lady of Lyon*; Knowles' *The Hunchback* and *The Love Chase*; Scott's *The Bride of Lammermoor* and Carlyle's *Past and Present* and *The French Revolution.* Again there was a preference for comedy and historical topics.

The group also favoured poetry as the records show fifteen nights devoted to genres of poetry such as 'The Lake Poets' and 'Living Poets' or they considered the works of poets such as Tennyson, Milton, Byron and Browning. On one occasion, however, Monday 18 March 1895, they deviated from their rule of British authors. On this evening the subject was 'American Authors; Prose and Verse'. The rules seem to have been relaxed on some occasions, further strengthening the idea that this was as much a social gathering as anything else. It is interesting to note that this particular reading club concentrated on British authors at a time when other groups in the city were engaged with the promotion of the Irish Literary Revival and nationalism in Belfast. Alice Milligan, for example, was involved in the foundation of the Henry Joy McCracken Literary Society and in the *Shan Van Vocht*, a newspaper established with Anna Johnston that promoted the setting up of home reading circles and recommended suitable Irish reading materials.[8] The choice of British authors was possibly a counter-reaction to nationalist cultural activity and an indication of the political allegiances of this particular group of middle-class Belfast men and women.

RULE FOUR

In common with other literary societies, regular meetings were held. Rule four outlined the arrangements for the meetings of Belfast Reading Club:

> The Club shall meet at the house of a member on every alternate Monday at 8 o'clock in the months of Jan, Feb, March, April, May, Oct, Nov, Dec unless it be agreed by a majority of members at a meeting to alter the date of subsequent meeting.

According to this rule the club was expected to meet on at least sixteen Monday evenings during the year. The minutes show that this rule was not strictly adhered to. In 1889 and 1891 there were fifteen meetings recorded, almost meeting the prescribed sixteen set down in the rule. In 1892 and 1894 the club met on twelve occasions but by 1897 there were only seven meetings held. The average number of annual meetings over the twelve-year period was ten, suggesting that members were perhaps not as enthusiastic as had originally been anticipated.

This point was raised in a discussion of the rules on 14 October 1895 when it was recorded that 'members should consider every alternate Monday an engagement'. After eight years and numerous changes in the membership, interest seems to have diminished even further. In the years 1897–99 the number of meetings dropped to under ten per year. The decline was recognized by the club, who held a meeting on 23 October 1899 in which they made changes to the format of the meetings. The changes in the names show that various members left and as they no longer appeared in later street directories it has to be assumed that they had moved away from the area.

RULE FIVE

According to rule five the host was to have absolute control over the meeting:

> The member in whose house the meeting is being held shall be the president of the said meeting, and shall have entire management of the selection of subject, arranging of parts, and making necessary cuts.

The Belfast Reading Club operated with a variable office bearer, the president, who had sole control of the individual meetings. The president changed for each meeting, members taking it in turns to host and chair the meetings. This democratic process was not typical of other book clubs, many of which operated with the input of a secretary and a treasurer as well as a committee who were appointed for a yearly term of office. Dunmurry Reading Society, for example, was run by a president, treasurer, secretary, librarian and committee of seven who were elected annually on the first Saturday of January, while Tandragee Reading Society had a president, secretary, librarian and a committee, again chosen at the first meeting of the year.[9] The rotation of presidential role was not unique to this club. The Belfast Medical Society operated the system whereby the fifth member entering the room acted as chairman for the meeting.[10]

Rotating the role of the president in Belfast Reading Club meant that the female members also had the privilege of hosting the proceedings. Within the Belfast Reading Club the president was responsible for the keeping of minutes, something that is evidenced by the changes in the handwriting styles, the different layouts and the type and amount of information included in the records of proceedings. The host also had to have sufficient ability to condense the reading material, a skill factor that has not been noted in connection with any other Ulster reading clubs. The role of treasurer was perhaps unnecessary in this club as there was no mention of membership subscriptions or joining fees in the minute book. It also has to be assumed that the members acquired their own copies of the books as there was no mention of book purchasing or loans of books.

It is interesting to analyse the meeting locations recorded in the minute book to see if they adhered to rule number five. Over the twelve years under examination the meetings were held at twenty-seven different locations. On seventeen occasions between 1889 and 1898 Mr and Mrs H.O. Lanyon hosted the meetings at 3 Castleton Terrace, Antrim Road. Their niece, Miss B. Lanyon of Lisbreen, Fortwilliam Park, hosted the meetings on sixteen occasions between 1891 and 1900. While these members hosted the meetings over a period of time, other locations were only used for a short period. For example, 8 Murray's Terrace, home of the Misses Ferguson and their brother Mr G. Ferguson, was used as the meeting place on three occasions in 1889, once in 1890, three times in 1891, twice in 1892 and once in 1893. The meetings were never held there again although all the Fergusons continued to be members until the close of the minute book in 1901. It is possible that during this intervening period the family moved to another address. Miss Gibson and Miss Blackley provided the meeting place at Laurine, Antrim Road on ten occasions between 1890 and 1895. Cluan in Donegall Park was the location for twelve meetings between 1894 and 1900. Eight locations were only used on one occasion. The only year where each meeting was held at a different venue every time was in 1897. It is evident, then, that the role of host, and therefore president, was not evenly distributed with each member getting equal representation, nor did the meeting location and the presidency run hand in hand as proposed in rule five.

The role of president and the organizational format was changed slightly on 23 October 1899 when the members agreed that an author was to be assigned for two meetings and the same person would host both nights. Therefore, the president and the location were to be duplicated rather than rotated each time and fewer people were involved. The minutes record that:

> The following members were appointed as presidents. Miss Clark for evenings to be devoted to Carlyle, Miss Lanyon for those to be devoted to Shakespeare, Mr. Brett for those to be devoted to Tennyson and Mr. Ferguson for those to be devoted to Ruskin.

However, the minutes show that this schedule does not seem to have been followed precisely over the course of the year. While the role of president was specified in advance it is interesting to note that the in the minutes of 11 December 1899 Miss Clark, who had been allocated president and host for the evening, was not recorded in the list of those present, although this may have been an oversight in her recording of the meeting. Miss Lanyon, Mr Ferguson and Revd Brett were all present on the dates they were assigned to act as president. However, the locations of the meetings do not correlate to addresses of these members. The Carlyle meetings were held at three different locations. The first was held at Miss Clark's, home at 13 Kinnaird Terrace,[11] but the subsequent meetings were either at Cave Cottage and at the home of Mr and Mrs Lloyd Campbell at Kenallen.[12] It has been established from newspaper reports that Cave Cottage was the address of Mr and Mrs John Bristow.[13] Miss B. Lanyon hosted both of her evenings at her own home, Lisbreen. While it is known that Mr Ferguson lived at 8 Murray's Terrace in 1891, the meetings he hosted were held at Cluan. The address given in the November 1896 minutes for Revd Brett was 1 Brookhill Avenue, yet the meetings he hosted were held at Hopefield and Cave Cottage. Hopefield was the residence of the Right Honourable Thomas Sinclair, later Deputy Lieutenant and a Privy Counsellor, a visitor to the reading club.[14] It appears that the meeting locations were therefore not linked to the presidential role; some members, such as Mrs John Bristow of Cave Cottage, enjoyed having the members round to their house. Sited on the Cavehill Road, this house was described as a 'superior house, containing three reception, five bedrooms, cloakroom, lavatory, bath ... plate glass windows. The grounds are neatly planted with shrubs'.[15]

Considering the geographical locations of the homes of the members hosting the meetings, it appears that many were located in North Belfast, the locus of the membership being around the Antrim Road. The following addresses were all in this vicinity: 3 Castleton Terrace, 8 Chichester Terrace, Hopefield, Joy House, Kenallen, Laurine and St James's Parsonage. Kenallen, home of Mr and Mrs Lloyd Campbell, was next to Ardrigh, the residence of Francis Joseph Bigger, a solicitor, editor of the Ulster Journal of Archaeology and a central figure in the Irish Cultural Revival and the Belfast Gaelic League.[16] Two houses, side by side, in one the visitors read books by British authors and in the other the visitors were interested in the Irish language, culture and history. Such were the diverse cultural interests of the protestants of Belfast. Other Belfast Reading Club members also lived in North Belfast at Donegall Park, Ben Eden Park, Fortwilliam Park, Hughenden Terrace off the Cavehill Road and numbers 1, 8 and 15 Brookhill Avenue. Another cluster of members resided in or near Queen's College in south Belfast. One member, Professor Purser, lived at Queen's College while other members lived nearby at 22 University Square and 37 Botanic Avenue.

Thus, to attend the meetings an element of travelling was required by some of the members on each occasion. It also suggests that other links, such as work or church, connected the members as they were not all from the same locality. This is reinforced when we try to construct the network of connections between the various members and visitors. In 1886 a fundraising stall was organised by members of St James's Parish Church. The list of helpers included Mrs Bristow, Miss Alice Bristow, Miss Hamilton and Mr John Bristow.[17] Thirteen years later on 15 December 1899 an evening of music and literature based entertainment was held at St James's Parish Church. Attendees were asked to wear fancy dress 'to represent characters from Shakespeare, Dickens, Scott or nursery rhymes'. The entertainment included a song 'My Love is an Arbutus' by Miss A. Bristow, a recitation 'By Special Desire' by Miss Lanyon and another recitation was given by the Revd C.W. Frizzell. The refreshments for the evening were 'under the management of Mrs John Lanyon'.[18]

It can, therefore, be assumed that these members knew each other from their church-based activities at St James's Parish Church. It also demonstrates members' interests and skills. St Anne's Parish Church, later cathedral, was where Mrs Thomas Andrews and Robert Garrett Campbell worshipped.[19] As Mr Campbell was 'a prominent linen manufacturer' in the family firm of Messrs. Henry Campbell and Company, he would have possibly known H.O. Lanyon, who was a flax merchant at John Olden and Company and was appointed as a director of York Street Flax Spinning Company in 1889, retiring from this post in 1895.[20]

Another way in which the members may have known each other was via educational connections. Queen's College was the workplace of Professor John Mallett Purser, who specialized in histopathology, Professor Fitzgerald was in the Engineering Department and Miss Cuming was the daughter of James Cuming, Professor of Medicine at Queen's College.[21] The Misses Knox: Mary and Kathleen, who resided at 11 Hughenden Avenue, were both teachers.[22] Social engagements also highlight the society in which the various members moved. On 21

October 1897 twenty-nine members of Belfast Reading Club attended the wedding of Miss Richardson of Lissue at Hillsborough Presbyterian Church. The bride was the eldest daughter of Theodore Richardson J.P. of Lisburn who was connected to Richardson Brothers and Company, flax and linen merchants.[23] The following Belfast Reading Club members were on the guest list: Mr and Mrs John Bristow, Canon and Mrs Bristow and the Misses Bristow, who gave silver photo frames as a wedding gift, Mrs and Miss Blackley and Mr F. Blackley, Mr Godfrey Ferguson and his sisters the Misses Ferguson, the Misses Kinahan and their brother Mr John Kinahan who gave a silver-mounted powder box, Mr and Mrs H.O. Lanyon and their son Mr C. Lanyon, Mr F. Platt-Higgins, the Misses Redfern, Mrs Sinclair and her children Mr T.C. Sinclair and the Misses Sinclair and also Mr Charles Slacke.[24] It can be presumed that at the club meeting on 27 November 1897 this event would have been one of the topics of conversation. Visitors and prospective new members were introduced to the group via invitation of the host so these and other avenues of contact might have been used. This social network will be explored further when the members and their occupations and interests are explored later in the chapter.

RULES SIX AND SEVEN

In some book clubs non-attendance at meetings would incur a fine. At Ballygan Book Club non-attendees were liable to a fine of three pence, which was doubled on each succeeding offence.[25] Harsher still, those who belonged to Trinaltinagh Reading Society faced a fine of 1s. for two absences and 'for 3 nights 2s. 6d. and the fourth night be expelled from the society'.[26] However, this was not the case at Belfast Reading Club as how the meetings were organized was determined under rule six:

> The parts shall be assigned to the members at least one week previous to evening of the meeting, and any member shall then give immediate notice to the President if he or she cannot attend.

The minutes do not always record the parts played or read by the members each evening. There are only fourteen meetings when this information was recorded. The notes relating to the meeting on 23 November 1896 were particularly detailed. The parts allocated to each member for the reading of Shakespeare's *Merchant of Venice* were noted.

> Cluan
> Members present
> Mrs. Lloyd Campbell – Nerissa
> Mr. L. Campbell – Lorenzo & Antonio
> Miss Clark – Portia
> Miss Ferguson – Salarino
> Miss M. Ferguson – Prince of Arragon
> Rev. A.G. Stuart – Bassanio
> Rev. H.R. Brett – Shylock
> Mr. G.W. Ferguson – Gratiano, Old Gobbo
> Guests
> Mrs. Hastings - Duke
> Mrs. Lanyon
> Miss Lanyon – L Gobbo
> Miss Hastings – Prince of Morocco
> Miss McFerran – Jessica
> Subject - Merchant of Venice.[27]

We are left to imagine how the meeting progressed, presumably with the members sitting in a circle and reading out their parts, using different emphasis or intonation appropriate to the activities of their character. It is also possible that the activity of play reading was the middle-class version of amateur theatre and they may have acted out their parts. They were, perhaps, inspired by the theatrical pursuits of the upper class. Rule seven describes how the evening should have progressed:

> At the close of the meeting a discussion on the subject of the reading shall be opened by the president or a member appointed by the president, and continued by the members as long as time shall permit.

The details about the discussions that followed the readings were never recorded in the minutes. It must have been felt that it was not important to record this information. The time at which the guests departed also remains a mystery. There is no indication about the interaction between the members of the club or the depth of their discussions on the books read.

RULE EIGHT

Rule eight of the Belfast Reading Club stated that members were allowed to bring guests to the meetings:

> The member at whose house the meeting is being held shall have the privilege of inviting a friend or friends to hear or take part in the reading, provided that the members shall not be deprived of any of the privileges of the Club in consequence.

This rule about inviting friends was extensively used with a total of 121 visitors attending the 134 meetings. Sixty-six people were found to have only attended one meeting as a visitor while thirty-nine visitors attended meetings between two and thirteen times. Twenty-two of this number attended meetings only twice, while Miss Lanyon, presumably a sister of Miss B. Lanyon, attended as a guest on thirteen occasions. Some of the invited guests must have been keen readers and sixteen of the visitors eventually became members. Six names only appeared in the minutes as a visitor on one occasion before becoming members. These include Mrs. T.J. Andrews, widow of Thomas J. Andrews, chemist and Vice-President of Queen's College who was a visitor on 5 December 1898 and elected as a member on 23 October 1899. She subsequently attended twelve meetings.[28] Mrs L. Campbell, née Ina Valentine, wife of Lloyd Campbell, was elected a member on 14 October 1895 and attended 32 meetings over the next six years.[29] However, others had to attend as visitors on numerous occasions until there was a resignation and they had the opportunity to join. Miss Florence Clark, sister of member Edith, lived at 13 Kinnaird Terrace and attended on six occasions as a visitor between 1892 and 1895 before being elected as a member in November 1896. During her membership of the Belfast Reading Club Florence was elected as representative on the Poor Law Board of Guardians for Cromac Ward in 1898.[30] Miss W. Blackley, daughter of Mr Travers Blackley, visited seven times before she was able to become a member in October 1891. She was a member until 14 October 1895 and attended twenty-four meetings during this time. Her sister Vera, her brothers and her mother were all listed as visitors when the meetings were held at Laurine, the family home. Four of the visitors who became members subsequently resigned and were then invited back as visitors on future occasions.

One example of this was Mr Charles J. Lanyon, son of Mr and Mrs H.O. Lanyon, who was recorded as a visitor on four occasions between 1892 and 1895 and was subsequently elected member of Belfast Reading Club on 14 October 1895. He attended eleven meetings as a member between 1895 and 1896 and then resigned in November 1896. His name thereafter appeared as a guest on five occasions between 1896 and 1900. It has to be said, however, that several members belonged to the Lanyon families so his relatives may well have invited him to attend when they were hosting the evening. The meetings on 7 December 1896, 8 December 1897 and 1 January 1900, attended by Mr C.J. Lanyon, were held at Lisbreen, the address of Miss B. Lanyon, who may have been his sister or his cousin. As there were only two Lanyon families listed in the 1895 and 1897 street directories, those of Mr J. Lanyon and Mr H.O. Lanyon, it is entirely possible that the Belfast Book Club members were all related. Sir Charles Lanyon, architect of many important buildings in Belfast including Queen's University, died on 31 May 1889, around the time that the reading group started. His will was witnessed by his sons John Lanyon of Lisbreen, Fortwilliam Park, a civil engineer and Herbert Owen Lanyon of Castleton Terrace, a merchant.[31] John Lanyon was in partnership with his father in the architectural company of Lanyon, Lynn and Lanyon. The Knockbreda Parish Graveyard archive confirms John Lanyon was the eldest son and Herbert Owen was youngest son of Sir Charles Lanyon. Furthermore, we learn the names of their wives: John was married to Hannah and Herbert Owen was married to Amelia. Although John and Hannah Lanyon were not members their home was used as a meeting place for the Belfast Reading Club by Miss B. Lanyon, presumably a daughter. Mrs Peacock, a visitor on three occasions, was Emma Hyde Peacock, elder daughter of John and Hannah Lanyon. Captain Peacock, later Major, was a visitor on one occasion and married to Emma. Both Herbert and Amelia were active reading club members.

Their eldest son, Charles James Lanyon, also attended the meetings. He died on 3 September 1905.[32] The Lanyons were not the only extended family group that attended the Belfast Reading Club. There were also various members from the Sinclair family who lived at Hopefield, the Travers Blackley family who lived at Laurine as well as the Campbell, Duffin and Bristow families. Some of the family were club members and they invited the extended family members as guests.

Interestingly, on three occasions: February 1895, 9 April 1895 and 10 February 1896, the visitors outnumbered the members. Some deductions can be made about how visitors were known to members of the Belfast Reading Club. For example, Miss Drennan was invited to a meeting at 22 University Square. As Maria Duffin was the granddaughter of William Drennan, the United Irishman, it can be assumed that she was Maria's relative. Belfast Reading Club members Mrs Adam Duffin, Miss B.H. Lanyon, Miss Gibson and the Misses Ferguson must have known visitors Mrs Thomas Sinclair and Miss Macpherson through their involvement in the Society for Providing Nurses for the Sick Poor.[33] Godfrey Ferguson, an original member, was an architect ,so he perhaps knew visitor Robert Graeme-Watt through professional connections.[34] Sporting connections may have also been utilized to recruit members. Thomas Sinclair has been 'credited as introducing golf to Ireland and was founder of Belfast Royal Golf Club' and Mr and Mrs Lloyd Campbell were keen golfers and members of Greenisland and Royal Portrush Golf Clubs.[35]

As the addresses of some of the members were recorded in the minutes this enabled a search to be carried out to discover whether the visitors also lived in the same areas of Belfast. *The Belfast and Province of Ulster Street Directory for 1897* showed that the following visitors to Belfast Reading Club lived in the Antrim Road area: the wife of Major J.L. Alison lived at Ardeen, Major and Mrs L.P. Ditmas lived at

2 Inver and Mrs Travers Blackley was at Laurine.[36] Visitors also lived at Fortwilliam Park: Miss Macpherson lived at St Oran's, Mrs O'Hara, wife of Canon O'Hara, lived at Glenview and Miss McFerran, possibly daughter of John McFerran, lived at Barnageeha.[37] All of these visitors attended when the meetings were held at Lisbreen, so it can be inferred that they were invited to attend by Miss B. Lanyon or were friends of the Lanyon family.

It also seems likely that members invited people from their work and social circle to attend the reading club. Looking at the occupations of some of the members and visitors it has been discovered that there were nine members of the clergy: Revd S. Carmody, Revd L. Drury, Revd E.T. Fripp, Revd F.T. Johnston, Revd J. Mervyn, Revd H.R. Brett, Revd Charles William Frizell, Revd A.G. Stuart and Canon Bristow all attended meetings. Both A.G. Stuart and H.R. Brett were Curates of St Anne's Parish Church in Donegall Street serving under the vicar Canon O'Hara.[38] Perhaps the vicar's wife, Mrs O'Hara, encouraged them to join the reading group. By 1901 Revd Henry Robert Brett had moved on and was listed as Rector of St Peter's Parish, Belfast.[39] The census records also show that in 1901 he was aged 32 and living at 15 Antrim Road. The Revd Charles William Frizell was a boarder at the same house and he was aged 52. Revd Frizell attended meetings between 1899 and 1900 first as a visitor and later as a member. The Revd E.T. Fripp was the minister at All Souls' Church, Elmwood Avenue, a non-subscribing Presbyterian congregation.[40] These Church of Ireland and various sectors of Presbyterian clergymen must have had a common interest in reading as well as involvement in the ministry.

The census information about the visitors and members also helped to establish a profile of the Belfast Reading Club in terms of ages and religious background. Thirty-one people have been positively identified in the census. Based on this sample the club had nine attendees who were aged under 35, twelve who were aged between 35 and 45, seven who were between 46 and 55 and three who were over fifty years of age when they attended. As several generations of family members were involved this may explain the variation in ages. Of the thirty-one attendees twenty-five were recorded on the census as Church of Ireland or Irish Church, Mr and Mrs Adam Duffin were Non-Subscribing Presbyterians, Robert Graeme-Watt and his wife were Church of England and Church of Scotland respectively, Mrs MacDonall was Presbyterian and Mrs Marcella Nagle, wife of Garret Nagle the Registrate Magistrate, was Roman Catholic.[41] As there was such a concentration of Church of Ireland members, unusual as Belfast was a predominately Presbyterian town, they must have known each other through various church functions and organizations.

It is also interesting to note the titles, gender and marital status of the members. Occupational titles included two professors, connected to Queen's College, two naval captains and an army major. Of the 141 names recorded 45 were males, while 35 of the female members and visitors were designated 'Mrs' Eleven of the married ladies from this number attended meetings with their husband, while another seven couples brought their sons or daughters to the meetings. Sixty-one of the names were prefixed with 'Miss'. It is particularly interesting that unmarried women were in the majority as this group was often under-represented in literary organisations. Some of the unmarried ladies were accompanied to the reading club by another family member such as the Misses Ferguson who attended with their brother, Misses Florence and Edith Clark attended with their mother, as did Miss Ashe, while Miss Alice Bristow attended meetings with her father Canon John Bristow. Three family groups consisted of two sisters: Misses Knox, Davison and Redfern. But twenty-four of the unmarried females attended without another relation. They must have been friends of the other members and felt quite comfortable attending the meetings on their own. Miss Eliza Eleanor Rollo Macpherson must have been good friends with the Sinclair family as Sir Thomas Sinclair of Hopefield was one of the executors of her will.[42]

RULES NINE AND TEN

The existence of the minutes on which this chapter is based is thanks to rule nine, which stated that:

> A minute book shall be kept, and the minutes shall be entered by the president of the meeting, and brought or lent to next meeting for inspection. The minutes shall consist of the subject & date of reading, names of the members and visitors present, parts assigned to different members, and any comments the president may think proper to make.

The minute book, unfortunately, does not contain as much information as this rule would suggest. Generally, the only information that has been recorded was the date, the location, a list of members present, a list of visitors and the subject. Only on eight evenings did the president see fit to make any comments, and two of these were preliminary meetings to organize the forthcoming sessions. Other notes recorded the elections or resignations of members.

Rule ten seems to be unique to the Belfast Reading Club. None of the other book clubs or reading societies examined in the course of my research have specified a dress code for members. Rule ten reads: 'Evening dress shall be optional'. As they do not record whether this rule was observed we have to imagine what they may have looked like heading through the streets of Belfast on a Monday evening to read their allocated parts of the play.

RULE ELEVEN

The final rule, number eleven, recorded the names of the original members, those involved in the creation of this organization. They were Miss Gibson, Mrs Parker, Mrs H. Lanyon, Mr H. Lanyon, the Misses Ferguson, Mr J. Bristow Jr., Mr Ferguson, Miss Cuming, Mr Pooler, Mr Cooper and Miss Davison. Only the two Miss Fergusons, their brother Godfrey, an architect, and John Bristow, a solicitor, were still members when the minute book ended on 5 February 1901. The other original members resigned in the intervening period. During the course of the minutes the Ferguson, Bristow and Lanyon families continued to play an active part in the proceedings and were also instrumental in many aspects of the development of the town of Belfast. Sadly, the reason for establishing the Belfast Reading Club remains unknown.

NUMBER 22

The final section of this chapter examines one family involved in the Belfast Reading Club and the extent to which they contributed to the development of social, cultural, commercial and educational life in Belfast. The Duffin family lived at 22 University Square, near Queen's College. It is interesting to speculate what the homes of the members were like and the surroundings in which the club members met. According to the description of the sale of the house in 1887, the house at 22 University Square, home of Mr and Mrs Adam Duffin, was a:

> ... very superior residence ... containing two sitting rooms, on ground floor; seven bedrooms, drawing-room and all necessary accommodation, together with stable and coach-house. The house has a frontage to University Square of 32 feet, and extends from front to rear 180 feet; is held for ever free of rent. The house is situate in a fashionable and

> healthy district of the town, facing Queen's College, and is quite close to the tram; is at present let at £92 per annum.[43]

Members were entertained on eight occasions between November 1891 and November 1896 at the Duffin home. From the above description of this member's home and the addresses of other members it is becoming obvious that the Belfast Reading Club was a select and elite group of citizens who lived in spacious properties and were from the more affluent mercantile and professional classes.

The census information shows that this family was part of this social group and had domestic servants.[44] Two ladies with the names of Fraulein Berger and Fraulein Helmkampf attended meetings as guests when the meetings were held at 22 University Square.[45] It was discovered that the reason why these German ladies attended was because the children 'were educated in a conventional middle-class fashion with governesses and several German Fräuleins' and so they accompanied the children to the meetings.[46]

Head of family, Adam Duffin, was elected a member of the Belfast Reading Club on 26 October 1891 and attended thirty-two meetings until his resignation at the age of 54 in November 1896.[47] Duffin was a stock and share broker and his business premises were located at 9 Waring Street.[48] He was also on the committee of the Belfast Royal Botanical and Horticultural Company and, on 10 April 1876, was elected as a member of the Belfast Literary Society, to which he gave papers based on his legal and business knowledge.[49] His presentation on 7 May 1877 was entitled 'The development of legal systems' and a second on 4 April 1881 was on 'Short-time as a remedy for depression in trade'.[50] He also became a director of the Commercial News Room, Waring Street, so clearly followed literary pursuits outside of this reading group.[51] He later pursued a political career with the Ulster Unionist party, being elected to the Northern Ireland Senate in 1921. Unfortunately this career was short-lived as he died on 13 March 1924.[52]

His wife, Maria, was daughter of Dr J.S. Drennan, physician for the Royal Hospital and a committee member of the Belfast Society for Promoting Knowledge. She was grand-daughter of United Irishman William Drennan, and grand niece of Martha McTier.[53] Mrs Duffin was elected a member of Belfast Reading Club on 26 October 1891 at the age of 36 and remained an active member attending thirty-one meetings until she also resigned in 1896. Maria, along with some of the female members of the Belfast Reading Club, was part of a deputation that approached the town's Parks Committee in 1889. The article in the *Belfast News Letter* on 3 October 1889 stated that the signatures in support of the memorial presented to the Parks Committee included a 'Mrs Cuming, 33 Wellington Place ... Miss Ferguson, Murray's Terrace ... Mrs Lanyon Lisbreen Fortwilliam Park ... Miss MacPherson St Oran's, Fortwilliam Park ... Mrs Parker, Methodist College and Mrs Sinclair, Hopefield...' These ladies saw 'the necessity in this large and rapidly growing city of making provision for open spaces to secure light, air and recreation to the inhabitants'.[54]

A number of the ladies belonging to Belfast Reading Club were known to each other through other organizations prior to their involvement in the Belfast Reading Club. Mrs Duffin and her daughters, Ruth and Olive, were also active in the Society for Providing Nurses for the Sick Poor. This organisation was presided over by 'Mrs Thomas Sinclair (Hopefield)'and other members included Mrs Alison, Miss Macphearson, Miss Ferguson and the Misses Clark.[55] Maria was also on the sub-committee for the rebuilding fund of Belfast Maternity Hospital in 1899.[56] Her public interests lay in the improvement of facilities for the welfare and health of the Belfast citizens. Maria inherited the manuscript documents of William Drennan, which she sorted and arranged. According to James Windor Good, 'Mrs Duffin's industry and insight triumphed over all obstacles, and she has completed her labours as editor by appending to the letters a valuable series of biographical and explanatory notes'. This document, although completed, was never published. To complete the story of this manuscript: 'Drennan Letters 1775–1793. A Transcription by Maria, Ruth and Dorothy Duffin' was auctioned in Dublin on 16 April 2011.[57] Mrs Duffin died on 14 October 1954 having reached the age of 100 and is buried at Dundonald Cemetry. One of her reminiscences was about Miss Mary Ann McCracken attending a party at her grandmother's house.[58]

Adam and Maria married in 1876 and had nine children.[59] According to the 1901 census the Duffin family were living at 22 University Square and had six daughters and one son. However, by the 1911 census, the family were living at 14 Cliftonville Road and the names of five daughters and two sons were recorded. Some children appeared on one census record but not the other. As well as attending the meetings of the Belfast Reading Club held at the parental home, the Misses Duffin also attended at other locations even when their parents were not present. For example, the Misses Duffin attended seven meetings during 1899 and 1900. However, it is not known which, or how many, of the Duffin girls were in attendance on these occasions.

Eldest daughter Ruth was born in 1878. She was educated at Cheltenham Ladies College and in 1914 was appointed as the first Warden of Riddle Hall, Belfast.[60] As she was educated in England between 1894 and 1896 this may explain why she only attended one meeting of the reading club on 13 February 1899 at the age of 22. In her job she was considered as 'austere, aristocratic and strict' but her diaries deposited in the Public Record Office of Northern Ireland show her personality as being 'pleasant and often humorous'. She was an author of several books of poetry. Copies of her poetry book titled *Escape* and

The Secret Hill written by Ruth and her sister Celia Duffin are available at the Linen Hall Library.[61]

Olive was the next child and she attended Belfast Reading Club on three occasions: twice in 1896 when she was 17 years old and once in 1900 when she would have been 21 years of age. Olive pursued a career in sculpture and was recorded as submitting items in local art exhibitions.[62]

Dorothea attended two meetings in 1895 and 1896 when she was respectively aged 14 and 15 years old. There were two boys in the family – Charles was born in 1882 and John in 1885. Masters Charles and John Duffin attended the Belfast Reading Club on 9 April 1895 when they were aged 13 and 10 and on 13 April 1896 when they were each a year older. In the 1901 census, 19-year-old Charles Edmund was listed as a clerk and ten years later he was listed as a stockbroker's assistant. It is probable that he was learning the trade from his father. He went on to pursue this career and became a stockbroker in his own right.[63] John Terence Duffin, at the age of 25, was an engineering apprentice. He later went on to serve in the army and his will records show that he achieved the rank of major. He later lived in Newcastle, Co. Down and died on 6 May 1936.[64]

Emma Sylvia, born in 1884, was also an author. She wrote *The Magic Glasses* and provided illustrations for Ruth's work.[65] Emma attended two meetings of the reading club in 1895 and 1896 when she was 11 and 12 years old. Emma later served as a voluntary nurse in Egypt and France. Extracts from her 1941 diary relating her experiences of the Belfast Blitz were published in an anthology of Irish women's writing.[66] Her diaries are now at the Public Record Office of Northern Ireland.[67]

Celia was born in 1888 and she attended Belfast Reading Club on five occasions between 1892 and 1900. Her parents must have brought her along as she would have been only four years old when she attended the first meeting, although she may have been able to participate when she was aged twelve at the meetings in 1900.

The *Belfast News Letter* dated 30 October 1890 announced in the births section: 'Duffin – 1 October at 22 University Square, Belfast, the wife of Adam Duffin Esq. of a daughter'.[68] This notice must have referred to Helen Duffin. She also followed the writing tradition of the family and had a book published.[69] Youngest daughter Sylvia was born in 1893.[70] Neither Helen nor Sylvia were mentioned by name as having attended any of the reading club meetings.

The Duffin family serve as a perfect example of the Belfast Reading Club members: they were middle class, involved in charitable endeavours, interested in literary and educational pursuits, they were involved in campaigns for health improvements and held strong political views. They had extensive family and social networks and they were active participants in local concerns and recreational interests.

CONCLUSION

Belfast Reading Club was unique. The members had the means to acquire their own texts and there was no mention of any payments to maintain the organization. A group of keen readers seem to have invited friends and family to join them in their literary enactments and the number of participants and frequency of meetings expanded and contracted over the years as circumstances changed. This society, in contrast to others, had a predominance of female members, especially unmarried ladies. They were particularly interested in reading Shakespeare, poetry and the more established authors of the nineteenth century. The members were predominately drawn from the Church of Ireland, but not exclusively, and many of the unmarried females had an income derived from dividends while the males were solicitors, architects, clergymen or owners of linen factories.[71] This was not a reading society that was set up for philanthropic purposes, nor was it governed by any religious or political organizations; it was purely for the recreation of a group drawn from the educated middle class in nineteenth-century Belfast.

5

The Belfast Natural History Society in the Nineteenth Century: A Communication Hub

Ruth Bowman Bayles

The Belfast Natural History Society (BNHS) was founded in 1821 at a time of expansion of similar societies in England. The society expanded and developed to become involved in the creation of specialist departments, a Botanic Garden (1827) and the construction of a museum (1831). A change of name also indicated a wider range of topics for investigation. It supported the founding of a field club in 1863 and hosted two prestigious meetings of the British Association for the Advancement of Science in 1852 and 1874. In 1910 the collections of museum specimens and artefacts passed into municipal hands, and subsequently to the present Ulster Museum. The Belfast Society, as it was later to be known, continues to meet in the Linen Hall Library on a regular basis.

During the nineteenth century, the population of Belfast increased rapidly as the town became industrialized and urbanized. While a proportion of the population constituted a poorly paid labour force, others prospered with new wealth from commerce and industry. In the main, it was from this latter group that the founders and first members of the Belfast Natural History Society came. Their purpose was to found a natural history society and to build a museum to raise even further the status of Belfast.

This chapter seeks to acknowledge the particular circumstances that indicated the uniqueness of this society and to demonstrate how it differed from similar societies in other British towns and cities. Science was not practised in isolation. Most of the members of the Belfast Natural History Society were from similar social and professional backgrounds, and were also involved in a number of other scientific societies at both a national and a local level. This chapter will situate the Belfast Natural History Society (BNHS) and its members within the network of scientific societies that spread across Belfast, Ireland, the UK, Europe and beyond during the nineteenth century.

Recognition of the significance of the local, the specific and the situated is an increasing feature of historiographic analysis. Studies by Withers, Finegan, Elliot, Naylor and others have been used effectively to contextualize provincial scientific societies.[1] Arnold Thackray suggests that such societies played a role outside the realms of the strictly scientific, and supported the civic empowerment of their members.[2] Others, such as Finnegan and Alberti, cite the expression of civic pride in the milieu of developing industrialization and urbanization as being a part of the driving force.[3] To quote Naylor, 'these studies show an appreciation of the relationships between science and the public and civic spheres'.[4]

The purpose of this chapter is to demonstrate how strongly the local affected the functioning of an individual society. By using the local as the main point of reference, the position of the society moves beyond place, as in geographical location, and relates to the broader historical and cultural contexts. It makes the move from abstract to concrete practical; in this case to place the BNHS and its members within a network of scientific societies that reached across Ireland, Britain, Europe and beyond.

THE BNHS IN AN IRISH CONTEXT

The natural resources of Ireland comprise 32,500 square miles land area, 3,000 miles of coastline, lakes, loughs and mountain ranges, along with boglands, beaches and forests. As well as the natural, the man-made resources that accompanied industrial and urban development such as railways, reservoirs and canals also gave opportunities for the study of natural history. The compact spread of resources and the networks of local societies also encouraged both competition and collaboration. James McAdam, founder member, used the formation of the railways with its blasting and construction of cuttings to further his geological research.[5] While not historians of science, the contribution of Irish writers such as Robert Lloyd Praeger and Estyn Evans (both members of the Belfast Naturalists' Field Club, sister organization to the BNHS) have also shown how fruitful location-centred work can be in Ireland. Their descriptions of the unique qualities, characteristics and personality of Ireland showed the richness of this approach.[6]

Publications such as *Nature in Ireland*, edited by John Wilson Foster, demonstrate the range and depth of recent work related this broad area of interest: in the histories of naturalists, physical resources, flora and faunae and the institutions involved in their study in a specific location and with local culture.[7] David Livingstone views the inclusion of additional characteristics, such as intellectual exchange, educational customs, cultural communications and religious beliefs as providing the unique regional psychology affecting the conduct and content of local scientific activity.[8] Natural History has, at times, been perceived as an informal and sociable branch of science, practised by amateurs rather than professionals. Up until the early nineteenth century the study of 'natural history' as compared to 'natural philosophy' was not generally seen as a serious scientific pursuit. It was to some extent a product of intellectual fashion, a fascination with nature associated with the Enlightenment, which saw the appearance in Ireland of 'romantically landscaped gardens, shell grottoes and rustic summer houses' in the late eighteenth century.[9] Botany and geology in particular became the subjects of natural history collecting. By the turn of the century, however, there was a change in orientation within the learned societies in London and Dublin, possibly linked to the greater involvement of the professional and middle classes. This was to lead to a particular strand of nineteenth-century science being identified as 'professional, systematic and specialized' while the other, usually identified as natural history, was frequently seen as 'amateur, descriptive and encyclopaedic'.[10]

While we now see the study of natural history as related to non-specialist and popular science, during the nineteenth century this was not the case. Natural history societies varied from the broad-based and eclectic to those that were more specialized, covering only one particular aspect of natural science such as bryology, conchology or ornithology. A number of natural history societies also included topics such as statistics and industrial processes within their remit. The name alone gave little indication of the broad areas of interest of these groups and their members.

Histories of the larger and metropolitan scientific societies in Great Britain have been the subject of some interest.[11] Comparisons have been made of their work, and also with the work of similar societies at an international level, emphasizing the role played by these societies and their members in the development of scientific practice and theories.[12]

By comparison, the smaller local and provincial societies, and the contribution of their members to the work of the scientific community as a whole, have largely been neglected until relatively recently.[13] The history of the successful provincial societies, their members and achievements, indicates amazing tenacity and resourcefulness. Even the short-lived societies also make a contribution to our insight into the position of science in the local and national setting.[14] For the significance and complexity of these activities to be appreciated, at both the local and the national levels, they need to be placed into a series of cultural and scientific contexts.[15]

It is estimated that during the nineteenth century over a thousand scientific societies were founded in rural and urban locations across England, Scotland and Ireland. Figures for Wales are more difficult to obtain. These provincial societies existed in small villages with populations of less than 1,000, for example Swaffham Prior with its population of 892, as well as in large towns and cities such as Manchester with a population of 108,000.[16] This type of scientific activity often reached across and between social classes and geographical locations, linking groups and individual members over a wide geographical distance.

A survey of Irish societies in the nineteenth century carried out by this author has revealed that over 250 named groups that studied natural history were founded. This included two national societies – the Conchological Society of Great Britain and Ireland (1876) and the Moss Exchange Club (1896) – which functioned across the whole of the United Kingdom. The rate at which societies were founded in Ireland was not distributed evenly across the nineteenth century with the effects of economic and social factors, such as the Great Famine (1845–50) possibly influencing developments. The overall rate showed an increase from 1780–1849 with a subsequent fall in newly-founded societies in the following decade. In Dublin, the number of new societies being established was highest from 1830–1849, while the provincial rate generally rose from 1780–1829, with a peak in the 1820s, the decade in which the BNHS was founded. Generally the increase in provincial foundations occurred earlier in Ireland than in England or Scotland.

Approximately a quarter of the total new societies being established during the nineteenth century were based in Dublin. The geographical distribution of the remainder varies throughout the century as more new societies were founded across Ireland. Those founded in the early nineteenth century were concentrated in Cork and Limerick towards the south, Mayo and Galway in the west and Tyrone, Monaghan, Louth, Antrim, Down and Co. Dublin in the east. By the end of the century the distribution was generally spread more widely across the country with the highest concentrations of new societies being founded in Co. Dublin (44), Co. Down (27) and Co. Antrim (56). That is, in the most industrial and urbanized areas of Ireland.

General factors cited as having influenced the distribution of new societies across time and place in Britain have included the foundation of the BAAS (1831); the 1843 Scientific Societies Act; the Great Exhibition of 1851 and the publication of *Origin of Species* (1859); however, these appear to have had little impact on the Irish situation. The distribution of Irish societies seems to have been related more to local issues such as the administrative change which accompanied the Act of Union in 1801, when Ireland's government was removed from Dublin to London; the impact of the Great Famine (1845–1850) on the mainly agricultural counties of south; and the rapid development of industry and commerce in Belfast relative to that in Dublin. A closer look at the situation in Belfast also identifies how the local situation affected the development of bodies that used and practised science.

BELFAST SURVEY

Even though large areas of Ireland remained rural, and despite political unrest, Belfast developed and expanded during the nineteenth century. The industrial, commercial and urban growth resembled that of many English towns during the same period and brought with it problems related to rapid population increase, such as poor housing, health, water supply and drainage.[17] It was here that science and scientific societies played a role. The majority of the members of the BNHS were also actively involved in a range of scientific societies and institutions in Belfast and Ireland that could be divided into four main categories: education, health, economics and personal interest. These included organizations such as the Belfast Medical Society, The Belfast Social Inquiry Society, The Chemico-Agricultural Society, the Naturalists Field Club and Ulster Statistical Society.

A survey carried out by the author has identified a hundred and one societies that were involved in the teaching, study or application of science in nineteenth-century Belfast.[18] These covered a wide range of public and privately funded bodies and ranged across all social classes. They included hospitals and dispensaries, schools, colleges and Mechanics and Workingmens' Institutes along with specialist societies, such as the Statistical Society, the Galvanic Society and the Phrenological Society. Generally, the trend in new societies founded in Belfast accelerated from the 1820s, with a peak in the 1870s, then falling away after this.

The societies have been divided into the four main categories related to functions centred on health, education, economic development and personal or group interest. Generally, the majority of the publicly funded institutions were concerned with health and education, while the greater number of privately funded societies centred on the interest groups. During the nineteenth century Belfast appears to have had two separate phases of scientific culture divided by a series of social crises in the form of medical epidemics and economic problems. The first phase dated from the late eighteenth century to the end of the 1830s and was characterized by a thirst for general knowledge, typically via libraries and reading societies, which held collections of scientific books and artefacts. These appeared to be suited to the needs of the wealthier citizens. The second phase was characterized by the use of science for civic purposes such as the amelioration of social problems related to industrial developments and rapid urbanization. This phase reflected the concerns of the wealthy Presbyterian merchants and businessmen who wished to influence the behaviour and education of the disadvantaged, as well as dealing with their social and medical problems.

The BNHS is an example of a society that adjusted its functions in line with the changes in the local scientific culture. In 1821, when the society was first founded, it comprised an interest group suited to the need of the wealthy middle-class Presbyterian members. Later the society provided a recreational and scientific facility for the members and for the invited and paying 'visitors' and 'scientific strangers' who were their peers. From 1833 the society offered a range of less expensive demonstrations and courses as well as reduced rates of admission charges to their museum in order to attract the middle classes who were not members. In 1842 the society included the term 'philosophy' in its title to indicate that a wider range of papers were now discussed at the meetings. Three years later, in 1845, admission charge to the museum was further reduced on Easter Monday Bank Holiday so that the mechanics and operatives could afford to enter for educational purposes. The following year the charge was again reduced to encourage the working classes to attend for 'moral edification'.

THE BELFAST NATURAL HISTORY SOCIETY

The BNHS was founded in 1821 and was the first named natural history society in Ireland. During its first fifty years the society founded a botanic garden (1827), built a museum (1831), changed its name to include the term 'Philosophical' to indicate the inclusion of discussion of a wider range of topics at its meetings (1842) and hosted a prestigious meeting of the British Association for the Advancement of Science, BAAS (1852).

The construction and opening of the botanic gardens and the museum was seen as an essential element for the developing town in a rapidly industrializing society. They were statements of culture, refinement and education. Exchange as well as construction of information was part of this identity. One of the ways that this could be seen was in the exchange of journals and specimens. There was also much competition to host the annual provincial meetings of the British Association for the Advancement of Science as this visit was seen as denoting scientific recognition. Hosting this visit gave a wide range of benefits that were also both scientific and non-scientific: these included trade and tourism, civic initiative and a building scheme, improvement to established resources, moral and intellectual interest as well as an acknowledgement of local scientific talents.

The first botanic garden in Belfast was opened by the Belfast Botanical and Horticultural Society in 1827 on an acre of land at Bradbury Place. Unfortunately the plot of land chosen proved unsatisfactory and was given up two years later. A committee was formed, subscription lists were opened and shares were sold to raise funds. By May 1829 over £1,200 had been raised. This was sufficient to lease a plot of land for 99 years and to plant a garden with an extensive range of shrubs and trees. In 1840 the Company received the title 'Royal' after the intervention of Lord Donegall and the term was added to the name of the garden.[19]

Access to the gardens was controlled by the amount the patrons had paid for their shares: basically, the higher the payment the more family members were entitled to visit and vote on the affairs of the garden. Funds were continually required to maintain the garden, so even casual visitors paid an entrance fee and further funds were raised from the sale of plants. In 1838 a decision was taken to hold a garden fête to increase funds. The event proved a great success and involved a balloon ascent, music, dancing, archery, boat trips and the sale of intoxicating liquor, making an impressive overall profit of £74.[20] The fêtes became a regular event.

Access to the garden was gradually expanded and became increasingly seen as a means of recreation for the working people, something that would provide them with 'improved moral status', as well as providing recreation for the wealthier middle-class shareholders. To facilitate this, it was agreed that the garden would be opened during the summer months without charge provided that 'No baskets, parcels or refreshment were brought into the garden'.[21] The Botanical Garden was becoming a public park.

In spite of the increased access, maintenance of the scientific element of the garden continued to be of the great importance. In 1829 a professional gardener was employed. Plants and seeds were collected and exchanged with other botanical gardens across the United Kingdom and beyond; for example Captain Portlock donated 100 papers of seed from Calcutta.[22] The educational function of the garden was not neglected and plants were arranged in the garden in order to demonstrate different species and their functions. The garden was designed to be suitable for both experts and non-experts and included collections of native pants, along with more specialized 'florists' flowers', which were arranged according to the popular Linnaeus system of classification. This would have been familiar to most of the educated middle-class patrons.[23] Financial difficulties had been reported for some time and by 1883 a decision was made to put the Company into liquidation. Part of the garden was sold to Queen's College (now Queen's University), and the rest of the ground to the town's Corporation. The Botanic Garden was renamed the 'Belfast Botanic Garden Park' in 1895 and opened free to the public.

The opening of a museum was also of great importance to the member of the BNHS. This would function as a depository for their library and collections of natural history artefacts as well as being a place to display these in order to confer status on the active members locally and within the wider scientific community. A local architect was employed and plans were drawn up, but the elaborate scheme was found to be too expensive and the project was postponed. By 1829 the committee felt confident enough to issue a pamphlet seeking financial support from members of the wealthy middle classes for the building of a museum. Shares and subscriptions were sold in a manner similar to the fund-raising for the Botanic Garden: basically, the more shares that were bought, the greater access the patron enjoyed. The architectural plans for the museum were elaborate, with the building to be in the classical Greek style – at that time a popular style for buildings of high status – and included large rooms that facilitated the holding of meetings, a library and rooms in which to display the collections.[24]

The foundation stone was laid at an elaborate ceremony on 4 May 1830 and building was formally opened on 1 November 1831. The collections comprised 'about 200 specimens of minerals, a nearly complete collection of native and considerable number of foreign shells, 200 native and foreign birds, about 300 insects, an extensive *Hortus Siccus* (dried garden) of indigenous, American and other exotic plants, about 200 snakes and lizards'.[25]

The funds raised were insufficient to fit out the premises with cases and cabinets to display the artefacts, so other measures were taken to raise money quickly: collectors were appointed from the members, local dignitaries were approached, duplicate specimens were sold to the London Zoological Society and the Royal Dublin Society, tickets were sold for classes and public lectures and a loan was sought from the Belfast Banking Company.[26] Rooms in the new building were also rented out to other local societies, such as the Medical Society, the Juvenile Natural History Society and the Belfast Literary Society. Even these actions did not eliminate the debt. Another effort to raise monies was made when a decision was taken to allow limited public access to the museum which had previously only been available to shareholders and other wealthy patrons.[27]

Public nights were introduced. These lectures were of a more popular nature; some with spectacular demonstrations, such as that given by Thomas Andrews in 1840 on 'The application of Galvanism in the Arts'. This featured an explosion to produce a column of water that rose some feet into the air in order to illustrate the use of galvanic electricity to destroy shipwrecks.[28] Public response was huge. Sometimes live animals were brought to these talks. In 1834 George Crawford Hyndman showed a live crocodile to the audience; however this was 'somewhat moribund as it had not eaten for three days'.[29] Gradually, access to the museum for the public, including artisans and the working classes, increased with an affordable admission charge.[30] In May 1845 arrangements were made for the Easter Bank Holiday with admission rates set at 'two pence for mechanics and their families and one penny for children'. This attracted large crowds, with up to 7,000 people admitted on Bank Holidays alone.[31] Despite these and other extensive measures, however, in the long term the society was unable to sustain an adequate income to maintain the premises and the collections in the museum. In 1901 the museum was eventually transferred to the Corporation of the city.

MEMBERSHIP OF THE BNHS

The 'eight youthful founders' of the Belfast Natural History Society, who had held the first meeting of the BNHS in June 1821, were almost exclusively from the local Presbyterian middle class in Belfast.[32] Two of the founders: Frances Archer and James Lawson Drummond, were in the medical profession; one: William McClure, in the Presbyterian ministry; one: George Crawford Hyndman, was a public notary; and the remaining four: Robert Simms, James Grimshaw, James McAdam and Robert Patterson, were businessmen involved in the flourishing textile industry. Their families had been established for at least one generation as important figures in the industrial, commercial and municipal expansion of Belfast, the local cotton and linen industries providing them, directly or indirectly, with their income. It was members of this social group who directed the society's affairs. The society was organized and controlled by a Council of ten men. This included a president, two Vice-Presidents, a Treasurer, a Librarian and usually six officers.

James Lawson Drummond (1783–1853) was the first President of the BNHS. He was born in Larne, County Antrim, and was educated at the Belfast Academy. He became an apprentice surgeon in the Royal Navy and then studied medicine in Edinburgh. In 1814 he was Physician to Belfast Dispensary and four years later was appointed Professor of Anatomy and Physiology in the Belfast Academical Institution. From 1835 to 1836 he was Professor of Botany, and was instrumental in founding the Faculty of Medicine of which he became the first President. He was the first President of the Belfast Natural History Society and founder of the Belfast Museum.[33]

The society was originally founded in 1821 to promote the study of natural history, 'for the cultivation of the science in its various branches, and more particularly for the investigation of the Natural History of Ireland'.[34] Within a year a committee was appointed to consider cabinets and cases for donated specimens. Six sections or departments had been established, each under the charge of a specialist: Dr Drummond dealt with Botany, Mr Archer with Conchology, Mr McAdam with Minerals, Mr Grimshaw with Ornithology and Mr Hyndman with Entomology.

Membership was divided into four categories: ordinary members, who were obliged to read papers at the meetings; visiting members, who did not read papers or attend the business meetings; honorary members, who held some scientific or social status, and corresponding members, who did not read papers. Papers were usually read at each meeting, with a fine being exacted for failure to do so.[35]

Items for the society's scientific collections, which had been received from the first meeting in June 1821, were held in the house of the then president, Dr J. Drummond.[36] Within two years the society had relocated to an apartment in newly built Commercial Buildings in the centre of Belfast. By 1827 it became obvious that this had also become too small to hold the growing collections and the library of the society. By the end of that year a campaign was established to raise funds to build a museum. In 1831 sufficient monies had been accumulated to open the new building.[37]

Further donations of artefacts were also received from local tradespeople with business connections abroad, from expatriates and from those employed by the various shipping companies that used Belfast's thriving port. Contacts and exchanges with other naturalists in England, Ireland and farther afield were an essential feature of the networks that were formed from the early days of the society.[38] William Hutton, secretary of the North West Historical Society, Newcastle-upon-Tyne, elected a corresponding member of the BNHS, exchanged geological and natural history specimens such as minerals, shells and insects from 1826 to at least 1829.[39]

The BNHS also received journals and proceedings from scientific societies within the UK, Europe, America and the Empire. This recognition from those they saw as their peers in the wider scientific community was a source of considerable satisfaction. But the BNHS members were not able to reciprocate fully in kind until the publication of the first bound volume of their own proceedings was produced in 1873, although these were printed in pamphlet form from 1850.

A CULTURE OF SCIENCE

Almost all forty-one members of the BNHS council between 1821 and 1870 were actively involved in a total of thirty-four other scientific societies or institutions in Belfast either before or after the foundation of the BNHS.[40] These societies represented the full range of functions. This involvement was outside members' activities in the BNHS and demonstrated both an individual and a collective commitment to the broader local scientific culture in addition to either their roles in the BNHS or their businesses or professional positions. As well as being members of other local groups, BNHS council members were also involved in scientific and learned societies outside Belfast. These included societies in Dublin (Royal Dublin Society, Royal Irish Academy, Geological Society) in London (Royal Society, BAAS, Linnaean Society); in Edinburgh (Royal Society of Edinburgh, Botanical Society, Royal College of Surgeons); and in Glasgow (Geological Society, Philosophical Society). By looking in closer detail at two members of the BNHS, it is possible to demonstrate the extent to which these people were involved in the world of scientific culture beyond the BNHS itself.

Robert Patterson (1802–1872) was born in Belfast and was educated at the Royal Belfast Academical Institution. He entered the family business and became the owner of a prosperous mill-furnishing business in Belfast. He was one of the eight founders of the BNHS, serving as its president on three occasions, a period covering seven years in total. He published numerous works, including *Introduction to zoology for the use of schools* (Belfast, 1849) and *First steps to zoology* (London, 1849). He also published *Letters on the natural history of the insects mentioned in Shakespeare's plays* (London, 1838). The extent of Patterson's wider influence beyond Belfast was demonstrated by the fact that he was one of the earliest members of the BAAS.[41] He was also a member of nine scientific societies in Belfast: the Belfast Literary Society, Belfast Society for Promoting Knowledge, Belfast Ladies' Institute, Belfast Municipal and Art Gallery, Belfast Society for the Prevention of Cruelty to Animals, Belfast Botanical and Horticultural Society, Belfast Naturalists' Field Club, Belfast Wardian Society and the Ulster Statistical Society. Beyond Belfast, but still within the United Kingdom, he also held membership of four additional scientific societies: the Royal Irish Academy, the Royal Society, the BAAS and the Entomological Society.

It would be inaccurate to view the BNHS as a purely provincial society. It should be noted that Belfast with its thriving commercial life and port enabled the Society's members to develop strong international links with similar learned bodies in France, the Netherlands and the German kingdoms. The membership pattern of another of the members of the BNHS, John Hodges (1815–1899), provides a good example of the kind of networks of which these people were a part.

Hodges was born in Downpatrick, County Down, and was educated in Dublin, Glasgow and finally in Giessen University, where he studied Chemistry. He founded the Mechanics' Institute in 1847 in Downpatrick and later became Professor of Chemistry at the Royal Belfast Academical

Institution and Professor of Agricultural Chemistry and Lecturer in Medical Jurisprudence at Queen's College, Belfast. He was president and a founding member of the Belfast Chemico-Agricultural Society and later chemical director of the Chemico-Agricultural Society of Ulster, whose journal he edited. He was one of the founders of the Royal College of Chemistry in London and was employed by the government as an analyst. He had honours conferred on him by Russia, Stockholm, Turin, Germany, France and Amsterdam, indicating the extent of his international recognition.[42] He also held membership of the BAAS, the Royal College of Chemistry and a range of medical societies in London. Outside the United Kingdom, he was a member of scientific societies in Sweden, Italy, France, Holland, the Netherlands and Germany and was a Fellow of the International College of Surgeons.[43]

This level of national and international communication is further confirmed by the journals and proceedings received in the library of the museum that the Society members built in 1831. A survey of these volumes, from national and international sources, included in UK journals from London, Dublin, Edinburgh and Glasgow as well as Cornwall, Lancashire, Cheshire and Aberdeen.

Figure 1 UK Journals and Proceeding received by BNHS

ENGLAND	
Metropolitan:	**Provincial:**
Antiquarian Society	Berwickshire Naturalists' Club
Astronomic Society	Cornwall Polytechnic Society
Entomological Society	Geological Society of West Riding
Geological Society	Historical Society of Lancashire and Cheshire
Linnean Society	Islington Literary and Philosophical Society
Numenistic Society	Leeds Literary and Philosophical Society
Phrenological Society	Liverpool Literary and Philosophical Society
Royal Society	Natural History Society of Northumberland,
Society of Antiquities	Durham and Newcastle
Statistical Society	
Zoological Society	

SCOTLAND **Metropolitan:** Botanical Society, Edinburgh Society of Scottish Antiquities Watt Club	**Provincial:** Philosophical Society of Glasgow Spalding Club, Aberdeen
IRELAND **Metropolitan:** Dublin Natural History Society Dublin Statistical Society Geological Society of Dublin Royal Dublin Society Royal Irish Academy	**Provincial:** Derry Natural History Society Cork Society Natural History and Philosophical Society, Armagh Ulster Journal of Archaeology

Outside the UK, journals were received for scientific societies in America, Canada, Austria, Australia, India and Norway, again emphasizing the wide communication networks in which the BNHS and its members were involved.

Figure 2: Foreign Journal and Proceedings Received by Belfast Natural History Society

USA	Academy of Natural History, Philadelphia Boston Natural History Society Catholic Union, Atlantis Connecticut Academy of Arts and Science Department of Agriculture New York Lyceum of Natural History New York University Orleans County Society of Natural History Silliman's American Journal of Science Smithsonian Institute, Washington
India	Calcutta Journal of Natural History Governor General Geological Survey
Norway	Meteorological Institute University of Christiana

Austria	Imperial Geological Society Zoologison Botanischen Gesellshaft, Vethandlurgen
Italy	Imperial Geological Institute, Verona Society Toscana di Scienze Naturali
Denmark	Royal University of Aarsberetning
Sweden	Royal Academy of Science
Germany	Natural History Society, Bremen
Canada	Nova Scotia Institute of Natural Science
Australia	Victoria Philosophical Institute,Melbourne

By putting these two sets of information together both numerically and geographically it is possibly to identify the extent of the network for the exchange of printed information by a natural history society with approximately 270 members. During most of the nineteenth century, a total of fifty-eight journals and proceedings from the UK and abroad were received. The exchange of information was larger and broader than had been expected, especially as there is no evidence of the BNHS being able to seriously reciprocate until they published their own work in the pamphlet form from 1850 and as bound volumes from 1873. However, this recognition by those that the members considered to be their peers in the wider scientific community was a source of considerable satisfaction.

Fig 3: U.K Journals and Proceedings received by Belfast Natural History Society

	Metropolitan	**Provincial**
England	11	8
Scotland	3	2
Ireland	5	4

CONCLUSION

This chapter has sought to demonstrate how local social, economic and intellectual conditions influenced the foundation and development of the Belfast Natural History Society. It has shown how strongly local culture has affected the foundation and development of the Belfast Natural History Society with the local resources, both natural and man-made, providing rich sources for its members. By centring this work on a single provincial society in nineteenth-century Ireland it has been possible to show the influence of contemporaneous local factors.

In Ireland it was local issues, rather than those affecting the rest of the UK, that influenced the distribution of their foundation over place and time. While the developments in Belfast resembled those of the industrial towns in England, the local societies were founded to deal with local requirements. The Belfast Natural History Society adjusted its functions over time in line with changes in the local culture, but these men also looked outwards. Journals and membership with similar bodies in the rest of the UK and farther afield clearly indicated this.

Situating a provincial scientific society within its own context is a valuable exercise to understand relationships with the local culture, but in order to tell the full story it is also necessary to investigate how this culture relates to the broader picture. To contextualize a single society in its own location in time and place does not indicate isolation from the wider world.

6

A Country for Young Men (Or Two Quacks and a Son of Dust)

Glenn Patterson

It is not often that you are able to put a precise date on the origins of a novel, but I can be quite specific and say that before 7 April 2006 I had not dreamed of setting a novel in the first decades of the nineteenth century.

At some point during that day, however, I came across 'Belfast Sixty Years Ago: Recollections of a Septuagenarian', a lecture by the Revd Narcissus G. Batt published in the *Ulster Journal of Architecture* in January 1896. Looking back to his boyhood in the 1830s, Revd Batt recalled an inn on the town's northern outskirts rejoicing in the name of the Mill for Grinding Old People Young and run by one Peggy Barclay.

It was the landlady's name, not the inn's, that first attracted me. In the late 1700s Peggy Barclay had, with her husband James, owned another inn, the Doctor Franklin, in Sugarhouse Entry, just off High Street. It was here under the quaint, and entirely ineffectual, disguise of the 'Muddlers' Club' that the Society of United Irishmen met in the years leading up to 1798 and planned their doomed rebellion in the name of 'Catholic, Protestant and Dissenter'. Several members of the club, including James Barclay, were betrayed to the British before the rebellion even began by one of the Doctor Franklin's own serving girls, Belle Martin.

To discover Peggy Barclay again, still a landlady, in the early decades of the nineteenth century was not only a delight, but also a reminder that all wars have their post-wars, all risings their settlings. We might not have been able to agree on what to call the events of 1969–1994 in Northern Ireland (the War? the Troubles? the Conflict?) but whatever they were called, there was good reason to hope by April 2006 that we were well beyond them.

My younger daughter was ten weeks old that first week of April, still sleeping in a Moses basket in our bedroom, still waking a couple of times a night for a feed or a chat. She awoke for the latter on the night of 7 April. I tried to get her to go back to sleep again, holding her in my arms, rocking from foot to foot, and repeating in my head, to keep the rhythm going, 'the Mill for Grinding Old People Young, the Mill for Grinding Old People Young…' It seemed to inflate like a balloon before my eyes, the novel that I might write, a novel about aftermaths and the accommodations required by the simple passage of time, with, at the heart of it, Peggy Barclay and her inn.

By morning, though, the air had gone out of the balloon entirely. I knew nothing worth knowing about the early nineteenth century. In the all-important matter of voice, I couldn't begin to 'do' 1830s.

As luck would have it, I had agreed to do a reading that night, 8 April, in Queen's University Belfast, at a conference, 'Cross Currents', organized by postgraduate students from Belfast, Dublin and Aberdeen. I had fully intended coming home straight after the reading (I had not, after all, slept much) but found myself instead, several hours later, with some of the conference's other participants in the Duke of York bar, barely one hundred yards from where the Doctor Franklin Tavern had once stood, although Sugarhouse Entry had long ago been downgraded to an unmarked alleyway up the side of the Northern Ireland War Memorial Building. I found myself, more to the point, in conversation with Suzanne O'Neill, now a lecturer in the Department of Classics at Trinity College Dublin then a PhD student at that university, who earlier in the day had delivered a paper called 'From Perikles to Presbyterian "Temples": Liberty, Democracy and Power Architecture in Nineteenth-Century Ulster'.

Suzanne O'Neill had, until a short time before, no particular interest in nineteenth-century Ulster, still less in Presbyterianism. She did, however, have an interest in columns, or to be precise in the form of Ionic columns found in the Temple of Apollo Epicurius, built in the fifth century BC at Bassai, in a mountainous area of Arcadia. So remote indeed was the temple that its ruins were only 'discovered' in 1765 by a French archaeologist who, on a return visit to explore the site, was murdered by bandits. Ill-luck befell the next archaeologist to reach the temple too, when the ship carrying the sketches he had made was wrecked off the coast of the Peloponnese. An 1812 expedition led by Sir Charles Cockerill had better fortune. The British Museum published detailed drawings of the temple in 1820 and in 1845 Cockerill himself designed the Ashmolean Library in Oxford, incorporating – for the first time since the fifth century BC, it was supposed – the Ionic columns *in antis* particular to Bassai.

In fact, as Suzanne O'Neill had discovered, Cockerill had been beaten to it by a full decade by the architect of, of all things, a Presbyterian Church in, of all places, the Castlereagh hills to the south-east of Belfast.

Bassai it is not, but Castlereagh Presbyterian Church is, easily missed today, now that the city has wrapped itself around the foot of the hills, though if you take the trouble to find it (right off the Ring Road, right again, stay in second gear: up) you will understand what a commanding position it once held: commanding enough for the O'Neill family, who ruled this part of Ireland before the Plantation, to have chosen the site for their castle, the so-called 'eagle's nest'.

(The story is often told here how, in a later century, the Marquis of Downshire, keen to preserve the castle's ruins, instructed his agent to build a wall around them; the agent passed on the instruction to a mason who proceeded to build the wall with stones from the ruins he was supposed to be protecting.)

The question Suzanne O'Neill had asked herself, the question that had led her to Cross Currents and thence to the Duke of York, was why that church – with those columns – had been built at that time in that place. The answer, as I understood her, was connected to the fall-out of the 1798 Rebellion, in which Belfast Presbyterians had played so conspicuous a part. In that instant I felt the balloon begin to inflate again. I had an inn on the north of the town, a church in the hills to the southeast, I had, somewhere in the background, by way of a third co-ordinate, the ghost of 1798.

There still remained the question of voice. I decided to adopt the narrative viewpoint of the essay that had got me started: that of an elderly man looking back from close to the end of the century to the Belfast of his youth. My grandmother, who was still alive, had been born in 1911. Her idiom would have been influenced, inflected by that of her parents, themselves born in the 1880s. I couldn't do 1830s, but between my great-grandparents and Narcissus G. Batt I thought I could make a stab at, say, 1898, or to take a little pressure off the date, the closing week of the year before that momentous centenary.

I also thought I could try to work the architect of Castlereagh Presbyterian into the plot.

His name was John Millar. His grandfather had a marble yard on Berry Street, off what is now Royal Avenue, one of Belfast's main shopping streets. Then it was Hercules Street, home to forty-nine of the town's eighty-odd butchers, 'an unhealthy and unsavoury area', according to Marcus Patton's *Central Belfast: A Historical Gazetteer*. Millar's father appears for a time to have managed the sandstone quarry at Scrabo, in Newtownards, far enough away from Belfast by the standards of early-nineteenth-century travel as to suggest a residence there.

According to Suzanne O'Neill, Millar had been a subscriber to the British Museum publication cataloguing the discoveries at Bassai. Before taking on Castlereagh, he had trained in London with Thomas Hopper, who throughout the 1820s and 30s (and on into the '40s and '50s) was overseeing the building of Gosford Castle at Markethill in Co. Armagh. Millar's first commission as an architect in his own right was for a pair of villas at Holywood, Co. Down, on the successful completion of which he entered, and won, the competition for another church, Third Presbyterian, on Rosemary Street, across Hercules Street from Berry Street. That was in 1829, and John Millar was eighteen.

What is remarkable, looking back over a distance of almost two centuries, is that John Millar's precociousness was not at all exceptional. If the past really is another country then Belfast-past was a country for young men. In 1823, a twenty-two-year-old, George Benn, had published (anonymously) a *History of the Town of Belfast, with an accurate account of its former and present state*, for many years after the standard work on the town. With his brother Edward, Benn was also a close associate of the group – several of whom were under twenty – that in 1821 established the Belfast Natural History and Philosophical Society. To begin with the Society met in its members' houses or in the premises of the Linen Hall Library, a.k.a. the Belfast Society for Promoting Knowledge, another legacy of the previous century's radical

Presbyterianism. By the end of its first decade, however, the Society was looking for premises of its own – a museum, no less – where it could display the many curios amassed and discussed by its members.

The building was paid for by public subscription – the first museum to be so funded in all of Ireland – and its design was entrusted to the partnership of Thomas Duff and Thomas Jackson. Jackson was a former pupil of Duff; and Duff, in turn, a pupil of Thomas Hopper. The Hopper connection might explain why John Millar, called away on who knows what business, shortly after winning the competition for Third Presbyterian, asked Duff and Jackson to oversee the actual construction of his church.

By the time I discovered this I was already well embarked on my novel. It is a fact that once you begin working on any book, you find out all the reasons why it is the very thing that you ought to be writing at that moment. Peggy Barclay had piqued my interest, John Millar had sharpened it, but what finally caused the novel to leap into life was the imaginative connections I had made reading around these two, in particular to the 1831 Port of Belfast Act, in the development of the town one of the most important pieces of legislation ever passed.

The passage of the Port Act, indeed, serves as a kind of foundation myth for the modern city of Belfast. Up until then, access to the town by water had been hampered by the tidal River Lagan, which meandered across extensive mudflats to join Belfast Lough. At the lowest tides water in the docks at the end of High Street dropped to a depth of only three or four feet. Larger vessels had to berth at the Pool of Garmoyle, three miles down river from the town, where their passengers and cargo were transferred to lighters, or 'gabbards', for the final leg of the journey.

Several plans for 'improvement' had been considered over the years and in the late 1700s a body known as the Ballast Board had been instituted to co-ordinate and advance these plans. (One early-nineteenth-century Board member was John McCracken, whose brother Henry Joy McCracken had led the Belfast volunteers in 1798 and had been hanged in the aftermath of their defeat.) The 1831 Act incorporated proposals made by the engineer James Walker for a series of cuts in the course of the Lagan below the town to create a straight channel into the Lough. The silt dredged up in the creation of this channel – named, on its completion in 1847, the Victoria Channel – helped to consolidate marshland on the east bank of the river giving rise in time to Queen's Island, which after a few years as a pleasure ground, the 'People's Park', complete with miniature Crystal Palace, became the home of Belfast's most famous shipyard, Harland and Wolff.

That, though, in 1831, was far in the future. The immediate concern for the promoters of the Bill was opening up Belfast to overseas markets. No one, it was thought, with the town's best interests at heart could object to a scheme that would benefit all its inhabitants. But objections there were, and from the highest echelon of society: Lord Donegall, principal landowner of the town, whose ancestor James Chichester had been granted the town's first charter, by James I, back in 1613.

The Chichesters or their appointees had supplied the town's MPs ever since, returned on a franchise of twelve. They now used their connections at Westminster to harry the Bill on its journey through the lower and upper houses. Lord Donegall had struggled for most of his adult life with gambling debts. The prospect – or rather near certainty – of reform threatened his family's continued influence in the town. There is reason to believe that his obstruction was motivated by nothing more than the desire to extract the best price he could for what were still officially his lands.

The lead-up to the Act, I had decided, was the ideal backdrop for the novel I had in mind to write and the Ballast Board, or rather the Ballast Office, at the end of High Street, the ideal place of work for my central character, a young man (as recalled by his older self) whom I named Gilbert Rice.

Orphaned at an early age Gilbert has been raised by his grandfather on Donegall Place (childhood home of Narcissus Batt), a few hundred yards from Berry Street and the marble yard belonging to John Millar's grandfather. Of course he and Millar meet; of course they become friends.

During the early months of 1831, which occupy the bulk of the narrative, Gilbert passes almost daily along Rosemary Street checking on the progress of Third Presbyterian Church which, in so far as he understands the meaning of the words, looks every bit as 'pure and massive' as his absent friend had intended. When at length Millar himself returns, however, he is appalled by what he finds: this is not the church he designed at all. A single day later and Duff and Jackson would have ruined it utterly. His ire extends to everything that those two 'architects' have touched and when Gilbert tells him, in passing, of the 'time capsule' they have had built into the foundations of the Museum for the benefit and enlightenment of future generations, he is rendered speechless.

The Mill for Grinding Old People Young is a work of fiction; its 'John Millar' is substantially a creature of my own imagination. The historical John Millar left almost nothing in the way of written testimony. Almost. As to the testimony of his architecture, J.B. Doyle, writing in 1854 in *Tours in Ulster* pronounced Rosemary Street a 'truly splendid building'. True its situation, in which Millar had no say, was 'unhappily chosen, the narrow street not permitting its proportions and elevation to be seen to advantage', unlike the building that precedes it in Doyle's tour, the 'very chaste and elegant' museum on the north side of College Square, but all else about it impresses. With its peripteral portico of twenty cast-iron columns (Doric, this time) each weighing two tons, it is in fact 'universally admitted to be the most gorgeously finished meeting-house in the kingdom'.

Charles Brett, whose seminal *Buildings of Belfast 1700–1914* was first published in 1966, three years before the start of the Troubles that altered the face of the city forever, remarks in a footnote to Third Presbyterian that Millar emigrated to New Zealand 'shortly after [the church's] completion' – the suggestion is still in high dudgeon at the havoc so nearly wreaked on his plans – but he was certainly in Belfast in 1835 when Castlereagh Presbyterian was completed on the site of the 'eagle's nest', and in 1841 when he built another Presbyterian church at Portaferry, once more making use of Ionic Bassai columns. It is more probable that he left Belfast in 1855. His name appears on Christmas Day of that year among the four hundred and thirty passengers on board the *SS Schomberg*, bound from Liverpool to Melbourne, when it ran aground at Peterborough on Australia's 'Shipwreck Coast'. The Captain, Forbes, had been below deck playing cards with two women passengers at the time. His ship, built by the Black Ball Line was considered the 'most perfect clipper ship ever', a curious prefiguring of another maiden-voyage wreck, the White Star Line's *RMS Titanic*, except that all four hundred and thirty of the *Schomberg*'s passengers were picked up unharmed.

John Millar made his way eventually to New Zealand's South Island where he became town engineer for Dunedin. The man who as a twenty-year-old tyro had got the jump on Sir Charles Cockerill and the Ashmolean ended his working life designing street lamps, on which he made sure that his name was embossed.

He died in 1876. Sixty-five years later, on the night of 15/16 April 1941, the Third Presbyterian Church was destroyed in a massive German bombing raid on Belfast. Inside one of the portico's columns a 'time capsule' was found in the form of an engraved slate, the DNA fragment from which I have grown my fictional character:

> "POSTERITY know ye that I a son of dust do cause this tablet to be here inserted that you may not attribute the design of this Building to others than myself which I designed in my Eighteenth year and third of my studentship 1829 During an absence from my native Belfast the superintendency was entrusted at its commencement to two quacks Duff and Jackson self-styled architects who so mutilated my designs as to make me almost disown them that portion of the dross you People of refined taste which I can foresee you must be can easily distinguish from the refined on my return I fostered my own child until it grew to what you now behold having begun and finished the Peripteral Portico under my own personal superintendence in the year 1831 JOHN MILLAR ARCHITECT."

The slate can be seen today in Presbyterian Church House, in Fisherwick Place, across the street from Jury's Hotel. A little up the street from Jury's, around the corner into College Square North, Duff and Jackson's museum building still stands. Until recently the 'Old Museum Arts Centre', it is still the home of the Belfast Natural History and Philosophical Society. And it was there – no longer by anyone's reckoning a young man – that I delivered this lecture in September 2011.

(Adapted from notes for a lecture to the Belfast Natural History & Philosophical Society, Old Museum, 7 September 2011.)

7

A City 'on the rise': Travel and Tourism in Nineteenth-Century Belfast

Éadaoin Agnew

> The Lonely Planet Bluelist, which features Northern Ireland on its "Go list" of hot destinations to visit in 2007, describes the six counties as "abuzz with life: the cities are pulsating, the economy is thriving and the people, the lifeblood that courses through the country, are in good spirits.
> The second edition of the annual guide ... also tips Belfast as one of the top 10 cities "on the rise", as well as Vilnius in Lithuania and Perth, Australia.[1]

In the same year that the Lonely Planet's Bluelist hailed the rising status of Belfast, devolution was restored to Northern Ireland, a seminal moment that marked a new and hopeful era for the previously troubled state. In this optimistic frame of mind, Northern Ireland embraced its position as an up-and-coming destination recommended by the well-respected global travel experts; and in 2008 just over two million visitors from the Republic of Ireland, Great Britain and overseas visited the province. It is not unreasonable to suggest that, along with Belfast's increased stability, the Lonely Planet's Bluelist was partly responsible for this influx of visitors. Being marked out as a 'City on the Rise' certainly indicated that Belfast was a favoured destination on the tourist trail; thus, it can be argued that travel guides and travel literature not only respond to an interest in a specific place but that they also help to create that interest. As such, it is a curious to note that in the mid-nineteenth century, Belfast was being drawn in terms very similar to recent tourist propaganda.

In 1855, the anonymous author of *Belfast and its Environs: The Strangers Pocket Guide through Belfast* noted that the city was developing and changing at a rather accelerated pace:

> Few cities have grown more rapidly than Belfast. The pressure of famine, and the consequent failure in trade and business, told fearfully on all commercial districts; but especially so in Belfast – whose very life is trade. The worst of the result, however, has now passed away, and fresh vigour pervades every department. It requires but a glance at its crowded streets, and rapidly extending suburbs, to anticipate what the future aspect of the city must inevitably be.[2]

Clearly intended as a practical guide, *Belfast and its Environs* was designed in such a way that it could be carried easily as the traveller traversed the streets of the city seeking out the recommended places of interest. Also published in the mid-nineteenth century, *Black's Guide to Belfast* similarly identified a 'city on the rise':

> Few towns have progressed in importance so rapidly as Belfast. It appears almost incredible that in the course of 30 years, the population should have increased nearly threefold; yet it is certain that in 1821 the inhabitants numbered only 37,000, while in 1851 they exceeded 100,000.[3]

The statistics offered by Black's are cited time and time again by various travel writers in numerous handbooks and guidebooks for the city. As noted in *Belfast and its Environs*, in the post-Famine years Belfast had made an enormous recovery and was attracting an ever-increasing number of inhabitants and travellers, both of which contributed to the life of the city. It is this curious parallel between the travel literature of the latter half of the nineteenth century and the early part of the twenty-first century that initially inspired this chapter, which seeks to explore the various ways that Belfast was viewed by visitors in the decades after the Great Irish Famine. By considering the various discourses through which Belfast was represented, it will be suggested that while particular places seem to have individual identities that are continually asserted, travel literature is also rooted firmly in the ideological apparatus of the author and the historical context. Thus, in order to fully understand the issues relating to travel in and around Belfast at this time, it will be necessary to first consider the broader political, cultural and ideological context.

The nineteenth century witnessed the birth of mass travel and tourism and Ireland as a whole enjoyed this boom. During this period, the vast majority of books published in English about Ireland were written by its British neighbours and Anglo-Irish settlers, although unsurprisingly there was also a number of Americans who travelled to Ireland, particularly in the post-Famine years. Prior to this, in the eighteenth century, it was generally expected that the British middle classes and upper-middle classes would satisfy their wanderlust by embarking on the Grand Tour, a rite of passage that was seen to complete their education and validate a sense of self through engaging with the antiquities of Europe. As a result, travel in Britain and Ireland was less popular. However, the Napoleonic wars (1790–1815) meant that British travellers were temporarily cut off from Europe; consequently, there were increasing numbers of British travellers who turned to their own and neighbouring countries.

The troubles in Europe also coincided with a reorientation of the notion of centre and periphery and as a result, as Glen Hooper informs us, parts of Scotland and Ireland were transformed from inaccessible and unattractive regions with little to recommend them to rediscovered venues of primitive delight.[4] Popular aesthetic concepts, such as the picturesque and the sublime helped to promote the 'undeveloped' nature of these places as they emphasized the beauty of awe-inspiring natural landscapes. In *Creating Irish Tourism*, William Williams claims that Ireland was among the first countries to be defined, at least in part, in terms of its scenic attractions, and Belfast's proximity to beautiful natural landscapes, such as the Giant's Causeway, meant that from the early nineteenth century it was a potential destination for those travellers seeking less-developed landscapes.[5] For example, in 1806, Richard Colt Hoare, having already explored Wales and Scotland, turned to the apparently 'unvisited and unknown' landscape of Ireland. Influenced by popular aesthetic discourses he revelled in the 'undeveloped' wilds of Ireland and praised its rugged and largely pre-industrial landscapes.[6] Yet it is interesting to note that on his way to explore the Antrim coast and discover these natural spaces, he briefly visited the 'manufactories' of Belfast; such industrial spaces would later become a destination in their own right.

By the early nineteenth century, romantic notions about Ireland's natural landscapes prevailed. However, these coexisted with a sense of shame at the impoverished lives of the Irish people. In this way, the underdeveloped state of the country was a source of beauty and of embarrassment for English visitors for whom Ireland was rather too close to home. As a result, the perceived lack of 'progress' contrasted with British imperial values and inspired a desire to improve the country to raise it to an acceptable level of 'civilization', a desire that can be seen as a direct consequence of the Act of Union in 1801. After this significant event, many English travellers were determined to view Ireland as a natural extension of their British State. While they recognized that Ireland was not entirely easily subsumed within the Union, it seemed to be taken for granted that it was merely a matter of time before this would happen. For many, Ireland was, for all intents and purposes, the same, while being different enough to warrant travel in the first place; this was a curious dichotomy that was humorously noted by the *Metropolitan Magazine*: 'Before travelling *in* Ireland, an Englishman must needs travel *to* Ireland'.[7]

Many of the Englishmen travelling to Ireland confronted Irish poverty with the Victorian values of improvement and civilization, which meant that they wrote about their experiences in terms of commentaries and analyses rather than literary descriptions of pleasurable holidays, a fact that is reflected in the titles of their texts; for example, Thomas Reid's *Travels in Ireland in the Year 1822: Exhibiting Brief Sketches of the Moral, Physical, and Political State of the Country: With Reflections on the Best Means of Improving its Condition*. Particularly in the early decades of the nineteenth century, such socio-economic narratives proliferated. These texts suggested that while Ireland was not already entirely known, it was seen to be knowable, which, as Thomas Richards has explained, was important for Britain's colonial project:

> From all over the globe the British collected information about the countries they were adding to their map. They surveyed and they mapped. They took consensus, produced statistics.[8]

Richards argues that as the empire grew so did Britain's need to control and construct it. Subsequently, the need to gather as much data as possible in order to gain and maintain power became paramount. In addition to supplementing official imperial drives for information such as the Ordnance Survey, there was also a more general move towards these imperialist ideals evident in travel literature throughout the empire, and Ireland's proximity ensured that it was open to being *known* by a vast number of travellers.

Thus, socio-economic commentators existed alongside those writers with a Romantic interest in the scenic. Together they encouraged increasing numbers of visitors to Ireland; this led to a subsequent demand for practical information in order to meet the needs of the travellers and tourists. Yet in the 1820s and 1830s there was often an articulation of the fear that Ireland had not been sufficiently stabilised by the Union to encourage tourism. In 1835 an advertisement for Cesar Otway's *Sketches in Ireland Descriptive of Hitherto Unnoticed Districts in the North and South* in the *Guide to Killarney and Glengarrif* claimed that it is 'An able and most delightful volume, which most certainly, if Ireland were in a tranquil state, could not fail to draw thither annual shoals of picturesque tourists'.[9] Already forming was the axis of trouble and tourism that has intermittently marked travel to Ireland, particularly to Belfast, where the 'troubles' have had a massive impact on the tourism industry of the late twentieth century. And in response to such concerns, the idea of gathering information gained even greater urgency in an effort to enable the Union to survive. One of the most popular travel books during this period was Henry Inglis's *Ireland in 1834: A Journey throughout Ireland in the Spring, Summer and Autumn of 1834*; it was clearly intended as more than a literary narrative of a leisurely tour as the two-volume work embarks on a systematic and wide-ranging account of social conditions, exemplifying the shared features of the pre-Famine travel text: poverty, dirt, beggary, oppression and obscurity. Inglis identified a general lack of information about towns in Ireland, but despite the fact that Belfast was 'a second-rate town', there was some knowledge of the northern city; this was in contrast to places like Kilkenny, Clonmel, Galway or Athlone, of which there were only vague descriptions.[10] Then of course, in the 1840s, came the Famine.

Perhaps contrary to expectations, the Famine did not entirely deter visitors from travelling in Ireland and writing about their journeys; it simply changed *how* they wrote about their travels. Indeed it almost seemed that poverty and devastation attracted visitors. It has even been suggested by Melissa Fegan that during the nineteenth century, the most cited reason for writing a travel narrative of Ireland was actually Irish poverty, as opposed to the beautiful scenery or cultural attractions.[11] Certainly British newspapers were full of Irish distress and unrest. Journalists, such as Harriet Martineau, were sent to Ireland to report directly from the scene. But such obsessive scrutiny of the situation was not purely altruistic. Clearly motivated by England's close relationship to Ireland, there was a discernible fear from the more prosperous, Protestant nation that the geographic and political proximity of a poor, populous Catholic country would prove to be a serious economic and social liability. Thus, the travel narratives in this period became a vehicle for the expression of British anxiety about Ireland.

While this was certainly not a time for leisurely holidays, during this period there was an influx of philanthropic travellers who wished to show the awful suffering of the Irish people in order to encourage attempts to alleviate it. In particular, many Anglo-Irish settlers wished to alert their English neighbours to the proximity of the tragic suffering in Ireland. Lord Dufferin of Clandeboye in Co. Down published his account of a journey from Oxford to Skibbereen in which he wrote:

> The scenes we have witnessed during our short stay at Skibbereen, equal any thing that has been recorded by history, or could be conceived by the imagination. Famine, typhus fever, dysentery, and a disease hitherto unknown, are sweeping away the whole population. The poor are not the only sufferers: fever is spreading to every class, and even the rich are becoming involved in the same destruction.[12]

Within two years of Dufferin's damning report, the Famine was deemed to have come to an end. Instigated by Queen Victoria's visit in 1849, assessments of the country presented Ireland as available for redevelopment and resettlement.

The Queen's Irish tour was intended to mark officially a change in Ireland's fortune and sought to reassure the travelling public about security in Ireland; thus, her published narrative focused on picturesque scenery, tourism and, perhaps most importantly, development; thus when she went to Belfast she visited the linen mill, the botanic gardens, and some places of architectural interest thereby initiating an itinerary that many travellers would follow. She restricted her visit to the major cities, Dublin, Cork and Belfast, which she only visited for a matter of hours. During this short period of time sectarian disputes were put to one side and the Queen was welcomed by Protestants and Catholics alike.[13] Interestingly, out of all the banners prepared for her visit, her published journal highlights one that read 'Cead mile failte,' which she translated for her readers as 'A hundred thousand welcomes' in order to underline the friendly reception she received.[14] But while she commended the generally affable nature of the people, she was rather less impressed by the women of Belfast, claiming that 'the female beauty has almost disappeared'![15]

The visit received extensive coverage in the British press, which certainly raised Ireland's profile in Britain and encouraged more visitors, particularly those with economic interests. In 1851, John Hervey Ashworth dedicated *The Saxon in Ireland, Rambles of an Englishman in Search of a Settlement in the West of Ireland* to 'persons looking out for investments or for new settlements'.[16] Yet for some politically conscious writers, such as Martineau, it was important to stress that such settlement would not necessarily be easy because of the inherent differences between the Irish and the English.[17] However, for those concerned about such disparities, Belfast's Scottish Presbyterian influence made the city more familiar to British travellers; this was seen as an attractive selling point. For some Anglophone travellers in the mid-nineteenth century the desire for the exotic was not as important as the replication of 'Englishness' elsewhere. In this way, Belfast was continually marketed as being distinct from the rest of Ireland. So while Ireland more broadly was seen as destitute and difficult, Belfast was depicted as more affluent. In 1854, Black's *Guide* remarked that in terms of poverty, Belfast suffered less than the rest of the country:

> It is but due to Belfast, however, to state that in no town in Ireland will the tourist be less pestered with crowds of beggars, and shocked with the squalid wretchedness of the supplicants. He may walk from one of the town to the other and never be once stopped by a beggar. Unfortunately, so much cannot be said for Dublin.[18]

The idea that Belfast was a haven from rural poverty was also put forward by Horace Grealy, who noted in a letter to the *New York Tribune* in 1851 that 'Belfast is a busy, growing town' amidst a sea of poverty. While travelling from Belfast to Dublin, Grealy commented that, 'Wretchedness, rags and despair salute me on every side'.[19]

Despite such positive impressions of Belfast in the first half of the century, the poverty-stricken south of Ireland seemed to awaken a morbid curiosity in people and the overwhelming majority of travellers to Ireland headed south on their journeys, only occasionally venturing north to take in the Giant's Causeway. However, Belfast came to be seen as an increasingly important city, which was largely a result of Victorian industrialization.

The industrial revolution changed how and why people travelled in Ireland. Not only did Belfast's industries become a source of interest to the average traveller, but the construction of the railways had a massive impact on the tourist industry. The rail networks of Ireland were developed throughout the 1830s and 1840s. In 1839 the Ulster railway opened its first line, which ran between Belfast and Lisburn, and in 1849, the Dublin and Belfast Junction Railway was opened; this had a major impact on the amount of ground a traveller could reasonably expect to cover in a single visit and helped to bring north and south closer together. As the Belfast bookseller and publisher William McComb noted in 1861 in a guide to his home city, the railways were integral to 'improving the acquaintance of the inhabitants of one district with the people, local curiosities, manners and habits of another; and dispelling the ignorance which previously prevailed as to those traits of Ulster, calculated amply to repay a casual excursion or an occasional sojourn'.[20]

Thomas Cook was one of the first to encourage casual excursions by capitalizing on the expanding rail network when he recommended short sojourns in Ireland in 1852. As we know, Cook played a major role in making tourism more widely feasible and he was instrumental in the construction of Irish railways. He supported the building of more and more track and he expanded his Irish business accordingly. In 1856, for example, Cook conducted about 1,500 tourists in sixty railway cars to some of Ireland's most beautiful spots. However, the railway companies soon began to take note of Cook's success and became convinced that they could increase their profit by organizing their own excursion trains; so, for a time, they refused to sell inexpensive tickets to Cook. For seventeen years Cook was unable to conduct tours in Ireland while the railway companies monopolized the package tour business. Eventually, the railways recognized that Cook's success actually contributed to their own and lifted their embargo. Cook then opened the company's first office in Dublin, and by the 1880s they enjoyed a lucrative business there.

Undoubtedly the railways and the tour companies did a lot to bring English travellers to Ireland, a fact noted by the *Belfast News Letter:*

> We understand that extensive arrangements for inducing English tourists to visit Ireland, during the ensuing summer, have just been completed by the Great Southern and Western and the Chester and Holyhead Companies, in co-operation with several of the other Railway companies both in England and Ireland ... The 'Irish Tourist Tickets', for so they are to be called, will be available for a month from the date of their issue. They will enable the holders to travel from the stations at which they are taken out to Bangor, to inspect the Britannia and Menai bridges, Holyhead and Dublin, and thence to Mallow or to Cork.[21]

There were various touring options available and Belfast, which became marketed as the gateway to the rest of Ulster, was an important attraction for those wishing to visit places like the Giant's Causeway or the popular seaside resort of Bangor. Indeed Belfast's fortunate location was frequently mentioned as one of its selling points:

> This city – metropolis of Ulster, and second to no city in the kingdom in commercial enterprise or manufacturing spirit – is situated at the embouchure of the river Lagan into the Belfast Lough; sheltered by Divis and the basaltic range of the Belfast mountains from the western and north-western blasts, ... and, though low in site, eminently fitted, by its facility of access from the surrounding agricultural districts and its nearness to Liverpool, to be, what it has become, the great outlet for the enterprise and industry of Ulster.[22]

Such recommendations and improvements certainly encouraged visitors, but for some travel guides, Ireland still had a little way to go:

> With the progress of time the inn accommodation in Ireland has considerably improved. Some of the local proprietors have erected handsome hotels on a most liberal scale. Nevertheless, if the facilities for travelling in Ireland were greater, and more attention were paid to order and cleanliness, by the Irish inn-keeper, he would have a fair chance of diverting into that beautiful island a large portion of the 'tourist flood' which now streams to the Continent.[23]

The expansion of the tourist industry meant that countries and cities had to compete for visitors and Ireland it seemed was comparatively late into the game: although John Murray began his series of handbooks in 1836, Ireland did not feature until 1864, by which time Belfast was established as a definite tourist destination.

By the 1860s there were periodicals that offered the tourist up-to-date travel information, such as *The Official Irish Travellers' Guide,* which included railway timetables, omnibus routes, and cab fares. And William McComb's *Guide to Belfast* aimed to provide all kinds of useful information, such as the prices for Belfast's Turkish baths. But in addition to such practical assistance, McComb offered a narrative that aimed to take travellers off the beaten track;[24] this implies that by 1861 there was a beaten track from which to stray, even though, as he admits, tourism in the north of Ireland was a relatively recent phenomenon. But as the railways suggested certain routes and the picturesque beauties of Ulster became more and more familiar to the tourist and the traveller, writers sought out new delights to justify their narratives.[25] Yet, for the most part, travellers and tourists noted the same points of interest.

Beyond its location, other popular selling points were price and the friendly people who welcomed strangers[26] with their combination of 'Scottish thrift and decorum with Irish impulsiveness and kindliness'.[27] Before long, the citizens of Belfast came to be depicted in terms that have become increasingly familiar: they were seen to display 'indomitable perseverance in spite of all obstacles', an 'unwearied industry' and 'intelligence, and keen-sighted sagacity'.[28] In fact, much of Belfast's rising status was attributed to the tenacity of its people:

> Belfast has not been nursed by government protection, or swollen to its present condition by government or any other patronage ... The sturdy independence of the people has been their might stay; and, under all chances, trusting to and in themselves, every adventitious circumstance has

> been turned to advantage, and difficulties have only called forth greater effort ... No city in Europe, is the almost universal opinion of the English papers, has made such rapid strides; and no city is less indebted to any extraneous aid.[29]

In the post-Famine years, as much of Ireland was being presented as some kind of outside investment opportunity, Belfast's industry was expanding under the watchful eye of local industrialists such as Andrew Mulholland.

From even before the Famine, Belfast had been working toward establishing itself as a centre for textile manufacture. In the 1840s, Andrew Mulholland had brought his son John into partnership and together they expanded the business, eventually opening branches in Paris, London, New York, Berlin and Melbourne. Linen lords such as the Mulhollands brought prosperity to the city and played an active role in Belfast's public life. For example, Andrew Mulholland, Lord Mayor of Belfast from 1845–6, donated the Grand Organ to the city's Ulster Hall, an organ now considered one of the oldest examples of a functioning English classic pipe organ. The fact that Belfast was really the only Irish city to experience fully the Industrial Revolution was, for many travellers and potential investors, a unique selling point. Furthermore, as part of the British empire, English travellers could share a sense of national pride in relation to Belfast's successes.

The keen interest in industry combined with the philanthropic spirit of the travelling Victorian middle classes meant that visitors to Belfast frequently stopped off at one of Mulholland's mills. In much the same spirit as they ventured to workhouses after the introduction of the Poor Law in 1838, the middle-class traveller exercised a sense of benevolence while indulging in a kind of 'poverty pornography' as it has recently come to be known. Factory workers were voyeuristically viewed by Victorian writers through rose-tinted spectacles; for example, in 1843 Thackeray saw Mulholland's 'millies' in rather romanticized terms:

> I have seldom, I think, seen more good looks than amongst the young women employed in this place. They work for twelve hours daily, in rooms of which the heat is intolerable to a stranger; but in spite of it they looked gay, stout, and healthy; nor were their forms much concealed by the very simple clothes they wear while in the mill.[30]

However, not all travellers were so naive. Notably, Washington, an American author, had a slightly more realistic view of the mill: 'The scene is almost terrific – machinery, steam; pretty, delicate, pale-looking young girls; old, horrid and hateful hags; spindles, noises – all more like a fevered dream than a fact. The women get wages ridiculously small, scarcely a dime a day'.[31] The divergence between these two descriptions may be somewhat explained by the national identities of the two authors and the potential readership of their texts. As noted above, British authors tended to place industry in high esteem, viewing it as marker of progress which brought Belfast more in line with English cities, inviting comparisons with Manchester and Liverpool rather than Dublin or Cork. William McComb and Queen Victoria were among those travellers who saw parallels between Belfast and these northern English cities. However, Thackeray was even more generous in his praise as he claimed that Belfast was the Irish London rather than the Irish Liverpool, primarily because it was hearty, thriving and prosperous.[32] On a similar note, John Murray wrote that 'The situation of Belfast is well adapted for commercial purposes, and it is rapidly rising, in enterprise, wealth and population, to the first place among

Irish cities'.[33] And Richard Harcourt went so far as to say that in terms of industry, 'Belfast is the great linen emporium of the world', and yet he noted that it is 'Strange that from the land where so many go shirtless, should come snow-white linen, to satisfy the want of the world'![34]

While industry does seem to have been a major reason for visiting Belfast, John Murray's guide is very clear that there was more to recommend the city: 'Nor is it only as a manufacturing centre that Belfast is pre-eminent; she is equally noted for the position gained by her inhabitants in literature and the arts'.[35] By the mid-nineteenth century, there were numerous attractions for those who came to Belfast. Visitors were encouraged to see the Belfast Bank, the Belfast Museum, St. Malachy's church, Queen's College, the Presbyterian Meeting house and the Botanic Gardens which were situated in the area of the city that received the most praise:

> This portion of the environs of the city exhibits remarkable taste in the edifices which line the road. They are generally very elegant – their style much varied; and being intermixed with handsome gardens, and agreeable promenades, and, as yet, with an open, smiling landscape behind them, present altogether a fine and gratifying appearance.[36]

While John Murray's guide did note that there were some fine commercial buildings, such as the Custom-house, the Ulster Bank, the Ulster Hall, the Music Hall in May Street, Queen's College, the Presbyterian College, and the Belfast Museum in College Square, he concluded that the Botanic Gardens were more impressive than much of the architecture on offer:

> The conservatories are excellent, well kept and contain a choice and rich collection of exotics ... The kindness of influential friends of the city is continually adding to the most valuable and rarities of foreign lands. Several fine specimens of the bird tribe are also to be seen. Altogether, it has been remarked by intelligent travellers, who have visited these gardens, that in no other of the kind has more taste and skill been displayed. The care, the spirited efforts continually in action for the increase and beautifying of the gardens just, indeed, when combined with taste and judgement, always produce such results. It may, however, just be observed, that the gardens are entirely too exclusive. They ought to be freer to the public; the price of admission ought to be lower. In Glasgow, since the price of admission to the Botanic Garden was reduced on half, the income from visitors has increased. Institutions of this kind, ought, indeed, to be, to a great extent, public.[37]

And as the Botanic Gardens' flowers and fauna were praised for the good taste by which they had been cultivated, many travellers were equally drawn to the natural beauty of the area. The natural landscapes of Belfast are what most impressed E.K. Washington who waxed rather lyrically about the beauty of Belfast and its environs:

> The morning is clear and delicious, but somewhat cool, and the dying summer smiles mournfully as the glistening, dried leaves fall around. Yet the general appearance of the country and the fields is worthy of the reputation of 'Green Erin'[38]

It was the wild and rugged Cave Hill that was most frequently singled out. It was the place upon which, according to Murray, the traveller can 'embrace a panorama of great beauty'.[39]

As noted above, dominant visual cultures played an important role in the discourses of travel literature, and in the later decades of the nineteenth century, influenced by panoramic pictures, travellers sought out positions from which they could gain a point of privileged viewing. This mode of representation has been discussed by David Spurr in his analysis of the explorer Henry Morton Stanley whose characteristic rhetorical strategy was to place himself on some 'noble coign of vantage' in order to survey the scene below in such a way as to combine spatial arrangement with strategic, aesthetic, or economic valorisation of the landscape.[40] For the imperial traveller in Belfast, Cave Hill offered an appropriate vantage point:

> The tourist should not leave Belfast without paying a visit to *Cave Hill*, which overhangs the city, at a distance of about 2m, and is interesting both in a geological and antiquarian point of view ... If the visitor be neither antiquary nor geologist, he will, nevertheless, be delighted with the view from any one of these heights ... At the foot lies Belfast, with its churches, mills and docks; the harbour, and the broad Lough of Strangford; the hills of Down on the opposite side, sprinkled with many a smiling village; while afar in the distance are the dim outlines of the Ayrshire coast, and on a clear day the cliffs of the Isle of Man.[41]

Yet for McComb, Cave Hill's empire-like vista was somewhat undercut by his rejection of the popular comparison between the outline of the hills and the Titanian profile of Napoleon the Great.[42]

For the most part, McComb's *Guide* delineated the usual excursions and attractions. Yet, he seemed to feel that Belfast broadly offered something for everyone and that his guide would be able to satisfy all their needs:

> The principal object of the present work is, to afford tourists and other strangers visiting the North-Eastern portion of Ulster, as well as to residents resorting to its numerous watering-places during the Summer season, accurate topographical, historical, antiquarian, and general information regarding the localities of leading interest – their scenery, inhabitants, natural curiosities, attractions to chose in search of pleasure or health, commercial, agricultural and social progress, industrial resources, &c.[43]

Perhaps unsurprisingly William McComb's guide was full of hyperbolic praise for his home city. He called to mind the rather grand appellation Belfast had apparently acquired:

> It is more than half-a-century since Belfast was first classically named 'The Northern Athens' from the distinction which it had gained, even then, in the cultivation of polite literature. The stranger who makes himself acquainted with encouragement of and progress in learning, and who secures for himself the pleasure of inspecting its literary and scientific institutions, will at once feel convinced that this honourable appellation was not injudiciously conferred.[44]

Murray's guide had similarly recognized Belfast's status as a cultural city, seeing it as second only to Dublin,[45] and had noted that the opening of the university, one of the Queen's colleges, had greatly consolidated Belfast's status in relation to its dedication to arts and learning. The American publisher/bookseller/periodical distributor William Fetridge confirmed this view by noting that Belfast was the first place in Ireland to print the Bible. However, having been sent around Europe by Harper's Publishing Company in 1865 in order to compile a travel guide, he was able to make comparisons with other European countries and thereby recalled that despite Belfast's Victorian advancement, there had been no printing press anywhere in Ireland until 1694, which was later even than Russia.[46]

For some travellers Belfast was a hot bed of arts and culture, but for others, Belfast seemed to lack cultural development. Thus, despite many allusions to art and literature in the city, Thackeray noted the lack of theatres and lack of talent:

> I found out the place where the poor neglected Dramatic Muse of Ulster hid herself; and was of a party of six in the boxes, the benches of the pit being dotted over with about a score more. Well, it was a comfort to see that the gallery was quite full, and exceedingly happy and noisy: they stamped, and stormed, and shouted, and clapped in a way that was pleasant to hear. One god, between the acts, favoured the public with a song – extremely ill sung certainly, but the intention was everything; and his brethren above stamped in chorus with roars of delight.[47]

It would seem unlikely that Thackeray would entirely agree with Belfast's appellation as the Northern Athens!

Certainly one stumbling block to the classical comparison is the fact that Belfast was consistently seen, even by McComb, as unfailingly modern:

> Belfast is, strictly speaking, a modern town. It possesses no relics of the dim 'long ago' – no hoary ruins – no time-defying monuments – not even a single fabric of respectable age. The antiquity of the oldest building in the borough does not, probably, exceed one hundred and fifty – certainly not two hundred years.[48]

Such modernity was set in direct opposition to much of the rest of Ireland and this was viewed as an antidote for visitors who may have tired of picturesque scenes of ruins and rolling hills. In 1860, E.K. Washington viewed it as a contemporary city, full of activity.[49] However, as in recent times, Belfast's modernity seemed to be in conflict with the rather entrenched religious attitude, which even the generally fervent Victorians found a little displeasing. Thackeray wrote in 1843 that, 'The stranger cannot fail to be struck (and haply a little frightened) by the great number of meeting-houses that decorate the town and give evidence of great sermonising on Sundays'; he also took note of various ongoing religious disagreements that he claimed would not translate for outside understanding.[50] He goes on to note that Belfast is 'a place that seems devoted to preaching, politics, and trade'[51] and it is fair to say that this is not an entirely positive observation, albeit one that has certain resonances with contemporary views of Belfast.

In fact, broadly speaking, it can be argued that many of the observations made by nineteenth-century visitors are echoed by twenty-first century travel guides. The city may have more pubs and clubs, and less industry, than its Victorian counterpart, but Belfast is still noted for the vivacity of the people, the beauty of its scenery and the various examples of fine architecture. However, it would be naive to see such parallels as evidence of Belfast's timeless spirit. We must remember Glenn Hooper's claim that 'each travel narrative was a response to, or attempt to understand, quite specific political and economic circumstances, rather than a mere record of wanderings by various routes across the country'.[52] The traveller is not an innocent wanderer devoid of motivation or ideology, and as we can see, nineteenth-century travel literature is continually informed by the ideologies of the time and the particular circumstances of the author. Such variables and personal differences can be detected even on the finer points of female beauty. While Queen Victoria was somewhat disparaging about the women of the city, Thackeray was rather impressed by the women he encountered:

> The stranger will be struck by the good looks ... of almost all the young women in the streets. I never saw a town where so many women are to be met – so many and so pretty – with and without bonnets, and good figures, in neat homely shawls and dresses. The grisettes of Belfast are among the handsomest ornaments of it; and as good, no doubt, and irreproachable in morals as their sisters in the rest of Ireland.[53]

Thus, just as the Bluelist encouraged a wealth of new visitors to journey to Ireland in 2008, perhaps Thackeray's recommendations were partly responsible for the increase in travel to Belfast in the latter half of the nineteenth century.

8

'A noble Church in the most Catholic quarter of a bitterly Protestant and Presbyterian city': The Church of the Most Holy Redeemer, Clonard, West Belfast.[1]

Caroline M. McGee

Some Lenten evening sharp, at five to eight,
pick a suburban road both long and straight
and leading – which do not? – to a Catholic church:
you'll see, whisked out through every creaking gate,
men only, walking all at the same brisk rate,
all in the same direction...[2]

Between the passing of the Catholic Relief Act in 1829 and the turn of the new century, the Irish Catholic Church conducted an intensive programme to build, renovate or extend church buildings throughout the country.[3] This investment in capital projects was carried out against the backdrop of adjustments to the practice of Irish

Catholicism. While Emmet Larkin has argued that these adjustments constituted a 'devotional revolution', increased mass participation in popular devotional practices during the second half of the nineteenth century is now considered to have been a more evolutionary process.[4] By the second half of the twentieth century, the period in which Hutchinson's poem is set, visiting priests from the many new religious orders who came to Ireland during the latter half of the nineteenth century with the blessing of Paul Cardinal Cullen were conducting regular 'missions' or retreats in Catholic parish churches around the country.[5] The objective of these retreats, which had their roots in a medieval tradition of worship and prayer, was to inculcate in those attending a devout adherence to the rules, regulations and traditions of the Irish Catholic Church.

The Passionist and Redemptorist communities were amongst the orders that came to Ireland at this time.[6] Both were instrumental in adding to the visual landscape of Belfast through the construction of impressive new churches built to accommodate ever-growing congregations. This chapter focuses on the architectural history of the Redemptorist order's church at Clonard Gardens, off the Falls Road, west Belfast: the Church of the Most Holy Redeemer.[7] A unified Romanesque design scheme for the new church and monastery complex was originally proposed, yet what stands on the site today is a large Gothic Revival church somewhat at odds aesthetically with the adjoining redbrick monastery. Recently discovered architectural plans drawn up in 1906 by the architect of both buildings, John Joseph (J.J.) McDonnell, may shed some light on how the present-day appearance of the Clonard Church came about and what an alternative Romanesque building might have looked like.[8]

BUILDING CATHOLIC IRELAND

The nineteenth century was a period of contest within the Irish Catholic Church, between a modern, centralist and homogenizing church and an older more independent tradition, rooted in monasticism. Important Irish prelates such as Cardinals Paul Cullen and Michael Logue oversaw the growth in status and economic power of the Church during the period. Over the course of the century the Catholic hierarchy used these processes of empowerment to achieve élite status. In so doing they brought along with them a wider Catholic political class. The labels 'Catholic' and 'Ireland' became fused with that of national identity.[9] While the extent to which Ireland can be considered a colonial society is critically contested, as it remained part of the Union with Britain until 1921, it may nevertheless be argued that the nineteenth-century Irish Catholic Church had colonial ambitions of its own and that church-building projects carried out during the Victorian period formed a key element of these goals. That they subsequently achieved their objective in the twentieth century may be seen in the role played by the Catholic Church in affairs of the nascent Irish State, and indeed beyond.[10]

From relatively low numbers in the 1820s, church-building projects doubled decade on decade until 1880 and continued, at a slow but steady pace, into the twentieth century. A subsequent critic considered that 'most of the rural Catholic churches were built in one of the worst periods of religious architecture, the nineteenth century'[11], but during this time the Irish Catholic Church managed to build an estimated average of two churches per week.[12] The hierarchy and key Catholic élites worked together on individual, local projects to build new churches and cathedrals. By the close of the century, in one single fund-raising event for decorating the interior of Armagh Cathedral, over £30,000 was raised.[13] Up and down the country Catholic merchants, solicitors, business-owners and landowners contributed their energies and resources to these projects with families and individuals making regular contributions to church-building committee appeals. A casual browse of dedicatory plaques in churches or of subscription lists in contemporary newspapers such as the *Freeman's Journal* serves to illustrate this point.

During the nineteenth century, Belfast grew rapidly as an industrial centre. The 1901 Census showed that the Catholic population had reached almost one hundred thousand, about one third of whom lived in the west Belfast area, then home to a fast growing labour force of mill-workers.[14] While capital development of church buildings was slow during the episcopate of Cornelius Denvir, it took off under the guiding hands of Patrick Dorrian and Patrick McAlister. By the time Henry Henry was appointed Bishop in 1895 the Catholic diocese of Down and Connor, which included the city of Belfast, had expanded dramatically. Thirty-five new churches had been built, fifteen of them in Belfast city. Convents, schools, hospitals and orphanages were also in train, and personnel to manage the running of these churches and institutions had increased accordingly.[15] But although there were three times more priests in the diocese than previously, it still was not enough. In an urban environment, where temptation might lie around the next corner, these rural migrants needed to be guided in the practice of their faith. Parochial missions were a means by which the Church could police this spiritual development, but they also offered Catholic communities an opportunity to publicly display their faith through attendance at weekly meetings, monthly communion services and sermons by visiting preachers. In the fifty years following the arrival of the Redemptorists at Clonard, throngs of people heading in the direction of the church became a regular sight.[16] The mission or retreat was one element of the new rules and regulations introduced to Ireland in 1850 for both priests and people, following the Synod of Thurles, which was convened by

Paul Cullen, then Archbishop of Armagh. Over the next three decades, adherence by Irish Catholics to Italian-inspired devotional models and practices was guided by his firm hand.[17]

One of the continental religious orders that came to Ireland to assist in Cullen's recalibration of Irish Catholicism was the Redemptorists, or the Congregation of the Most Holy Redeemer (C.Ss.R.) as they are officially titled. The order was founded by Saint Alphonsus Liguori in 1732 at Scala, near Naples. The Redemptorists' arrival in Ireland in 1851, just as the Synod of Thurles changes began to gather speed, put them in an excellent position to implement their Congregation's driving goal of

> … forming and consolidating strong Catholic communities by confirming the resolute, reviving the languid faith of the spiritually negligent, recalling the lapsed, and evangelizing the ignorant.[18]

A Redemptorist house was founded in 1853 at Limerick and was followed quickly by the construction of a monastery and church.[19] In 1876 the community was encouraged by Archbishop of Armagh Daniel McGettigan, to found a second house in Dundalk. In 1892 a fine Romanesque church by George Coppinger Ashlin replaced the temporary one that had initially served the area.[20] From these two bases Redemptorist priests were dispatched to as many parishes as possible around Ireland to offer salvation to the faithful through their preaching.[21] As soon as he was appointed Bishop of the Diocese of Down and Connor in 1895, Henry Henry approached the Dundalk community imploring them to found a monastery in his diocese. The Belfast General Mission was held in October 1896; both Passionist and Redemptorist priests preached at it. In the meantime, official sanction by Rome for a new foundation by the latter was almost complete. The

Falls Road neighbourhood of Belfast was chosen by the Bishop as the area most in need of the Redemptorist ministry due to the high concentration of Catholics in the area and the poor ratio of priests to people there.

Soon after their arrival the Redemptorist community established sodalities and confraternities for men, women and later boys, to cater for and nurture the spiritual needs of migrant, rural Catholics who had flocked to the vibrant city of Belfast at this time in search of work.[22] Bishop Henry provided the wherewithal for the foundation of the new community, which was led by Fr. Patrick Griffith. The place in which they would live and minister was to be Clonard Street, adjacent to the linen and flax mills on the Falls Road.[23] The three-acre site and its dwelling, Clonard House, was purchased from local estate-agents-turned-developers R.J. McConnell and Company, who had built many of the terraced houses in nearby streets. The house provided the Redemptorist priests with a residence and a place of worship until such time as a monastery building and church were completed.[24] The first mass was held on 1 November 1896 and within a month the community had engaged Belfast architect J.J. McDonnell to design a temporary church while plans for a monastery complex with a permanent church were conceived.[25] The Redemptorists sought a Romanesque design for the new church, but their Bishop wanted a Gothic one, and so ensued a local, ecclesiastical version of 'The Battle of the Styles'.[26] A brief look at the means by which ownership of the medieval past became a badge of identity for both the Protestant and Catholic traditions will provide some context for how Clonard Church came to sport a predominantly early French Gothic aesthetic.

RECLAIMING THE PAST

The progression of Catholic ecclesiastical architecture from simple mass houses to barn chapels to elaborate buildings even for small communities during the nineteenth century was testament to the growth in strength and confidence of post-emancipation Irish Catholicism. The popularity of a classical idiom for new churches was a consequence of the education received by Irish priests at continental seminaries. This style prevailed in Ireland until greater numbers of priests began to be trained at Irish seminaries and gradually, as was the case elsewhere in Europe, medieval models for church designs began to be revived in Ireland. Over the course of the century, the symbolic or cultural currency of Irish medieval ecclesiastical buildings took on more significance with different architectural styles meaning different things to different groups at different times. Both Protestant and Catholic churches competed for exclusive rights to claim the religious heritage of Ireland as theirs alone. Following the Anglo-Norman conquest in 1169, the occupation and use of ancient medieval ecclesiastical sites became a key element in a struggle to establish who would be accepted as representatives of the 'true' church in Ireland. New buildings for what became the 'established' Church of Ireland were often located on the site of an existing medieval structure. Following the repeal of the Penal Laws and into the early part of the nineteenth century, newly-built Catholic churches were either tucked away out of sight of the main street, or later located on the margins of settlements.[27]

As the century wore on antiquarian societies were established with a view to studying ecclesiastical culture, including that of medieval liturgy. In 1842, the Church of Ireland founded the Down and Connor and Dromore Church Architecture Society; this was followed not long after by the Catholic Irish Ecclesiological Society, which was established in 1849. Both groups drew their inspiration from the achievements of the Cambridge Camden Society, a body founded in 1839 by a group of Cambridge scholars. Their goal was to reform church building design, making Gothic the pre-eminent style for Anglican churches. Later renaming themselves the 'Ecclesiological Society', they published their views in a periodical, *The Ecclesiologist*, and in a number of pamphlets.[28] Supporters of each of the Irish societies strove to apply what had been learnt through their studies to new Irish church-building projects, vying for the honour of being the first to produce a building that was true to the models of the past. In 1846 James Joseph (J.J.) McCarthy, Ireland's foremost architect of Catholic churches and a founding member of the Irish Ecclesiological Society, confidently claimed the Church of St Kevin at Glendalough, Co. Wicklow as the first 'uncompromisingly true church of the old type'.[29] Twenty years later, the design of the Church of St Patrick (Church of Ireland), Jordanstown, Co. Antrim by William Henry Lynn, which was inspired by tenth-century Irish medieval architecture at Clonmacnoise, was described as 'The first attempt in modern times to revive the ancient ecclesiastical architecture of Ireland'.[30] The dilemma of which style was appropriate for new churches – the thirteenth-century Gothic model used at St Kevin's, with its pointed arches, lancet windows and spatial relationships that expressed liturgical order, or the revived Hiberno-Romanesque design of St Patrick's with its rounded forms and tenth-century inspired belfry – was a dilemma that would continue to provoke debate over the next half-century.

That Gothic Revival architecture became a popular choice for many nineteenth-century Irish Catholic churches owes much to the architects who followed the lead of its principal proponent, Augustus Welby Northmore Pugin.[31] Pugin left a lasting legacy in his Irish work that was continued by his son Edward Welby Pugin and others such as George Coppinger Ashlin and J.J. McCarthy. The latter was influenced by Pugin's ideological treatises, *Contrasts* and *True Principles of Pointed*

Architecture,[32] which argue for the moral and aesthetic superiority of Gothic architecture over Classical styles. This influence can be seen in a paper McCarthy published under the auspices of the Irish Ecclesiological Society in 1851 entitled *Suggestions on the arrangement and characteristics of parish churches*.[33] McCarthy's manifesto first examined the evolutionary styles of Catholic parish churches, before going on to advise on the most suitable design for country churches. He also provided a checklist of recommendations for architects of city churches including a directive that 'the decorative character of the Church will equal, if not exceed, that of secular buildings, and that it will, as far as possible, harmonize with them.' He gave precise dimensions for different parts of the building: 'make the side walls from 25 to 30 feet high (so as to remove the windows from the reach of the people on the outside)' and he specified materials that were most suited to urban church design: 'dressed stone, "clean-hewn ashlars" … very desirable in town Churches'.[34] Visually impressive as the Gothic Revival design of Clonard Church is, the rusticated limestone and sandstone brickwork contrasts with the polychrome redbrick appearance of the adjoining monastery buildings. This locally sourced, easily worked material was also used for the temporary church in order to curtail the cost.[35] As will be seen, brick might also have been McDonnell's choice for the main church had his original plan for a Romanesque design been used. However, as well as dictating the style of the new building, Bishop Henry also stipulated that it was constructed in stone and not brick.

CLONARD CHURCH: A NOBLE CHURCH

J.J. McDonnell trained in the offices of Timothy Hevey before setting up his own practice in 1881 and being elected to the Royal Institute of Architects in Ireland three years later. Hevey, an accomplished architectural draughtsman, had worked in the Dublin offices of Augustus Pugin's son Edward and his partner George Coppinger Ashlin prior to returning to Belfast and setting up his own architectural practice.[36] During his brief career (he was just thirty-three at the time of his death), Hevey was responsible for designing many Catholic churches but the bulk of his ecclesiastical work was for the Diocese of Down and Connor. Two of the many commissions Hevey received from Bishop Patrick Dorrian included St Joseph's Church, Prince's Dock Street, (1877–79)[37] and the Church of St Patrick in Donegall Street, which replaced an earlier building (1873–77). Both were planned in a Romanesque revival style, the former Italian. Another Romanesque revival design by Hevey, this one more self-consciously Irish, was for the Church of the Sacred Heart, Dunlewey, Co. Donegal (1876–77). Like Lynn's work at Jordanstown the belfry is also housed in a round tower. This church was constructed for Belfast city councilor William A. Ross, who owned lands at Dunlewey.[38] Belonging to a Catholic élite of Belfast, described by Hepburn as the 'millocracy', Ross' flax mill was adjacent to the site on which the Redemptorists built their monastery and church.[39] McDonnell is likely to have remained on as a pupil in Heavey's practice after the latter's death in 1878, working under Hevey's partner Mortimer H. Thompson, who completed the work on St Patrick's. McDonnell's many ecclesiastical designs included the Romanesque Church of St Brigid, Derryvolgie Avenue, Belfast (1891) in polychrome blue and red brick (later replaced by a building of modern design).[40] McDonnell's first church commission to use a Gothic Revival style came in 1884 when he designed the Church of St Paul on the Falls Road, just a few minutes walk away from the Clonard site, for the parish priest Fr. Pat Convery.[41]

According to the community's house archivist and record-keeper, Bishop Henry's intervention prevented the Redemptorists from building 'a noble Church in the most Catholic quarter of a bitterly Protestant and Presbyterian city'.[42] The Bishop imposed his architectural preference on the community – Gothic Revival – and even dictated the size of the church and the construction materials. The recent discovery of some previously unseen architectural plans and drawings by McDonnell permit conjecture as to what a fully worked up Romanesque-style design for Clonard might have looked like.[43] McDonnell may have used Romanesque design concepts worked out in original sketch plans for Clonard Church in a similar scheme he drew up for Reverend Henry Laverty in 1906.[44] Laverty, until the previous year had been a leading member of Bishop Henry's Catholic Association, of which McDonnell was also a member.[45] In 1905 Laverty was appointed parish priest of St Matthew's, a wealthy Catholic area in east Belfast.[46] The drawings are labeled 'Proposed new church – St Anthony, Willowfield, Belfast' and show a Romanesque design in polychrome red and yellow sandstone that would have blended very well with the monastery buildings at Clonard. The west façade features a large rose window with bar tracery surmounting a band of blind arcading in sandstone (also repeated at the apex of the façade) over the double entrance doors. McDonnell appears to have been still working out the client's potential options for the interior as the drawing shows the aisled six-bay nave carried on columns with foliate capitals on the north side of the nave while the south shows cushion capitals, quite similar to those he used at St Paul's on the Falls Road. The apsidal east end of the basilica plan shows three lights resting on a string-course surmounted by a coffered ceiling. Round-headed arches are used throughout and window openings are paired on the clerestory and aisles. The side elevation view shows buttresses that provide bay definition to the exterior façade. Single lights pierce the polygonal belfry, located to the northwest side of the front elevation. The red brickwork is punctuated by a sandstone string-course and the round-headed windows are positioned alternately within the bands of brickwork. This lends a jaunty visual rhythm to the tower, which terminates in an open arcade of foliate capitals topped off with conical roof, all in sandstone.

In contrast, the executed design of Clonard Church is constructed of regular coursed, rock-faced rusticated blue limestone blocks, complimented by dressed sandstone features and topped by a slate roof. The basilica-plan building seats about a thousand people. It is described as being in the early French Gothic style owing to the prominence in the front façade of the signature rose window with bar tracery, triple entrance portals surmounted by blind arcading and twin turreted towers.[47] J.J. McCarthy used these features extensively, and there is a noticeable similarity between Clonard's west façade and that of the chapel of St Patrick's College, Maynooth, which was completed to McCarthy's design by William Hague after McCarthy's death.[48] At Clonard, McDonnell develops the Maynooth motif, employing three entrance portals featuring moulded jambs and arches arranged in receding orders of red polished granite shafts on moulded bases with carved foliate capitals. The symmetry of the west elevation is completed with matching side chapels and forward projecting octagonal turrets terminating in pillared and gabled niches with conical caps that are indebted to a number of Pugin and Ashlin churches in the Dublin area.[49] A copper-topped square-base belfry, with pointed twin lancets and a corbel table under the eaves, is located beside the sacristy at the southeast corner of the building. The five-bay aisled nave is forty-six meters long, with shallow transepts, a semi-circular apse, side chapels and a crypt beneath the sanctuary. Flanked by lean-to side aisles with triple lancet windows, the nave arcade is carried on pillars of polished red granite with marble bases and foliate capitals of Portland stone rising to a clerestory with paired lancet windows beneath a barrel-vaulted, coffered ceiling.

As well as forcing the Redemptorist community to accept his preferred choice of architectural style, Bishop Henry also insisted that the overall length of McDonnell's design for the nave be shortened by more than six meters as he feared that a church of greater length, 'on the full lines of M[oun]t St Alphonsus, Limerick' would create the impression of Clonard as 'the Cathedral or ... the "basilica" of Belfast'. Henry is said to have taken a pencil and simply drawn a line through the plan thereby drastically altering the proportions of McDonnell's design.[50] Comparing the front elevation of Clonard as built with the Willowfield drawing suggests that McDonnell may have redesigned the entire building, delivering one that looks similar to the Willowfield proposal, save for the fact that it is executed in stone and not redbrick. Comparing the extant plan for Clonard Church as executed with the plan that Bishop Henry is said to have tampered with we can see that his amendment resulted in the loss of one entire nave bay and its accompanying side aisle chapels and a radical altering of the overall proportions of the nave.[51] Following this intervention, McDonnell redesigned Clonard Church: the new plan saw matching octagonal turreted towers replace the tower and spire that was originally intended for the northwest corner of the west elevation. A less ostentatious tower was situated at the southeast corner of the church with the intention of bridging the gap between the sacristy and the main monastery building. Although it serves a function it is somewhat visually awkward and would perhaps have benefited from having a spire.

Both plans put forward by McDonnell for Clonard Church, the first in the Gothic design that Bishop Henry so disliked and the second for the church as executed, were acceptable to the Rector, Patrick Murray. How did Bishop Henry so successfully manage to impose his architectural preferences for Clonard Church on the Redemptorist community? He had paid for the site, it is true, but the cost of building the church fell fairly and squarely on the shoulders of the community and local people who were members of Clonard's confraternities and attended services in the church.[52] A more pertinent question that might be considered is *why* the Bishop so deliberately and drastically altered the dimensions and balance of McDonnell's Gothic plan? The Redemptorists were given strict instructions by Bishop Henry not to get into debt when constructing the church. Much of the funding for building the monastery, the temporary church and its successor was raised through subscriptions and collections. The priests were seen as a positive influence on the area; consequently members of the confraternity and sodality memberships were diligent in their efforts to extract whatever amounts they could from Belfast's Catholics for the building fund. Early on, the female members founded a group to raise funds for the monastery project: while the contributions were encouraged to be modest, the 1897 account books of the 'Pious Union of the Most Holy Redeemer' show that its contribution to the building fund ranged from £11–17 per month.[53] Clonard Church had an initial price tag of £20,000 but by the time the church opened in October 1911, it had exceeded this budget considerably.[54] The main objective of the Redemptorist mission in Clonard was to minister to the large numbers of Catholics who worked in the linen mills of the area, thereby promoting religious practice and preserving cultural identity; they were repaid with profound loyalty in a practical way – raising money and attending services.

Conflict between bishops and religious orders is not unknown although the Redemptorist community in Ireland was, for the most part, highly regarded by respective bishops. The community's record-keeper was confident, however, that envy over the Redemptorists' confident plans for a grand new church was the reason for the Bishop's veto on the design. Given his close working relationship with Henry Henry, Fr. Pat Convery, parish priest of nearby St Paul's, was suspected of having a hand in encouraging the Bishop in his objections.[55] Between 1882–95 Fr. Convery worked as the administrator of the parish church of St Peter's, which later became the Pro-Cathedral of Belfast, a period that covers the episcopates of Patrick Dorrian, Patrick McAlister and Henry Henry.[56] St Peter's was also located off the Falls Road within a stone's throw of Clonard. Both St Peter's and St Paul's therefore, drew their congregations from the same pool of mill-workers who worked so tirelessly to raise funds for the new Redemptorist church. Convery relied on the monies generated by parish collections for an income and may have felt that the limited funds of his parishioners might be diverted to support the building of Clonard Church. Bishop Henry himself cannot have been impartial: his seat was located at St Peter's, which was designed by the priest-architect Fr. Jeremiah McAuley in 1866, while Patrick McAlister held the office. The spires were added to the towers of the west façade in 1886, increasing the verticality and visual presence of the building while strengthening its links to French Gothic architecture.[57] Given its location on a more elevated part of the Falls Road, could McDonnell's ambitious original design, complete with tower and spire, for Clonard Church have threatened the visual primacy of St Peter's on the skyline of Belfast? Would this by extension have challenged the Bishop's authority?

While it is possible that Bishop Henry was reluctant to let a mere order of mission priests have a more elaborate church than his own episcopal seat, an alternative explanation, proposed by Grant, concerns the relationship between the Bishop and the brothers at Clonard, which cooled somewhat in 1906. This was due to events surrounding the general election that year, which were played out locally in a row over votes between candidates supported by the Bishop and local nationalist Joe Devlin. The latter received significant support from the Redemptorist community, something the Bishop could have seen as a direct challenge to his authority.[58] It may be that Fr. Murray and his community acquiesced to Henry's demands in regard to the design of the church in order to dissipate any ensuing friction, as less than harmonious relations might have hindered the continuance of their work in Clonard. Direct confrontation over which design might be sanctioned therefore was not an option. This was more difficult when dealing with secular clergy who frequently felt undermined by the popularity of mission work by orders such as the Redemptorists. The confraternities that were established as an integral part of the Redemptorist ministry to the Catholic community drew large memberships that often affected attendance at parish masses, as well as drawing on funds. Fr. Convery therefore may have welcomed, if not actually encouraged, Bishop Henry's veto of McDonnell's first Gothic plan that ensured a less grand structure was built for the Redemptorists at Clonard. They do not explain why he would have rejected a Romanesque design. Bishop Henry may simply have wished to exercise a degree of control over a community of priests who seemed set to gather a large loyal congregation around them. However, a look at building activity by other Belfast faith communities at this time and the complexities associated with the politics of architectural styles are also worth considering.

ARCHITECTURE AND COLLECTIVE IDENTITY

The battle for hearts and minds over the most appropriate style for churches conducted by respective Church architecture societies was played out against a backdrop of national identity in architecture with all parties claiming to have the monopoly on Gothic. For J.J. McCarthy and the Irish Ecclesiological Society, this meant rooting designs in Ireland's medieval Celtic past although it was, in fact, French Gothic that came to dominate his later work. For the most part, however, style choices still came down to the tastes of architects and patrons, and of course, cost. Thomas Drew's original thirteenth-century English Gothic design for St Anne's Cathedral, Belfast (1898–1910) was passed over for a Romanesque plan on the basis that it would be less expensive to construct. In addition, as we have seen, the medieval model offered by Hiberno-Romanesque designs was considered to give the stamp of authenticity in terms of religious pedigree.[59] Dissenting church architecture suffered the same funding issue as that of the Catholic Church at this time, that is to say, lack of state support. It is noteworthy therefore that Fisherwick Presbyterian community were able to raise the substantial cost (£16,000) of their impressive sandstone Gothic Revival church at Malone Road (1898–1901).[60] Similar in size to Clonard Church and also on a cruciform plan with an apse, the Gothic Revival style used moves away from the classical models associated with earlier meeting house architecture. Instead it combines Scottish baronial style circular poches and perpendicular window traceries, the latter medieval motifs, identified by Thomas Rickman as quintessentially English.[61] At exactly the same time as the Redemptorists arrived in Clonard, Reverend Henry Montgomery founded an evangelical congregation, the Shankill Road Mission. This group had similar goals to the Redemptorists as each sought to improve the welfare of the community in which they ministered. Montgomery's focus was on a number of locations in Belfast he considered to be 'plague spots' of such inappropriate social behaviour as public intemperance and gambling.[62] Under Montgomery's direction the Shankill Road Mission funded the construction of new premises for their congregation, to the designs of W.J.M. Roome.[63] The building's frontage took up an entire block. The Mission only closed in 2009 but the building still exists. Its conventional four-storey Queen Anne Revival style redbrick and sandstone exterior gave little clue to the interior, which contained a central octagonal hall with galleries that could seat two thousand people. The design of the façade has more affinity with public building design and little association with the classical idiom of any nineteenth-century Catholic churches and, by extension, little connection with Rome.[64]

Could the reason for Bishop Henry's objections to the original Romanesque plan for Clonard have been influenced by the use of the same style for a prominent Church of Ireland building nearby? Moreover, was his insistence on a French Gothic model, albeit one with a scaled down tower, a way of distancing Belfast Catholics from all things English? Can we in fact, read collective identity through architecture? William Whyte argues that, for the architectural historian, the most useful approach considers this question from the perspective of transpositions or translations. Multiple meanings may be then interpreted in a building as it moves from the architect's design concept to eventual completion, use and reception.[65] As Clonard Church moved through these phases, it came to mean different things to different agents at different times: the Redemptorist priests, who wanted a church design that expressed the continental origins of their congregation; Bishop Henry, who wanted to make a mark architecturally on his diocese without detracting from the importance of his own episcopal seat; local secular clergy, who resented the potential that Redemptorist rituals and groups might have had for reducing the numbers contributing to their parishes; the confraternity and sodality membership, whose urban collective identity was integrated with and dependent on the church building in which the activities of their groups were enacted, and finally the subsequent generations of Catholics who have continued to support and worship with the Redemptorists at Clonard.

As Claire Mitchell has noted, the interrelationships between religion and identity, communities and politics, may be seen in the way that communities self-fashion collective identities through religious observances, ideas and symbols.[66] The medieval tradition of lay confraternities in Ireland can be traced back to the fifteenth century and Colm Lennon describes the means by which they were instrumental in 'forging and sustaining communal identities at a time of heightened ethnic sensibilities' during that era.[67] Although confraternities were active in Belfast prior to the arrival of the Redemptorists,[68] once established they set about forming a number of such lay groups at Clonard – the men-only Confraternity of the Holy Spirit, the women's Confraternity of Our Lady of Perpetual Succour and a separate one for young boys. Participants attended weekly and sometimes daily devotions in the church, annual retreats and pilgrimages as well as holding processions and events to mark important dates in the liturgical calendar. Membership thus permitted confraternity members to publicly display their status as ethnically separate.[69] Furthermore, as Connolly has suggested, access to services provided by churches such as Clonard may have given rural migrants to the city a sense of belonging and 'the basis of a social network, in the harsh and unfamiliar environment of an early industrial town'.[70] In the eyes of the clergy, this had the additional benefit of protecting the participants from damaging outside influences, such as 'company keeping' with non-Catholics or from becoming involved with anti-social behaviour.[71] Nevertheless, in spite of substantial local sectarian tensions, where there were serious riots in the 1880s and '90s and again in 1907, the confraternities and sodalities enjoyed a high profile on the streets during this period, especially at times of major religious Catholic celebrations including that of the titular feast of Clonard Church, which falls on 15 July, during the loyalist marching season.[72]

From small beginnings in 1896, the Redemptorist congregation grew and grew. The lay confraternities they established, initially for men and later for women and boys, fostered a spirit of belonging, community and commitment in the large group of rural migrant Catholic workers living around the Clonard area. Within a decade their increasing numbers necessitated the building of a large neo-Gothic style church. Alterations to the original brief for Clonard Church were accepted by the Redemptorists, although these alterations changed the overall look of the building dramatically; however appeasing their Bishop seemed to be the wisest option. The official opening of the Church of the Most Holy Redeemer on 1 October 1911 was covered in a two-page spread in the *Irish News and Belfast Morning News.* It was, said one report, attended by visiting religious and secular dignitaries including 'nearly all the Catholic and Nationalist representatives on the local public boards' as well as the local people who paid a shilling, if they could afford it, to hear the dedication sermon made by Bishop Henry's successor, Revd Dr John Tohill. The collection that was taken up that day yielded some £2,000.[73] That the people who had already contributed so much to the raising of this church were willing to pay an entrance fee at all is a measure of their loyalty and commitment to the Redemptorist community. The Bishop's sermon recalled the original ancient Irish Christian monastery of Clonard saying 'There once was another Clonard in the territory of Meath, near the Banks of the Boyne. Its monastery was one of the most celebrated of the sixth century …

The spiritual glory of the ancient Clonard, we feel confident, will be revived in this new Clonard of St Alphonsus … and perfection will be well and faithfully done.'

CONCLUSION

Over the course of the nineteenth century Irish Catholics countrywide saw a dramatic expansion of the Church's capital investment programme. By 1900 almost every town and village in the country could boast a substantial newly built, extended or renovated Catholic church. A great number of these were in a French Gothic idiom. Like their predecessors, the people of Clonard were proud to see the wealth and status of their community expressed in bricks and mortar. Historians have debunked the perception that nineteenth-century Catholic churches were built with the pennies of the poor. Nevertheless, the funds to build the Redemptorist church at Clonard were largely generated, if not actually supplied, by many working-class Belfast Catholics. Had it been a parish church, the people might have been less closely involved in its construction. Had Bishop Henry not intervened, the church might have been a redbrick building in a Romanesque idiom. (The construction material, it has to be said, would have been a better aesthetic fit with the monastery building.) As late as the 1940s, the changes that were made to shorten the length of J.J. McDonnell's Gothic design still rankled with the lay groups who had contributed so much financially to the building programme: in fact, they even sought the then Bishop's permission to reinstate the lost bay.[74] Oddly enough the request was granted, although it is impossible to see how this could have been carried out. Nonetheless, it demonstrates the strength of feeling and commitment local people still had towards Clonard Church even after many years.

On 5 May 1898, not long after the Redemptorists held the first mass in the 'tin' church, an *Irish News* reporter wrote: 'In this noble pile

God's work will go on, it is to be hoped, for centuries to come, from it spiritual blessings will flow forth on our people'.[75] In 2011, for the first time in its one-hundred-year history, the 'tin' church's successor was closed to facilitate an extensive refurbishment programme that cost over £1.5 million. A range of options allowed people to contribute to the renovation costs at whatever level their particular financial circumstances permitted, thus maintaining a link to the past and to those who contributed to the original construction costs, some of whom are the ancestors of today's contributors.[76] While the refurbishments were being carried out a temporary building was erected in more or less the same location of the 1897 church, enabling continuity of religious services by the Redemptorists while the refurbishment works were completed. This temporary structure had the same capacity as the main church, ensuring that the novena was as well attended as previous ones, with over 10,000 attending the opening day of the 2011 Novena.[77] The commitment and loyalty demonstrated by all agents associated with Clonard Church, past and present, indicates the enduring power of architecture in forming and maintaining collective identity.

GLOSSARY

APSE	Circular or polygonal extension to the choir (sanctuary).
ASHLAR	Blocks of masonry with smooth sides and square edges (as opposed to rubble blocks straight from the quarry). Also known as 'dressed stone'.
BAR TRACERY	Window with thin stone mullions that allows more glass to be used and gives a more delicate appearance.
BLIND ARCADE	A row of decorative arches applied to a flat surface.
BUTTRESS	Masonry support that counteracts the lateral thrust of an arch, roof or vault.
CAPITAL	Portion of a supporting pier that separates the pier (or column) from that which it supports. May be carved with foliage (foliate capitals) or plain (cushion capitals).
CHOIR	Area between the transept and apse where services are performed. May also be called the chancel or sanctuary.
CLERESTORY	Upper story of the main walls of the church with windows piercing adjacent aisle roofs.
CORBEL	A projecting feature, sometimes used as a support for a structural member. Multiples may also be used to highlight elements (corbel table).
JAMB	Vertical element in an opening (door or window).
MULLION	Vertical structural support in a window.
POLYCHROME	Use of multiple colours in, for example, brickwork.
RUSTICATED	Large rough-hewn masonry blocks that either come straight from the quarry or appear to do so.
STRING-COURSE	A continuous horizontal band of masonry.
TRANSEPTS	Rectangular spaces bisecting the main axis of a building. In a basilican plan they separate the nave from the apse.
TRIBUNE	Upper storey over an aisle with an opening (sometimes screened) to the nave or choir.

9

Edwardian Belfast: Marriage, Fertility and Religion in 1911

Liam Kennedy
Lucia Pozzi
Matteo Manfredini

Ireland is of particular interest to social scientists and historians because of its outlier status within the West European demographic system. The city of Belfast, in the north of Ireland, has its own distinctive demographic features, though intriguingly in quite different ways. In part this distinctiveness derives from the ethnic mix of the population. While in many respects a Presbyterian-dominated city, Belfast also housed a large Anglican population and a substantial Roman Catholic minority. Put crudely, each traced its ethnic origins back to Scotland, England and Ireland respectively, with the seventeenth-century Plantation of Ulster as the fountainhead of so much subsequent change. Belfast was remarkable also, in the Irish context, as it was Ireland's only industrial city. The political and administrative capital, Dublin, it is true had a substantial proportion of workers who were classified as 'industrial'. These accounted for more than one out of every two, or

54 per cent of those with occupations. But these were mainly old-style craft and unskilled workers, with low levels of productivity. By contrast, three out of every four in the workforce in Belfast pursued an industrial occupation, many in modern industry where productivity levels were high.[1]

The interconnections between industry and demography have been the subject of a huge literature.[2] So, it might be, for all its claims to a unique identity, that Belfast has much in common with other industrial towns and cities. Might the social and industrial structure of the city have implications for fertility, gender ratios, internal migration and marriage patterns, in a fashion that mirrored patterns elsewhere, or could it be that Belfast ploughed its own demographic furrow?

This chapter focuses on Belfast at the end of the Edwardian era and before the outbreak of World War I.[3] The primary sources used to address a variety of social and demographic issues are the manuscript returns of the Census of Ireland for 1901 and 1911. But first the historical evolution of Belfast, from early settlement to modern industrial city, is sketched. This is followed by a discussion of social conditions in the city, including wage levels, housing and literacy. The methodology used to explore various dimensions of demographic behaviour is then outlined, and finally a series of results arising from the census-based explorations is presented.

HISTORICAL BACKGROUND

Belfast is a latecomer in the story of European urbanization. Unlike many towns and cities, it does not have deep medieval roots. Its origins as an urban settlement only stretch back to the early 1600s and the Plantation of Ulster by English and Scottish settlers.[4] Situated strategically at the mouth of the river Lagan, the town enjoyed vigorous though hardly spectacular commercial growth during the course of the eighteenth century. Its vibrant civic culture earned it the title – half-serious, half-mocking – of the 'Athens of the North'. Thus by 1800 it was a thriving market centre and port town, with a strong merchant community serving the agricultural and handicraft industries of its hinterland in east Ulster.[5] Its population, in round figures, was about 20,000.[6] In religious terms it was overwhelmingly Protestant, though there was a small minority, perhaps 10 per cent, that was Roman Catholic.[7] It housed the beginnings of a factory-based cotton industry, though this would be superseded within a few decades by mechanized linen manufacture. When the Halls visited the town at the beginning of the 1840s, they described it as 'Ireland's only manufacturing town':

> It was something new to perceive rising above the houses numerous tall and thin chimneys which are indicative of industry, occupation, commerce and prosperity, with the volumes of smoke that issued from them giving unquestionable tokens of full employment.[8]

During the course of the nineteenth century Belfast grew phenomenally, with its population multiplying more than fifteen fold. This was on the back of linen manufacturing, shipbuilding and a range of engineering and other industries.[9] Belfast is thus an outstanding example of the transformative power of modern industrialization: in a very real sense it was a child of the British Industrial Revolution. Its progress bears comparison with the growth of other industrial towns in the north of England and the west of Scotland. In some decades of the nineteenth century it was the fastest-growing town in the United Kingdom. Within Ireland it was the undisputed industrial capital, beginning to challenge Dublin in terms of size, if not social and political prominence. Marking its transition from a provincial town to a modern Victorian city, it was accorded city status in 1888. By the eve of the First World War the city hosted a range of internationally-competitive firms in linen manufacture, shipbuilding and engineering. The port of Belfast was the nerve centre of a global set of connections, linking the city to sources of raw materials for its industry and final markets for its sophisticated products.

The population of the city stood at 387,000 in 1911. The gender division was distinctive: more than half (53 per cent) were women.[10] In the working and largely unmarried age group of 20–24 year olds, the imbalance was greater still, with women accounting for 56 per cent of this age category. This female surplus had its basis in the opportunities for female employment in the city. The linen industry, the largest employer of labour, was dominated by women, though the supervisory and managerial roles were largely reserved for men.[11] In 1911 some 53,000 persons were employed in textiles and clothing, most of these in the city's linen mills and factories. Three out of every four of these employees were female, thereby contributing to the gender imbalance in the city.

Gender ratios had implications for marriage opportunities, as for much else. The marriage prospects for men in the city were much better than for women, or indeed as compared to their male counterparts in the Irish countryside. In Ireland as a whole in 1911 some 29 per cent of men and 25 per cent of women in the age group 45–54 years were unmarried and were unlikely ever to marry.[12] Viewed in international context, Irish society was remarkable for the restraint shown in relation to marriage. In Belfast, however, only 13 per cent of males remained unmarried in this older age range, which is less than half the celibacy rate for Ireland as a whole. The prospects for women in the marriage stakes were less good, though, with one in five (21 per cent) unmarried in the 45–54 age category. To some extent, of course, spinsterhood may have been by choice. The urban economy furnished economic niches that could sustain women living independently, much more so than rural Ireland where there was a deficit of women relative to men. Single or widowed women with some financial resources could take in boarders or engage in retailing, while working-class women might find employment in the mills and factories, and in domestic service. Within marriage, the shadow of death wasn't far away. Infant and child mortality was an ever-present danger, while one in five (19 per cent) of all women were returned as widows at the time of the 1911 census. Most of these were in the upper age range, and often heads of households in their own right, such as Frances Sarah McIlvenny of the Falls Road, Belfast. Frances was 61 years old in 1911, a spirit grocer and Catholic, with three surviving children.[13] Occasionally, though, one comes across a very young widow, such were the vagaries of the times in terms of disease and industrial accidents. Margaret McCartney, who worked as a living-in servant and cook for a Presbyterian minister in the Malone area of Belfast, was only thirty years of age and widowed at the time of the census.[14] Her religious background was Church of Ireland and she apparently had no children.

SOCIAL CONDITIONS

Contrary to popular impression, working-class housing was both affordable and of good quality. Only a tiny proportion of families huddled together with another family. In most instances this was a temporary economy measure, at an early stage in married life or as a result of a downturn in employment. So we find Jonathan Burns, a 'gate man', and his wife Catherine mentioned in the household schedules for 1911 as sharing their four-roomed rented house in Dewey Street in west Belfast with their married daughter, also named Catherine, and her husband Robert Murdie, a general labourer.[15] The younger couple had been married for less than one year, and as yet had no child. The presumption must be that this co-residence was a brief stage in the life cycle of the Murdie couple and that they got rented accommodation of their own not long afterwards. The overcrowding to be found in the slum dwellings of Dublin or Glasgow was largely unknown in Belfast, while the suburbs of Malone and Belmont catered for an expanding middle class.

Houses were graded as first to fourth class in the Irish census reports, fourth class being the most undesirable. Four out of every five houses in Belfast were graded as second or third class, with most of these dwellings falling into the second-class category. These were the rows of redbrick terraced houses – often in the shadow of a great mill or factory – that characterized much of the city's streetscape. In all, out of a housing stock of 75,172 inhabited dwellings in the city, only 288 were one-roomed tenements occupied by two or more persons. A quarter of these one-roomed tenements were clustered in one ward alone (out of fifteen), this being the Dock ward. The strong supply of housing, relative to demand, which was the product of speculative building in the 1890s, meant a good range of rented accommodation and house rents that were among the lowest in the United Kingdom.[16] Suffice it to say that some of the photographic evidence of extremely poor housing that can be found for the period – for example, a grim image of Mitchell's Court, Brown Square, which features in the Hogg Collection – is untypical of working-class housing in general in Edwardian Belfast.[17]

Belfast was a city of in-migration. The proportion of people with birthplaces in counties Antrim and Down (including Belfast), who were resident in the city on census night, was typically three in every four during the period 1851–1911. But this understates the extent of movement as many of these inhabitants had made short-distance migrations from the other towns, villages and rural areas of counties

Antrim and Down to the city. Belfast, it should be explained, was largely located in County Antrim but the city expanded across the river Lagan into County Down during the course of industrialization. Unfortunately the census report only gives birthplaces for the gross entities of County Antrim and County Down, whereas ideally one would like more geographically detailed points of departure.

In addition to those who migrated to the city from counties Antrim and Down, most other migrants came from the other counties of the province of Ulster. This conforms to a larger British pattern of internal migration occurring over short distances. Thus, 78 per cent of the inhabitants of the city in 1911 were born either in Belfast or in other parts of counties Antrim and Down, and a further 11 per cent came from the other Ulster counties.[18] A tiny 3 per cent came from elsewhere in Ireland but perhaps the really striking figure is the 7 per cent whose birthplace was across the sea in Britain. McRaild makes the point that one of the largest concentrations of Scots living outside of Scotland was to be found in Belfast.[19]

Few of the city's inhabitants were born outside of the United Kingdom, less than 1 per cent in total. This tiny stream of newcomers included 424 Russians, mostly Jewish migrants it may be surmised.[20] These were followed in descending order of importance for European immigrants by 151 Germans and 149 Italians. America supplied 867 foreign-born residents, most of whom were from the United States and a majority of whom may be assumed to have been of Irish extraction.[21] We may sum up by saying Belfast was a city of in-migration, largely from the Ulster countryside, but not of immigration from distant parts.

Inevitably of course some departed the city, for one reason or another. It might be trade depressions, for instance, in which case skilled labourers might well migrate across the channel to the shipyards on Clydeside or Merseyside, returning again when employment picked up. Others might be permanent migrants to North America, to Canada in particular where the links with Ulster were strong. But unlike most of Ireland, where emigration was endemic, the outflow of people was small compared to the inflows. Emigration from counties Antrim and Down (including Belfast) totalled 3,628 in 1910. Three-fifths of these were male, a further confirmation of the opportunities for work for women in Belfast.

Many commentators have remarked on the Presbyterian character of Belfast, and this is borne out by the demographic facts as well as by architectural features of the city. The largest denominational grouping was Presbyterian, accounting for 34 per cent of the population, closely followed by the Protestant Episcopalians, or members of the Church of Ireland, at 31 per cent. The Roman Catholic share was lower at 24 per cent. Significantly this had been falling during the second half of the nineteenth century. In 1861 its share had been as high as 34 per cent but while the Roman Catholic population had grown in absolute size in each successive decade, the proportion of Roman Catholics within the city's population was in long-run decline. (This trend towards relative decline would be reversed, ironically enough, after the formation of the Northern Ireland state and during the course of the twentieth century.) Whether this was due mainly to discrimination against Catholic job-seekers or informal recruitment mechanisms that favoured labour market 'insiders' and their kinfolk, or still other factors, is not clear.[22] Outside of the big three churches, Methodists accounted for a further 6 per cent of the population. In line with other protestant nonconformist groups, the Methodists had grown in strength since 1861 (the first year in which a question on religion was included in the Irish census). This suggests some fragmentation of the Protestant denominational bloc during the course of rapid urbanization and industrialization. The quest for low-church or more fundamentalist forms of religious devotion may in turn have been associated with the stresses and strains affecting the lives of the recently-recruited industrial proletariat.

Table 9.1: The Changing Religious Composition of Belfast, 1861–1911.

	Catholic	Anglican	Presbyterian	Methodist	Other
1861	33.9	24.6	35.2	4.1	2.2
1881	28.8	28.1	34.4	4.4	4.3
1911	24.1	30.5	33.7	6.2	5.5

Source: Census of Ireland, 1861, 1881, 1911.

Literacy is one of the concomitants of economic and social development and also a measure of the human capital embodied in the population. On this count, Belfast scored well by comparison with other parts of Britain and Ireland. If the census report is taken at face value, then 96 per cent of Belfast inhabitants aged nine years or over in 1911 were literate. This is in the sense of possessing basic skills in reading and writing. One of the limitations of this and other censuses, however, is that personal characteristics were self-reported. Signing up, as it were, for illiteracy was not an attractive proposition and no doubt gave rise to some social embarrassment. We know from examining the original census forms that a household head who claimed to be able to read and write on the census return – completed by another member of the family or perhaps more likely by the census enumerator (a member of the Royal Irish Constabulary) – was occasionally unable to sign the form. The "X" signatures amounted to 4.1 per cent of the households in our sample, which tallies well with the overall results for Belfast.[23]

There is some minor variation in literacy by geographical area, by social class, by gender and by religion. For instance, in west Belfast, almost five per cent of people were returned as illiterate, whereas in more affluent south Belfast the corresponding proportion was less than half this. In terms of social class, there was virtually no illiteracy reported for the 7,300 males in Class 1 – this census classification refers to the professional stratum in the social hierarchy – whereas among the 20,000 or so general and factory male labourers the reported level of illiteracy was as high as 7 per cent. When illiteracy is viewed along exclusively gender lines, a small advantage in favour of men emerges: only 2.8 per cent of men were illiterate as compared to 4.3 per cent of women in the Belfast population.

Table 9.2: Illiteracy by Gender and Religion in Belfast in 1911.

Denomination	Male (%)	Female (%)
Roman Catholic	5.4	8.6
Protestant Episcopalian	2.8	4.1
Presbyterian	1.5	2.2
Methodist	1.1	1.7
Other	1.1	1.7
Total	**2.8**	**4.3**

Source: Census of Ireland, 1911: Province of Ulster: City (or County Borough) of Belfast, British Parliamentary Papers, [Cd. 6051], 1912, p.37.

The higher incidence of illiteracy, or at least reported illiteracy, among women could have demographic as well as labour market implications in relation to fertility, child care and child mortality. Illiteracy also varied by religious persuasion, affecting 7 per cent of Roman Catholics but less than 2 per cent of Methodists (to take as reference point the most literate of the major denominations). Still, to use Akenson's felicitous phrase, while patterns of variation are apparent, we are dealing with 'small differences' in levels of illiteracy within the population, be it broken down by area, social class, religion or gender.[24] The fact remains that more than 90 per cent of people in *all* social categories were literate, as reported to the census enumerators.

The language of Belfast was of course English, as it had been since its foundation in the seventeenth century. A tiny minority, a mere 2 per cent of the population, claimed an ability to speak Irish or Gaelic in 1911. According to the census of that year, some 7,591 people, divided roughly equally between males and females and most of them under the age of thirty, could speak the language.[25] This was in addition to English as there were no monoglot speakers of Gaelic (if one discounts a handful of children aged under ten years). Ironically, among the most fluent Gaelic speakers were members of the Royal Irish Constabulary, some of whom had been recruited from the West of Ireland where a knowledge of *An Gaeilge* was still widespread. Thus Neal Gallagher, an RIC (Royal Irish Constabulary) constable born in County Donegal but living with his family in the Shankill area of Belfast in 1911, put himself down as Gaelic speaking on the census form.[26] Others who did so, however, may have been expressing an aspiration as much as an ability. The recorded numbers of Irish speakers in Belfast doubled between 1901 and 1911, which raises the suspicion that the activities of the language revival movement had led, not just to an increase in Irish speaking, which was undoubtedly the case, but also to some inflation in the numbers of Irish speakers.

One measure of extreme poverty, or destitution, was the number of people accommodated in the Belfast Union Workhouse. This was a Victorian institutional building located on the Lisburn Road, at some distance from the centre of the city. The number of inmates varied according to the season, the trade cycle, business conditions in the city, and the proportion of older people in the population. On the night of the 2 April 1911, there were 3,426 inmates in the Workhouse, a majority of them being men. This represents just under 1 per cent of the population, suggesting buoyant trading and employment conditions in the city, as well as care by family and kinfolk of the elderly and the frail in the community (a burden lightened by the granting of Old Age Pensions to the over-seventies in Lloyd George's 'People's Budget' three years earlier).[27]

What of the age structure of the population? While the city boasted six inhabitants aged 100 years or over, Belfast was a comparatively youthful city in 1911. More than half the population (52 per cent) was aged less than 25 years. This also implies a low dependency ratio. Belfast was a city of work, indeed of long hours of work. Engineering and shipyard employees, for example, worked an average of 53 hours per week, not counting meal times or overtime.[28] For skilled workers, wage rates were high, amongst the highest in the United Kingdom.[29] Nor were these high wages confined to a small section of the workforce. The proportion of skilled workers was relatively large. Gribbon concludes it was as high as one quarter of all male workers, which meant that the 'labour aristocracy' was more developed in Belfast than in most comparable industrial towns (where the proportion was much lower at 10 to 15 per cent of the male workforce).[30] In Belfast most craftsmen and mechanics were in high-technology industries such as shipbuilding and engineering, bringing home wages of around forty shillings per week.[31] To place this in context, the rent of a five- or six-roomed terraced house, the kind of housing such households would have occupied, was five or six shillings per week, and so amounting to 15 per cent or less of weekly earnings.[32]

The position of unskilled workers was very different, however. Housing costs were low, admittedly, with a modest kitchen house renting for three to four shillings per week. But a surplus of labour in the Irish countryside kept wages low, at well under half the rate paid to skilled workers.[33] Some working-class families were obliged to send their children out to work on the half-time system (half time spent in school and half time in the work place). It was only in 1901 that the legal starting age for work was raised from eight to twelve years.[34] In the poorer families married women, particularly those within walking distance of a spinning mill or weaving factory, combined work and child-rearing so as to make ends meet. Life was a hard grind. Yet despite the unhealthy working conditions of the many women who worked in the textile industry in Belfast, many recall the camaraderie, singing and storytelling of the workplace with affection.[35]

SOCIAL CLASS, RELIGION AND SECTARIANISM

The rewards of work and enterprise were unequally distributed. As in other industrial cities, society in Belfast was stratified along the lines of social class. In the words of Sybil Gribbon:

> The hierarchy of class dominated Edwardian society. At its apex were the three hundred families, whose households at Strandtown or on the high ridges of the Antrim and Malone Roads contained a gardener and coachman as well as several indoor servants.[36]

These were the captains of industry and commerce, including a handful of self-made millionaires, and a sprinkling of the landed gentry. Beneath these were the middle classes, a diverse category that included top surgeons and lawyers as well as lowly clerks and commercial travellers desperately clinging to the coat-tails of respectability. The skilled working class we have already encountered, involved in church and trade union, trading at the Belfast Co-operative Society, and proportionately larger than in many other industrial towns. At the broad base of the social pyramid, if one excludes vagrants and the destitute, were the masses of semi-skilled and unskilled labourers. Among women these included female spinners and weavers, living-in servants, washerwomen, charwomen, machinists and factory labourers. The male occupations included carters, porters, coal heavers, male servants and over 20,000 general and factory labourers.

Paradoxically, modern industrialization co-existed with pre-modern forms of social conflict. Belfast was deeply divided, not just along class lines but along lines of religion and nationality as well.[37] There had been instances of united working-class action to demand higher wages, such as the Dockers' Strike of 1907, and this spread quickly to other sections of the workforce.[38] But the more pervasive and enduring divisions were those revolving round religious and political identity. Simplifying, but only a little, Catholics and nationalists sought Home Rule for Ireland while Protestants and unionists were determined to maintain the union with Britain. Sectarian and communal conflict was the outcome of these contradictory political aspirations.

Social and economic differences as between Catholic and Protestant exacerbated but did not cause these divisions. The ownership of industrial capital was overwhelmingly in Protestant hands; Catholics were underrepresented relative to their share of the population in law and medicine but were overrepresented among general and factory labourers.[39] We can get a summary view of social stratification by religion for 1901 from the work of A.C. Hepburn (see Table 9.3), where OD stands for Other Denominations or denominations other than Catholic:[40]

Table 9.3: Social Class by Religion (Male Household Heads).

	RC (%)	OD (%)	Britain (%)
Classes 1 and 2	13	13	15
Class 3	8	12	7
Class 4	31	35	33
Class 5	44	36	45
Not Classified	4	4	0
	100	100	100

Source: Hepburn, A Past Apart *(1996), p.64.*

Classes 1 and 2 refer to the high end of the income and wealth distribution: professionals, higher civil servants, successful entrepreneurs and business managers. Class 3 is at least as heterogeneous, and is comprised of lower white-collar occupations and skilled (manual) workers. Class 4 refers to semi-skilled workers, many of whom were to be found in the shipyards and building trades. Class 5 was the most numerous and contained the teeming population of unskilled and casual labourers. Two points in the table are worth underlining: the Catholic population was disadvantaged relative to the Protestant population of Belfast; it was not, however, disadvantaged relative to British society as a whole. Thus, in Catholic-Protestant relations a sense of *relative* deprivation was a divisive force in Belfast social life, notwithstanding the fact that in absolute terms most poor working-class people came from Protestant backgrounds.

METHODOLOGY

A number of writers have commented on the apparent similarities in demographic behaviour as between the Catholic and Protestant populations. As Collins and Hepburn show, mean household size was much the same in 1901. The age of male household heads, on average, was broadly similar; as were the proportions of households with children, corresiding relatives and lodgers.[41] But fertility might be a different matter. Nuptiality might also vary by religion and social class.

To explore these issues in greater detail we have constructed a database of Belfast households in 1911. This, the BelFam database, consists of some 40,000 individuals or just over 10 per cent of those enumerated. While it is not, strictly speaking, a random sample, the major geographical areas within the city are represented, as are middle-class and working-class districts.

The sample used in this study, however, is a smaller one, and is really a subset of our larger BelFam database. It is composed of the thousand or so couples (1,016), where the wife was aged 50 years or over in 1911. We have been able to trace almost nine hundred (894) of these married couples back to the 1901 census as well, even though in many instances the couple had changed addresses between census dates. Changes of address, it is worth noting, indicate high levels of residential mobility in the Edwardian city. The reason the sample was restricted to couples in which the wife was 50 years of age or older was to get at completed fertility. The husbands were typically a few years older than their wives but in a minority of cases were less than 50 years of age. We are also interested in seeing each couple in 1901 as well as in 1911 for a specific reason. This is because doubts surround the accuracy of the ages of older men and women, as reported in the 1911 census.[42] The introduction of Old Age Pensions a few years earlier gave older people an incentive to exaggerate their age, and this could skew badly the study of fertility and age at marriage. Richard Rice of Foxglove Street in east Belfast, to take but one example, aged inexplicably from 47 to 65 years, a difference of eighteen years, over the intercensus decade of 1901–11.[43] Rice's occupation was given as labourer, and he could read and write as is evidenced by the fact that he was able to complete and sign the census form, so illiteracy is not the obvious explanation.

Table 9.4: Age Discrepancies: Comparing Reported Ages in 1901 and 1911 in the Matched Sample.

	Males			Females		
	Mean	**St. Dev**	**N**	**Mean**	**St. Dev**	**N**
Catholic	3.13	3.68	226	3.68	3.94	242
Church of Ireland	1.80	2.45	226	2.31	2.61	238
Methodist	1.23	1.93	79	1.65	2.00	80
Presbyterian	1.71	2.41	297	1.93	2.52	281
All Prots	1.68	2.36	646	2.01	2.51	645
Overall	2.06	2.84	872	2.47	2.32	887

Source: Dataset of Matched Couples, Belfast 1901 and 1911 (using absolute values).

Table 9.4 shows one summary measure of the extent of inconsistency in the reporting of ages by individuals, as found in the censuses of 1901 and 1911. The sample consists of the same couples, compared at these two moments in time, and is made up of 872 husbands and 887 wives. At one census or other a husband or wife might happen to be absent from the household on census night, perhaps visiting elsewhere or absent because of the kind of work he or she was engaged in. Interestingly, absence seems to be particularly noticeable in relation to Catholic and Church of Ireland males, perhaps pointing towards more itinerant or migratory work patterns. Building labourers, seamen, commercial travellers, shipyard workers (during cyclical downturns in the industry), are among those who might be taken away from home by economic circumstances. Other possibilities include abandonment, in a period when divorce was the preserve of the relatively affluent.

Using absolute values, rather than pooling positive and negative age discrepancies, which would tend to cancel each other out, we find in Table 9.4 that Belfast Catholics were much more likely than Protestants to show inconsistent ages as between the two census dates. Where there was a discrepancy, it tended to be in the direction of overstating one's age in 1911 as compared to 1901. In a smaller number of cases, it is true, individuals apparently 'aged' by less than ten years.

So, the mean difference between Catholic males and Protestant males in terms of age discrepancy, and using absolute values, was 3.13 years as compared to 1.68 years. Standard deviations are also presented in the table, indicating the degree of spread round the mean value. The size of the standard deviation relative to the mean suggests the spread of aberrant ages was wide. Methodist males seem to have been the most accurate, or at least the most consistent, in reporting ages. Turning to gender differences, the discrepancies were more pronounced amongst women. Again Catholics were the least consistent and Methodists the most consistent in reporting ages to the census takers, with Anglicans and Presbyterians located in between. Put another way, we find that of those who added on more than ten years between 1901 and 1911, those most likely to do so were Catholics. This is not inconsistent with the fact that the economic status of Catholics was lower than that of Protestants, hence the gains from deliberate age misreporting would have been higher. Furthermore, women were more likely than men to do so, stereotypes about women and ageing notwithstanding.

Lying seems to have been a deliberate strategy in some cases. Otherwise it is hard to understand why the great majority of those giving inconsistent ages should have added to rather than subtracted from their expected age in 1911. Thus, as many as 8 per cent of men and 11 per cent of women had apparently aged by more than 15 years between 1901 and 1911, which is quite a substantial leap in years and possibly imagination.[44] Of course some of these individual discrepancies may be put down to illiteracy: illiterates were likely to produce less accurate ages and durations of marriage, while higher status individuals showed greater consistency across the census decade.

In general, we have assumed that the ages reported in 1901 are the more accurate of the two. We cannot of course discount the possibility, indeed the certainty, that some of the ages reported in 1901 were not accurate either, but on balance the likelihood is that 1901 is the better benchmark. In a small number of cases, though, where the internal evidence on duration of marriage and age at marriage suggests that the ages in 1911 were closer to the mark, then we have made a judgement in favour of the ages reported in 1911. Including or excluding these doubtful cases makes little difference to the results.

The evidence on age reporting, and misreporting, is of interest in its own right. It bears on issues that have been discussed in relation to census data both for Ireland and for other countries.[45] But the issues have a specific relevance to the remainder of this chapter. The summary statistics in the next section and the econometric tests in a later section, make use of the dataset on couples in 1911 but subject to a major qualification: ages have been corrected using age information from the 1901 census.

MARRIAGE, RELIGION AND SOCIAL STATUS

By the early twentieth century the Irish were famed for their late age at marriage and a low propensity to marry.[46] But Belfast had many of the features of an industrial town of the kind found in the north of England or the west of Scotland, so generalizations about Ireland do not necessarily extend to Belfast. As we saw earlier, marriage rates for men were much higher in Belfast as compared to Ireland generally. Permanent celibacy was correspondingly lower, with only 13 per cent of Belfast men in the age group, 45–54 years of age, not married in 1911. This was much the same as in England and Wales.[47]

One in five women in Belfast, however, remained permanently celibate, which is a high proportion forsaking marriage, even if the countrywide average was higher still at one in every four women. The corresponding proportion for women in England and Wales was considerably lower at 16 per cent.[48] So, men in Belfast approximated to the English standard while women in Belfast were situated mid-way between the Irish and English levels.

The proportion marrying is only one dimension of nuptiality. Age at marriage, which varies over time, is important, not least because it had major implications for the number of children likely to be born. The published census does not, however, present marriage ages broken down by religion, social class or locality. The aggregate picture though is that Irish men in 1911 delayed marrying, on average, until their early thirties while Irish women were not far behind at around 28 years.[49] By international standards these were late ages at marriage, contributing to the image of Irish society as the demographic freak of Western Europe. But what of urban Ireland, and of Belfast in particular? Our sample of older couples in 1911 provides a window on marriage age in the city. In view of our earlier discussion, it is important to bear the problem of age misreporting firmly in mind. Table 9.5 displays average age at marriage (AAM) for men and women in our Belfast sample, using age information for the same individuals from the 1901 census and the 1911 census.[50]

Table 9.5: Average Age at Marriage of Older Men and Women by Religion in Belfast in 1911.

	Male AAM		Female AAM	
	1901 Age	**1911 Age**	**1901 Age**	**1911 Age**
Catholic	26.49	28.17	22.98	25.48
Church of Ireland	26.15	27.31	23.54	25.11
Presbyterian	27.29	28.18	24.10	24.96
Methodist	25.42	25.94	23.22	24.26
Protestant	26.61	27.55	23.77	24.93
Overall	26.62	27.77	23.62	25.11
No. of Cases	854	873	866	873

Source: Dataset of Matched Couples, Belfast 1901 and 1911.

First, the differences between the 1901 and the 1911 estimates are striking. Correcting for age – assuming age in 1901 is the more accurate of the two reported[51] – makes a difference, and this is especially so in the case of women. So, on average, Catholic women married two and a half years or thirty months earlier than is suggested by the uncorrected information taken from the 1911 household schedules. Catholic men married some twenty months earlier. *These are worryingly large discrepancies*, and they apply to other denominations as well, though to a lesser degree.[52] Second, corrected age at marriage for men was broadly similar for all denominational groups, though Presbyterians appear to marry a little later in life. Third, Catholic women are shown to marry at an earlier age than other denominations, and more than a year earlier than Presbyterian women for instance. This could have important implications for completed family size, among other issues. Finally, and most importantly perhaps, it is clear that both men and women married at much earlier ages in Belfast than in Ireland generally, the heavily rural character of the latter carrying much of the explanatory weight for that curious state of affairs. Belfast was different.

FERTILITY AND FERTILITY DIFFERENCES

A frequently noted feature of life in later twentieth century Northern Irish society has been the contrast between Catholic and Protestant fertility. In 1971 Catholic fertility was two-thirds higher.[53] But were there visible differences a half century or more earlier in time? The historical origins of this divergence – one replete with political as well as social and demographic significance – are not well understood. Perhaps it was the case that some Ulster men and women were less 'tardy and unenthusiastic participants in the European fertility transition' than is sometimes imagined.[54]

Fertility might be related to social class as well as religion, and within classes to particular occupations. The evidence from some industrialized regions of Europe is that fertility was influenced by occupational structure and the possibilities of female employment.[55] Thus women in English textile towns had relatively low fertility while, for example, women in rural coal-mining communities had relatively high fertility.[56] At first sight the economic rationale underpinning such differences in behaviour seems straightforward enough, though Garrett counsels that the relationship between 'a couple's employment histories and their family building can be … an extremely complex one'.[57] Moreover, could religious belief and practices trump economic and economically-related considerations? The Belfast region was the great textile centre of Ireland in the early twentieth century, hosting the largest linen industry in the world. Its labour force was predominantly female, with some 80 per cent of the workers in the industry being women. Belfast was also a city renowned for its religious loyalties, not to say zealotry, and its commitment to Christian marriage and family life was second to none. On the face of it, there may have been a conflict between material considerations and religious conceptions of the optimal family size.

To test these possibilities further we have related fertility, in the form of completed family size, to a range of explanatory variables, using standard regression analysis (Table 9.6). In the first and simplest version of the model fertility is related to membership of different Protestant denominations. A negative coefficient suggests that a Protestant affiliation implied lower fertility within marriage as compared to Catholics. So the finding in this simple model is that Presbyterians had, on average, almost one child (0.8) fewer per family than Catholics (the reference group). Where a finding is statistically significant, that is, unlikely to have happened by chance, the coefficient is placed in bold. The coefficients for membership of the Church of Ireland and the Methodist church are also negative but not statistically significant at the 95 per cent confidence level.

Table 9.6: Explaining Variation in Fertility by Reference to Religious Affiliation and Other Variables.

		Model 1	Model 2	Model 3	Model 4	Model 5
Variables	**Freq**	**Rel.risk**	**Rel.risk**	**Rel.risk**	**Rel.risk**	**Rel.risk**
Religion F (ref. Catholic)	26.4					
Church of Ireland	29.5	-0.662	-0.441	-0.257	**-0.829**	**-0.882**
Methodist	10.1	-0.719	-0.605	-0.318	**-0.941**	**-0.897**
Presbyterian	34.0	**-0.795**	-0.413	-0.149	**-0.872**	**-0.868**
Woman's age at marriage			**-0.344**	**-0.332**	**-0.323**	**-0.320**
Housing Points (ref. <7 pts)	18.1					
7-11 pts	52.2			0.459	0.477	0.502
12+ pts	29.2			-0.562	0.069	0.407
Unknown	0.5			-1.890	-1.109	-1.182
Ward (ref. Falls)	24.7					
Pottinger	5.2				0.332	0.343
Shankill	33.8				**1.273**	**1.226**
Windsor	36.3				0.030	0.224
Social status (ref. Unskilled & semi-skilled manual workers)	37.4					
Professional, Clerical, Higher White-Collar	15.7					**-0.944**
Proprietors, Commercial, Farmers, etc.	14.3					-0.233
Skilled Manual Workers	18.1					-0.086
Textile Workers	12.2					0.582
Unknown	2.3					0.153
Women's education skills (ref. Not able to Read or Write)	84.6					
Read & Write	15.4					0.394
Constant		**6.746**	**14.707**	**14.183**	**13.792**	**13.622**
Observations		729	729	729	729	729
Log-likelihood		-1964.7	-1868.7	-1861.2	-1852.8	-1844.8
LR test - chi square			192.0	15.0	16.9	12.0
LR test - p-value			0.000	0.002	0.001	0.062

This simple variant of the model does not control for other influences that might be shaping fertility. We next introduce age at marriage for women into the equation, the expectation being that the longer the duration of the fertile period the greater the risk of pregnancy. In this variant of the model it is noticeable that the coefficients for religion sink into statistical insignificance, though the negative signs remain for all three Protestant affiliations. As expected, age at marriage is negatively related to fertility.

A further possibility is that fertility is related to wealth. We do not have any monetary measures of wealth so we have to make do with a proxy or stand-in measure. In a rough-and-ready fashion, the quality of housing should give some indication of relative wealth positions. The census authorities allocated housing points to each house, on the basis of the number of rooms, the building materials used and other physical properties. A score of less than seven housing points indicates poor housing conditions, and that is the reference category used here. A score of seven to eleven points suggests an intermediate level of housing, while twelve points or more implies a very substantial habitation and hence a wealthy householder. Somewhat surprisingly, none of the coefficients for the housing variable turn out to be statistically significant, nor for the religious variables either. The signs of the coefficients are generally negative, however, which offers faint hints at a negative relationship between protestant religious affiliation and fertility, and also between wealth and fertility.

The fourth version of the model introduces geography into the explanation, using the ward as the spatial unit. These are: Falls and Shankill in west Belfast, both heavily working-class areas; Pottinger in east Belfast, to some extent associated with higher-paid skilled workers in engineering and shipbuilding; and the largely middle-class ward of Windsor in south Belfast. There is no evidence of a direct geographical effect, with the exception of the Shankill ward – and the positive coefficient is hard to explain for such a largely Protestant area – though it may well be that the spatial units are too large and amorphous to hold much explanatory power. We do not, therefore, rule out neighbourhood effects, believing this should be explored using more refined geosocial units. The coefficients on all three categories of Protestant affiliation, it will be noted, now appear as statistically significant.

The final version of the model, in addition to the variables discussed so far, adds social status and women's literacy to the brew of possible influences on family size. Literacy does not appear to matter, but it is noticeable that again the influence of religion comes through. Lower fertility relative to Catholics is associated with membership of the three main Protestant churches, and the earlier findings regarding the impact of age at marriage are also confirmed. Social class matters, though only in relation to the top social group, which is composed of members of the professions and higher white-collar employees. Membership of this category is associated with smaller family size.

The model also included *male* textile workers as a separate category but no statistically significant relationship emerged. We surmised earlier that family size among textile workers might have been smaller because of the opportunity cost of child care. This, however, is a very weak test. Women rather than men are the important gender in this context (though where the husband was employed in textiles this might suggest the likelihood that his wife had been employed in textiles at one time or other). A limitation of the census data on occupations, however, is that wives are returned almost invariably as housewives, though some may have been outworkers. More importantly, though, the information we really need is a past history of work in the textile industry on the part of these older women.[58] A snapshot view of older couples at a moment in time – 2 April 1911 – is less than revealing, given that decisions about participation in the labour force or not, and decisions about more children or not, would have been taken many years earlier. Economic circumstances, including family earnings and spells of unemployment, may also have changed over time. As things stand, we can draw no firm conclusions. On economic and financial grounds, there is some reason to expect a negative relationship between female involvement in the textile industry and fertility. But it might be profitable also to speculate as to why this might *not* be the case. Possibly alternative child-care arrangements, through kinfolk and tightlyknit neighbourhoods, were more readily available in Belfast than in industrial cities elsewhere, for example. Varying levels of infant mortality may also have mattered, as might income from child labour. Or it could mean simply that married couples were indifferent to, culturally averse to, or ignorant of the possible trade-offs between earnings and additional children. For the present it is best to remain agnostic on this intriguing cluster of possibilities.

CONCLUSION

Belfast occupies a unique position within Irish economy and society, principally because of its status as the lone industrial outpost of any scale on the island of Ireland. There were other industrial towns in Ulster but none was remotely comparable to Belfast in terms of size and range of industries. We can get a sense of this by comparing Belfast with Derry, the second most important industrial centre in the north of Ireland. Derry had grown fourfold between 1821 and 1911 but the already larger town of Belfast grew tenfold in the same period.[59] In 1911 Belfast had ten times as many industrial workers as Derry.[60] This is testament to the extent to which Belfast dominated the industrial landscape of Ulster and Ireland in the early twentieth century.

Consistent with this commanding position it attracted short-distance migrants to the city, and hence its youthful population, its low levels of emigration and a gender ratio biased towards women. By virtue of its high-technology industries, which were geared towards exacting export markets, the city housed a substantial 'labour aristocracy', with up to a quarter of male workers in 1911 classified as skilled workers. To pursue the demographic characteristics of Belfast in more detail it was necessary to turn to the single most revealing set of sources on Belfast society during the Edwardian period, that is, the manuscript returns of the censuses of population for 1901 and 1911. They are generally believed to be reliable across a range of categories of information, from birthplace and religion to literacy, occupation and marital status, and this indeed appears to be the case. However, we can be less sanguine about the ages reported in 1911, which in turn are vital to the study of issues such as fertility, mortality, age at marriage, age differences between spouses, and the age structure of the population in 1911. One of the principal findings of this chapter is that age misreporting at the time of the 1911 census was serious for older people, particularly so when one seeks to compute measures such as the mean age at marriage of men and women, either for the population as a whole or broken down by religious affiliation. The misreporting of ages seems to have been most acute in the Catholic community, and particularly amongst women. We have, therefore, corrected the age information reported in 1911 by reference to the ages recorded against the same individuals in 1901, when the distorting effect of the introduction of the Old-Age Pensions Act of 1908 was not operative.

Having corrected the age information, it is apparent that Belfast does not fit neatly an Irish template of demographic behaviour. The frequency of marriage was higher and age at marriage was appreciably lower than in Ireland generally. Broadly speaking, these variables conform to English and Scottish patterns, though the high incidence of non-marriage among women in Belfast is worth highlighting, being somewhere between Irish and British levels.

The fertility of married couples in Belfast deserves closer examination than is possible here. Fertility was generally high, though somewhat lower than in Ireland generally.[61] Fertility varied by age at marriage, something that might be expected. But it also seems to have varied by religious background. There is some evidence that Protestant couples in Belfast had smaller completed family sizes, as compared to Catholics, which suggests that the great fertility divergence between Protestants and Catholics – so evident in Northern Ireland in the later twentieth century – had its origins a century earlier.

10

'The Family Wage' – A Factor in Migration?

Lesley E. E. Donaldson[1]

'Why move to Belfast?' This is a question that must have been asked by many skilled shipbuilding workers in the late nineteenth century when debating the wisdom of moving, with their families, to Belfast from any of the other shipbuilding areas in Britain. Although these skilled workers were so vital to the development of Belfast's shipbuilding industry very little appears to be known about them or their families. Previous research by this author into the migration of Scottish skilled shipbuilding workers to Belfast widened out to include migration from England and outside Britain, and also internal migration from other parts of Ireland.[2] People migrate, or move permanently, for a wide variety of reasons. It has been known since the nineteenth century, however, that a major cause is the hope or expectation of economic and/or social improvement in the place of settlement.[3] The distance travelled could be as short as to the next townland or across the oceans to the far side of the world.[4] This chapter examines two possible reasons for the decision of skilled, shipbuilding workers to move to Belfast in the late nineteenth century: female employment in Belfast in 1901, and the idea of the 'family or household wage'[5] as a motivating factor in the decision to migrate.

In the early years of the nineteenth century Belfast's population rose steadily as factory-based manufacturing of first cotton and then linen became increasingly concentrated in the Belfast area; this coincided with a decline in both the profitability of the rural, domestic linen industry and in agricultural prices after the Napoleonic wars.[6] The linen industry was the largest employer in Belfast by the late nineteenth century with a labour force of nearly 70,000, of which the vast majority was female.[7] The engineering industry developed to service the needs of the textile industry and, by the middle of the nineteenth century, this was allied with small-scale shipbuilding. By the end of the century, however, Belfast had become a major centre of heavy engineering and shipbuilding.[8]

Belfast had no natural advantages when it came to the development of the shipbuilding industry; in particular there was a notable shortage of the necessary skilled labour.[9] This shortage of skilled labour was largely made good by the immigration of skilled shipbuilding workers from England and Scotland, especially from Barrow-in-Furness or Clydeside – the Belfast/Barrow/Clydeside triangle (hereafter shortened to B-B-C) (See Fig. 10.1). This triangular migration circuit around the northern part of the Irish Sea was another example of how this area had been criss-crossed by transport links for millennia.[10]

Figure 10.1: The Northern Irish Sea Showing the Belfast/ Barrow-in-Furness/Clydeside Triangle.

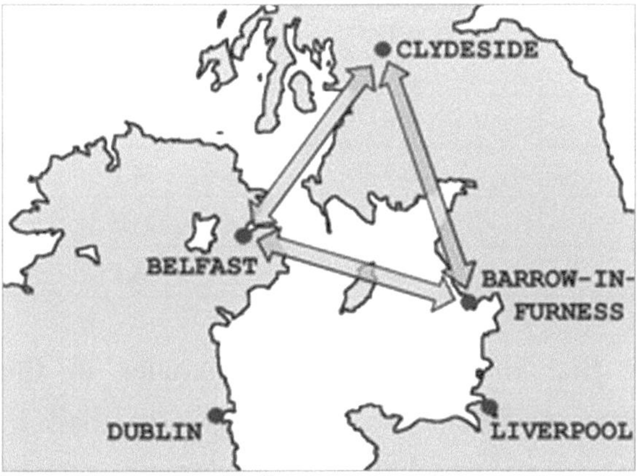

Although these skilled workers played such a vital role in the development of Belfast's shipbuilding industry, relatively little is known about them, and especially why they would chose to come to Belfast, a city which, even in those days, had a reputation for sectarian conflict.[11] Lynch has examined wage rates, housing costs and conditions and food costs, and has argued that a skilled man would have a higher quality of life in Belfast compared to his contemporaries in England or Scotland; however, there was a higher risk of unemployment in Belfast due to the lack of a wide industrial base so the question remains: 'Why come to Belfast?'[12] It has been suggested that the greater opportunity for female employment in Belfast compared with the other main shipbuilding areas around the northern Irish Sea might have been a significant factor in the decision to move to Belfast.[13]

Which other areas might Belfast have been compared with? This chapter singles out Barrow-in-Furness in Cumbria and Glasgow and Greenock on the Clyde as earlier research into the place of birth of immigrant shipbuilding workers in Belfast has revealed these to be two of the largest donor areas.[14]

Table 10.1: Male and Female Employment in Selected Shipbuilding Areas, 1905.

Town/Area	Total Manufacturing Labour Force	Male (%)	Female (%)
Belfast	100,890	55.6	43.7
Barrow	17,787	85.9	14.1
Glasgow	203, 752	69.0	31.0
Greenock	19,390	78.4	26.1

Table 10.1 shows clearly that the proportion of females in the manufacturing labour force in Belfast was much greater than in either of the donor areas of Barrow or Clydeside, the difference being particularly marked in the case of Barrow.[15]

In this 'B-B-C triangle' Belfast had a more broadly based economy than either of the other two areas. This was possibly due to Belfast's long-established textile industry, which had a predominantly female labour force. Linen was the largest employer in Belfast and of its labour force of approximately 60,000 in 1896, 68 per cent were female and 26 per cent juveniles under 18 years of age.[16] As well as linen production, rope manufacturing, textile making-up, printing, tobacco manufacturing and food processing were important industries in Belfast in the late nineteenth century.[17] Belfast was also a major commercial centre servicing the surrounding areas and, with the city's rapid population growth, there were increased employment opportunities in the service industries. The more broadly based economy that was emerging in the later years of the nineteenth century would provide much greater employment opportunities for anyone who settled in Belfast. In Barrow, by comparison, there was a narrow industrial base comprised of heavy engineering and jute and flax works; these last were specifically created in the 1860s to provide employment for anyone other than working-class males. By the end of the nineteenth century that employment was dominated by migrants from Dundee. The ensuing lack of permanent employment for other family members discouraged the permanent settlement of labour.[18]

Migration from Scotland to Ulster was a continuation of a centuries-old pattern.[19] Similar employment opportunities, combined with the possibility of a higher standard of living (the result of wage and housing differences) made it a natural move to cross the North Channel to Belfast;[20] for many families crossing and re-crossing the North Channel was the norm, often associated with cyclical movements in the economies on both sides of the North Channel.[21]

BOUNDARIES OF STUDY

For the purpose of this chapter, microstudies have been used to examine the migration of shipbuilding workers. The main sources are the individual household returns from the 1901 Census of Ireland; these returns include the name, age, occupation, marital status and the place of birth of every individual in each household.[22] As this research is focused on the migration of shipbuilding workers, a selective approach has been taken when deciding which Household Returns to examine.

Areas of working-class housing have been chosen but main arteries are avoided as they had a predominance of shops rather than residential accommodation.[23] Two areas have been selected on the County Down or south side of Belfast Lough where the shipyards were concentrated, and one on the north or County Antrim side; although this area was farther from the main shipbuilding area on Queen's Island, Workman Clark had a shipyard on the north side of the river, there is also photographic evidence of transport links between the areas.[24] Streets have been picked at random within these areas and are allocated to three blocks:

Block A was located between Newtownards Road and the Belfast and County Down Railway line and included Chadolly Street, Church Street East, Dee Street, Island Street and Mersey Street: there were 410 households with a total population of 2,071 in this block._

Block B (between Newtownards Road and Albertbridge Road) comprised Beechfield Street, Belvoir Street, Bryson Street and Madrid Street: there were 391 households with a total population of 2,079 in this area.

These two blocks were dominated by the shipyards, which at that time employed about 9,000 men, and where it was thought the immigrant shipbuilding workers would settle.[25]

Block C, which comprised Silvio Street, Snugville Street and Tennent Street, was located on the County Antrim side of Belfast Lough in an area dominated by the linen industry but with many engineering businesses[26] and transport links to the shipbuilding yards. This area had 510 households with a total population of 2,557.

These three blocks had a total population of 6,607, which represented 1.7 per cent of Belfast's population of 349,810, with a weighting towards the industrial areas. These Census Returns indicate that employment, equated with 'stated occupation' for the purpose of this research, was the norm for males.[27] Female employment, thought to be a reason for migration, is examined here in detail.

FEMALE OCCUPATION IN SELECTED AREA

The patterns of female occupations have been determined by a careful examination of the occupation of females from the Household Returns; however, some guidelines are necessary in order to ensure consistency. Females, both those who gave 'housekeeping', or a variant thereof, as well as those where no occupation was stated, are allocated to 'housekeeping'; however, this presumed lack of a stated occupation would not have excluded them from being economically active. Many of them, for example, might have been engaged in looking after a neighbour's children, or taking in lodgers.[28]

Where females have stated occupations there are some ambiguities. Machinists and reelers were employed in the linen as well as the rope and textile industries. If there is any doubt about which sector these females worked in they have been allocated to the rope/textile group. Women who worked in warerooms have also been included in the 'rope/textiles' group. These allocations probably resulted in an under-estimate of the numbers employed in the linen industry. Mantle-makers, or dressmakers, have been included in the retail group as, in contrast with those who stated that they worked in a 'wareroom', they were more likely to be working in a domestic rather than a factory environment, and may have been supplying individual clients.

Using these guidelines a number of aspects of female occupation have been examined. The first of these is the place of birth related to occupation (see Table 10.2).[29]

Table 10.2: Place of Birth and Occupation of Females.

Females - Place of Birth and Occupation - numbers in each category					
Place of Birth	Housekeeping	Rope/Textiles	Linen	Retail	Total Nos by P of B
Belfast	59	38	25	10	132
Co Antrim	56	11	5	3	75
Co Down	110	36	16	9	171
Rest of Ulster	52	8	10	4	74
Non-Irish	61	25	13	3	102
Total - Block A	338	118	69	29	554
Place of Birth	Housekeeping	Rope/Textiles	Linen	Retail	Total Nos by P of B
Belfast	71	54	4	29	158
Co Antrim	45	12	1	13	71
Co Down	156	41	4	19	220
Rest of Ulster	28	6	2	12	48
Non-Irish	72	30	3	2	107
Total -Block B	372	143	14	75	604
Place of Birth	Housekeeping	Rope/Textiles	Linen	Retail	Total Nos by P of B
Belfast	71	52	86	26	235
Co Antrim	166	41	96	29	332
Co Down	86	9	38	14	147
Rest of Ulster	59	9	32	13	113
Non-Irish	22	7	9	0	38
Total - Block C	404	118	261	82	865

Source: 1901 Census of Ireland, Household Returns.

The most obvious feature of Table 10.2 is that 'housekeeping' was the major occupation in all three blocks, with employment in rope/textiles being the most important in terms of wage earning in Blocks A and B and the linen industry being the major employer in Block C. These figures reflect the industrial make-up of each block; there were at least five ropeworks adjacent to Blocks A and B, whilst Block C was in an area dominated by linen mills.

Immigrants from England, Scotland, Wales and farther afield comprised just 7 per cent of Belfast's population in 1901. 76 per cent of Belfast's population was born in Belfast, Co. Antrim or Co. Down including siblings of the non-Irish-born. 12 per cent came from the remaining seven of the nine counties of Ulster with only about 2 per cent from the rest of Ireland.[30] These internal migrants were found to have similar employment patterns to the immigrant population;[31] therefore *all* females have been aggregated in further analyses. An assessment of any correlation between age and employment has been carried out and the results demonstrated in Table 10.3.[32]

Table 10.3: Female Age and Stated Occupation.

	STATED EMPLOYMENT										
Age Group	House-keeping	Dom Service	Linen	Rope/Textile	Retail	Clerical	Printing	Prof	Other	Total stated occupation	Total in age group
Block A											
15-30	108	8	58	93	12	0	3	2	14	190	298
31-50	169	5	7	11	13	0	4	0	3	43	212
61-65	51	4	0	3	1	0	0	0	2	10	61
66+yrs	9	1	0	0	0	0	0	0	1	2	11
Total each Occupation Group	337	18	65	107	26	0	7	2	20	245	582
Block B											
15-30	102	10	12	117	52	12	14	11	19	247	349
31-50	166	5	2	8	18	40	3	4	4	84	250
61-65	94	7	0	4	3	0	1	2	5	22	116
66+yrs	20	2	0	1	1	0	0	0	1	5	25
Total each Occupation Group	382	24	14	130	74	52	18	17	29	358	740
Block C											
15-30	125	9	180	57	48	5	0	3	8	310	435
31-50	192	9	59	15	24	1	0	0	7	115	307
61-65	73	4	5	3	2	0	0	0	2	16	89
66+yrs	24	0	1	0	1	0	0	0	0	2	26
Total each Occupation Group	414	22	245	75	75	6	0	3	17	443	857

Source: 1901 Census of Ireland, Household Returns.

It can be seen from Table 10.3 that most females between 15 and 30 years of age had a 'stated occupation'; also that there is a precipitate fall between that group and the next oldest, i.e. 31–50. The total numbers in either age group are not so different as to account for this difference. The numbers of women allocated to the 'housekeeping' group rises between 15–30 and 31–50 but the rise is not as dramatic as the fall in stated occupation in the same age groups. In an attempt to see when this fall in stated occupation occurred, and if it was related to marital status, a more detailed study of the 15–30 age group was carried out.[33] This time the age ranges were much narrower, being 15–20, 21–25 and 26–30 and the group was further divided by marital status into 'Not Married', 'Married' or 'Widowed'.

Table 10.4: Marital Status, Stated Occupation and Age in Females Aged 15–30 Years.

	Single		Married		Widowed		
	Stated Occupation	Housekeeping or No Stated Occupation	Stated Occupation	Housekeeping or No Stated Occupation	Stated Occupation	Housekeeping or No Stated Occupation	Total Numbers in 15-30 age group
BLOCK A							
15-20	129	6	3	8	0	0	146
21-25	54	2	6	39	0	0	101
26-30	11	1	3	52	2	0	69
BLOCK B							
15-20	116	22	2	0	0	0	140
21-25	111	16	1	25	0	0	153
26-30	43	9	3	32	0	0	87
BLOCK C							
15-20	131	10	0	3	0	0	144
21-25	109	9	8	42	1	0	169
26-30	67	2	10	51	4	2	136

Source: 1901 Census of Ireland, Household Returns.

In each group 'stated occupation' predominates in the age group 15–20; in Block B there is a greater number of single females in the 'housekeeping' group. This could be because in some households in this Block there were a number of boarders and these single girls, with no stated occupation, could have been helping with the running of the house (Figure 10.4).[34]

Table 10.5: Extract from Household Return for 130 Madrid Street, Belfast.

130	William Beattie	Head	48	M	Shipwright	M	Co Down
	Agnes	Wife	51	F	----	M	Co Down
	Ellen	Daughter	21	F	----	NM	Belfast
	Francis	Son	14	M	Scholar	NM	Belfast
	Emily	Daughter	11	F	Scholar	NM	Belfast
	John Palmer	Boarder	19	M	Carpenter	NM	Co Down
	William Palmer	Boarder	17	M	Apprentice fitter in s'yard	NM	Co Down
	David Pyper	Boarder	18	M	Apprentice Iron turner in s'yard	NM	Co Down
	Archibald Robinson	Boarder	28	M	Factory foreman	NM	Co Derry

Source: 1901 Census of Ireland, Household Returns.

For other young girls, the daughters of widowers or widows, they were looking after the household; as in the case of Joseph Cooper's daughter following the death of the mother (see Table 10.6).[35]

Table 10.6: Extract from Household Return for 90 Chadolly Street, Belfast.

90	Joseph Cooper	Head	49	M	Store assistant	Widower	Co Tyrone
	James	Son	20	M	Machine man	NM	Co Tyrone
	John J	Son	19	M	[-------------machine?]	NM	Co Tyrone
	Alfred	Son	17	M	Apprentice machine man	NM	Co Tyrone
	[-----?]	Daughter	14	F	Housekeeper	NM	Co Tyrone

Source: 1901 Census of Ireland, Household Returns.

For Violet Dunlop this situation followed the death of her father, probably between 1900 and the date of the Census; Mrs Dunlop appeared to be carrying on her late husband's business[36] (Table 10.7).[37]

Table 10.7: Extract from Household Return for 11 Madrid Street, Belfast.

11	Jane Dunlop	Head	57	F	Sand merchant	Widow	Co Antrim
	James	Son	19	M	Apprentice engineer in s'yard	NM	Co Antrim
	Violet	Daughter	17	F	Mother's help	NM	Co Antrim
	Margaret	Daughter	16	F	Milliner	NM	Co Antrim
	Alicia Jane	Daughter	14	F	Scholar	NM	Co Antrim
	Alexander Kirkwood	Brother	54	M	Clerk	M	Co Antrim

Source: 1901 Census of Ireland, Household Returns.

An examination of the occupations and ages of the non-Irish-born females was also carried out (Table 10.8).[38]

Table 10.8: Occupation/Age of Non-Irish-Born Females.

		House-keeping	Rope/ Textiles	Linen	Retail	Others
Block A	15–30	15	23	10	-	1
	31–50	39	1	2	3	-
	51–65	4	-	-	-	-
	66+	3	-	-	-	-
Block B	15–30	16	26	3	2	11
	31–50	37	3	-	-	4
	51–65	16	1	-	-	3
	66+	3	-	-	-	-
Block C	15–30	8	6	8	-	3
	31–50	12	1	-	-	-
	51–65	2	-	-	-	-
	66+	-	-	-	-	-

Source: 1901 Census of Ireland, Household Returns.

Block A contained forty-nine women in the 15–30 age group, i.e. mainly the daughters of the skilled workers who had come to Belfast. Ten (20 per cent) of these women were employed in Belfast's linen industry and twenty-three (47 per cent) were in the rope/textile industries; both these sectors were large employers of female labour.[39] It is notable that only fifteen (30 per cent) were listed under 'housekeeping' and one was still at school. In the age group 31–50 the figures are thirty-nine (86 per cent) housekeeping and only six (13 per cent) in employment. In Block B the difference between the age groups is also marked: of the fifty-eight females in the age range 15–30, twenty-six (45 per cent) were employed in rope/textiles, with only three (5 per cent) in linen, and thirteen (22 per cent) found employment in the retail, clerical, and professional (teachers or nurses) sectors. In the older age group (31–50) thirty-seven (86 per cent) were listed under 'housekeeping' and only seven were in employment. In Block C the numbers of non-Irish-born is small but again employment is more important in the 15–30 age group and housekeeping in the 31–50 age group.

In all areas employment was the norm for the 15–20 age group, including the daughters of the immigrant shipbuilding workers who were located predominantly in Blocks A and B.[40] These figures indicate that marriage usually occured in the twenties rather than in the late teens; when combined with the results of the analysis of age and stated occupation this would tend to suggest that once a woman married she withdrew from the labour force. This pattern was seen also in Block C, where the number with a stated occupation dropped from 159 in the younger age group to only fifty-nine in the 31–50 age group, which was surprising as Block C was dominated by the linen industry where women were the major element of the workforce.

This availability of employment for females in Belfast, with the high rate of employment of females aged 15–30 seen in this selection, would tend to confirm the hypothesis that the availability of employment for the daughters of the skilled men was a factor in their decision to migrate to Belfast.

MULTIPLE WAGE EARNING IN THE SELECTED AREAS

The availability of these opportunities for females coupled with full male employment meant that for many households 'multiple wage earning' was possible and a high incidence of multiple wage earning per household was observed during census analysis.

The level of multiple wage earning was analysed, but first it was necessary to decide who was a 'wage earner'. Anyone who gave a stated occupation on the census form was deemed to be a potential wage earner and hence a contributor to the total household income unless they were one of the very few actually listed as 'unemployed'.[41] There were, however, some anomalies.

Some men, mainly the joiners and carpenters in the selected population, were recorded as 'on strike'; there had been a strike of carpenters and joiners in Belfast since the beginning of May 1900.[42] It was still not settled on 8 March 1901, census night, and they were not counted as 'wage earners', being deemed not to have been bringing a wage into the household at that time.

Another area where a distinction between 'occupation' and 'wage earner' had to be made was where a person gave an occupation that was complementary to that of the Head of the Family. The Head of the Family, for example, is listed as a 'Grocer' and his wife as a 'Grocer's assistant'. One such case is James and Letitia Bell of Silvio Street who both recorded their occupation as 'Shopkeeper Grocery'.[43] In such cases, for the purpose of this research, one was excluded as a 'wage earner' as they were not bringing an additional wage into the household. It could be argued, however, that the participation of these household members meant that more income was kept within the household rather than being disbursed in the form of wages to a third party, but this could not be deduced from the Census Returns. Those not included as wage earners for this reason included wives, sons, daughters, relatives, and the occasional servant. Another excluded category was people who gave an occupation as 'domestic servant' *and* their relationship to the Head of the Family as 'servant'. Again no additional income would be brought into the household; in fact it was a household expense. Bearing these caveats in mind, and the illegibility of a very few Census Returns, detailed analysis was carried out and the results are set out in Table 10.9.[44]

Table 10.9: Numbers and Percentages of Wage Earners Per Household.

	No of House-holds	5 wage earners		6 wage earners		7 wage earners		8 wage earners		9 wage earners	
Block A											
Chadolly Street	96	0	0.0%	0	0.0%	0	0.0%	0	0.0%	0	0.0%
Church Street East	77	3	3.9%	0	0.0%	2	2.6%	0	0.0%	0	0.0%
Dee Street	80	6	7.5%	7	8.8%	3	3.8%	0	0.0%	0	0.0%
Island Street	102	3	2.9%	2	2.0%	0	0.0%	0	0.0%	0	0.0%
Mersey Street	55	6	10.9%	2	3.6%	1	1.8%	0	0.0%	0	0.0%
Total	410										
Block B											
Beechfield Street	98	6	6.1%	2	2.0%	4	4.1%	0	0.0%	0	0.0%
Belvoir Street	57	2	3.5%	0	0.0%	0	0.0%	0	0.0%	0	0.0%
Bryson Street	78	9	11.5%	3	3.8%	1	1.3%	0	0.0%	0	0.0%
Madrid Street	158	19	12.0%	8	5.1%	1	0.6%	4	2.5%	0	0.0%
	391										
Block C											
Silvio Street	145	7	4.8%	0	0.0%	0	0.0%	0	0.0%	0	0.0%
Snugville Street	184	14	7.6%	5	2.7%	5	2.7%	1	0.5%	0	0.0%
Tennent Street	172	12	7.0%	8	5%	2	1.2%	1	0.6%	1	0.6%
	501										

Source: 1901 Census of Ireland Household Returns.

The results reveal that single-earner households were the *minority* in each street (16.7–49 per cent) with two or more wage earners the norm. Two-earner households constituted between 19–33 per cent of the households per street, with the remainder made up of three, four, or five or more wage earners per household. The households where there are five or more earners are either houses with large families i.e. five or more children, or with a large number of lodgers, for example Madrid Street. There was no direct correlation between house size and number of occupants, as shown by some notable cases of large numbers of occupants in houses containing three rooms plus kitchen. There were no great differences in the patterns of wage earning per household between the streets, or blocks.

It can be seen in Table 10.9 that there were a few households where there appears to be no wage earner, these were often 'female-headed households' where there were no children old enough to be employed. However, when the valuation notebooks, the street directories and the census returns were looked at together it became obvious that, in some cases where the Head of the Family was 'married', the Householder was the husband and he was not in the house on the night that the census was taken. One example is Mrs Etta Rosenberg of Snugville Street; her husband, Joseph, was listed as the Householder in the valuation book,[45] he was a 'Baker'[46] and was probably at work on census night. Alternatively the 'head of the family' was a widow with a lodger who had submitted a separate return, for example Mrs Sarah Cheshire of 3 Beechfield Street, who submitted one return for herself and her two children, while her lodger John McKee, a Presbyterian Clergyman, submitted a separate return. The presence of her lodger must have been critical for Mrs Cheshire as her son, who was 16, could neither read nor write and had no stated occupation and her daughter was only 9 years old.[47]

In contrast to those households where there were no wage earners recorded there was a group of households where the number of wage earners was five or more. This group was further examined and this produced some truly surprising results (Table 10.10[48]):

Table 10.10: Incidence of Households with Five or More Wage Earners.

	No. of House-holds	5 wage earners		6 wage earners		7 wage earners		8 wage earners		9 wage earners	
Block A											
Chadolly Street	96	0	0.0%	0	0.0%	0	0.0%	0	0.0%	0	0.0%
Church Street East	77	3	3.9%	0	0.0%	2	2.6%	0	0.0%	0	0.0%
Dee Street	80	6	7.5%	7	8.8%	3	3.8%	0	0.0%	0	0.0%
Island Street	102	3	2.9%	2	2.0%	0	0.0%	0	0.0%	0	0.0%
Mersey Street	55	6	10.9%	2	3.6%	1	1.8%	0	0.0%	0	0.0%
TOTAL	410										
Block B											
Beechfield Street	98	6	6.1%	2	2.0%	4	4.1%	0	0.0%	0	0.0%
Belvoir Street	57	2	3.5%	0	0.0%	0	0.0%	0	0.0%	0	0.0%
Bryson Street	78	9	11.5%	3	3.8%	1	1.3%	0	0.0%	0	0.0%
Madrid Street	158	19	12.0%	8	5.1%	1	0.6%	4	2.5%	0	0.0%
TOTAL	391										
Block C											
Silvio Street	145	7	4.8%	0	0.0%	0	0.0%	0	0.0%	0	0.0%
Snugville Street	184	14	7.6%	5	2.7%	5	2.7%	1	0.5%	0	0.0%
Tennent Street	172	12	7.0%	8	5%	2	1.2%	1	0.6%	1	0.6%
TOTAL	501										

Source: 1901 Census of Ireland Household Returns.

Although the numbers of households involved and hence the percentages would not be significant in statistical terms they lend support to the theory put forward by Lynch that one reason for coming to Belfast was employment opportunities for all family members of employable age.[49]

A great many of the households of all sizes contained 'Kin' as well as 'Boarders or Lodgers' and their effect in multiple wage earning in a household was determined by examining the individual returns. 'Kin' were divided into two groups – 14 years and under or 15 years and over – and this was used as a proxy for their potential earning power. It did not follow that because a person was 15 or over they were in paid employment; there were numerous incidences of widowed mothers, unmarried aunts or nieces with no stated occupation living in the household. It is probable that their presence allowed for greater wage earning in the household as these female relatives would have provided domestic assistance, thus enabling a young daughter to go to work rather than helping her mother in the house. Where the head of the family was a bachelor or widower it was assumed that these female relatives would have been the 'housekeeper' either paid or unpaid – this last information cannot be gleaned from the census returns.

No particular patterns of the incidence of 'Kin' or 'Lodgers' were noted, but observations indicated that the number and percentage of households with either 'Kin' and/or 'Lodgers' was low in each wage-earning group. The number of Lodgers declined as family members entered the workforce. 'Kin' and 'Lodgers' were often a feature of widow-headed households; here they would be a valuable source of additional income, thus enabling a widow to maintain her independence, especially if her children were too young to work.[50] Some households included 'Kin' under 14 years and it was impossible to tell from the records if they were visiting or if they lived in the household; if the latter the head of the household may have received some financial assistance for their board and lodging. Whilst 'Kin' or 'Lodgers' could provide vital additional income to the household it must be borne in mind that there were also additional costs and work involved.[51]

MULTIPLE WAGE EARNING IN INDIVIDUAL HOUSEHOLDS

As a further test of Lynch's theory that the 'family wage' was a motive for migration it had been hoped to examine the numbers of wage earners per household of the non-Irish-born. This was not possible, however, as many of these had parents, children or siblings who were Irish-born and the number of totally non-Irish households was limited. As a result household income reconstruction was felt to be more useful as a guide to the effects of multiple wage earning on a household's resources.

As a point of comparison, the Belfast Board of Guardians estimated in 1909 that the *minimum subsistence income* for a family with three children was 22s.5d. per week. This allowed 12s.8d. for food, 3s.6d. for rent, 2s.3d. for clothing, 2s. for fuel and cleaning materials and 1s. for luxuries, e.g. tram fares, newspapers and tobacco.[52]

Seven households were selected at random and, using available knowledge of wage rates, an approximate weekly income was deduced for each household; the house rent (per week) was also noted.

1. One wage earner

William Beer was a shipwright who lived at 33 Chadolly Street with his wife and four daughters aged between three months and eleven years; they were all English born.[53] His weekly wage was between £1.18s.3d. and £2.0s.8d.,[54] their rent was 3s.6d. per week for the house and yard;[55] the house was newly built and had three rooms and a kitchen. If the figures suggested by the Board of Guardians is taken as a gauge it is probable that this household had more than sufficient income to maintain a reasonable standard of living for the period with the possibility of spending some of their spare cash, maybe between 8s. and 10s. per week in any of the numerous shops that lined the adjacent Newtownards Road. These shops included house-furnishers, drapers and confectioners.[56]

2. One wage earner

David Gray of 36 Island Street was a Co. Antrim-born shipyard labourer, his wife had been born in Co. Antrim and their daughter, aged one year, was born in Co. Down.[57] His wages were 15s-18s.6d. for a full 54-hour week but this figure could be drastically reduced.[58] The house was newly built with three rooms and kitchen, and the rent was 3s. per week.[59] Mrs Gray has no stated occupation on the Census Return but this does not mean that she was economically inactive: she might have done 'out-work' for a local textile factory, taken in laundry, minded children or carried out other services for her neighbours.[60] Equally important in keeping the household economically viable was Mrs Gray's ability to manage the household income in terms of outgoings; although this aspect of history is less visible to the local historian, household economy and budgetary management are both important in social and economic terms.[61]

3. One wage earner and one boarder

William Thompson of 24 Belvoir Street was a thirty-seven-year-old joiner in the shipyard and his wages were £1.18s.3d. per week.[62] He had a wife and three daughters aged 3 to 11 years. This family came to Belfast from Scotland between 1891 and 1898; there was one boarder, James Marten, 25 years old, a Scottish-born plumber[63] earning £1.18s.3d. a week.[64] Their house had three bedrooms and one sitting-room, was between seven and ten years old and the rent was about 5s. per week.[65]

4. Three female wage earners

Thirty-year old Martha McKendry lived in 39 Beechfield Street with her three sisters aged between 19 and 24 years. They had all been born in Co. Down. The three eldest sisters were machinists, the youngest was the housekeeper;[66] wages for each woman would depend on the sector in which she was employed: average wages in linen in 1906 were 10s.9d. per week, 18s.8d. in cotton, 13s.10d. in wool or 11s.2d. in silk.[67] The rent for a house in Beechfield Street was between 7s. to 8s. per week, and the house probably had one sitting-room, a kitchen and three bedrooms.[68]

5. Eight wage earners

Joseph Cunningham of 137 Snugville Street was born in Co. Antrim and, after a number of years in Uttoxeter, England,[69] returned to Belfast some time between 1887 and 1889. Apart from Joseph Cunningham, his wife and seven children (five in employment), two male, Belfast-born boarders, and a Co. Armagh-born widow (with no stated occupation) were also living in the house – twelve people in all.[70] The house had two storeys and an attic, with five rooms plus kitchen, gas was fitted, the rent was 4s.9d. per week.[71] Household income per week could have included two iron turners each earning c£1 18s.3d.,[72] three ship platers each earning between c£1 19s. 8d. and £1 18s.3d. per week,[73] two carpenters each earning c£1 18s.3d.[74] and a junior clerk (wages unknown).The total wages coming into the house could therefore have been between £12 and £13 per week. It was not possible to tell how much the lodgers contributed to the household or if they were remitting money to their own families.

6. Three wage earners

Thomas Ferguson was a Foreman Iron Moulder living in 118 Madrid Street with his wife and eight children who ranged in age from 3 to 21 years.[75] The parents and their six eldest children were born in Scotland, the family came to Belfast sometime between 1892 and 1896, the two youngest children were born about 1896 and 1898 in Belfast. Their house was 16 years old, had two storeys and a dormer window, there were four bedrooms and a sitting-room, gas and a bath were fitted and there was hot water to the bath; the rent was £23 per annum.[76] As well as Thomas Ferguson, his eldest daughter (21) was employed as a 'clerkess', and his eldest son (18) was a pattern maker, there were four children still at school and two not yet of school age. As the eldest son was only 18 it is assumed he was an apprentice, probably fourth year, and would receive about 8s.0d. per week,[77] the wages for his father and his sister are unknown.

7. Two wage earners

John Aicken of 167 Madrid Street was a Constable in the Royal Irish Constabulary, earning between £1.1s.0d. and £1 7s.0d. per week.[78] He was born in Co. Antrim and his wife was an American-born National School teacher.[79] The pay scale for teachers would have ranged from 19s.6d. to £2 18s. per week, however, the census data gave no indication where she would be on these pay scales.[80] They had two daughters aged four and two years. Their house had two storeys, with three bedrooms and one sitting-room. There was gas and a bath, and it had been built in 1900. The rent was about £1 5s. per month (6s. per week).[81] This family would appear to be relatively well off in that they had a larger house, had no lodgers and, unusually in this research, they employed a domestic servant.[82]

These are just a tiny sample of the hundreds of households included in this research but they demonstrate the potential income generation of some of the possible combinations of multiple wage earning per household. It was impossible to estimate how much of the potential income arrived into the house and how much, if any, was diverted to the local licensed trade, but it was noticeable that nearly every street corner had its spirit grocer, or public house.

Multiple wage earning was the major financial resource for the majority of households in this selection and could have had a positive effect not only for the individual household but probably for the wider economy. In multiple wage earning we have seen that there was potential for considerable surplus to spend on non-essential consumption compared with a one-earner household. This non-essential consumption could create greater consumer demand, possibly leading to increased employment opportunities in the service sector such as retailing, entertainment and travel. These employment opportunities would be a draw not only for immigrants from Britain but also for internal migrants from elsewhere in Ireland and *all* members of the industrial labour force able to benefit from this feature of the Belfast economy in the years around 1900.

CONCLUSION

This work is based on a series of microstudies and, although limited in extent, it does illustrate some of the potential in Belfast in 1901 for employment for the working class. Different areas might produce different results, and certainly if a middle-class area was subject to this close analysis the results would in all probability be very different.

The starting point for this research was a study of the immigration of skilled shipbuilding workers to Belfast and Lynch's suggestion that the opportunity for employment for daughters as well as sons was one of the reasons why such men moved to Belfast. In this study we have seen that for young women employment was the norm and on marriage they disappeared from the statistics of the economically active; this did not mean, however, that they did not play a major role in the economy of their own households. The availability of ample female employment linked to 'full' employment for males meant it was normal for a household to contain more than one wage earner with some households having more than five people each bringing in a wage. This potential for additional family resources, allied with plentiful housing, could be a powerful incentive to move from the north-west of England, or Scotland, to Belfast.[83] It would certainly qualify as improving a family's economic and social position,[84] and enable the skilled shipbuilding worker to say 'That is why we came to Belfast'.

11

Migration in Belfast History: Trajectories, Letters, Voices

Brian Lambkin
Patrick Fitzgerald
Johanne Devlin Trew

Migration – the process of 'moving place of residence' – still needs putting into the history of Belfast. Not that Belfast is alone in this respect. Historians worldwide until recently tended to neglect the phenomenon of migration, which comprehensively understood includes not only immigration, internal migration, emigration, return migration and the dynamic interaction among all these aspects, but also the formation of 'diasporas' (scatterings of people who are resident outside their common home place of origin), and the 'family' type of relationship that connects diasporas and their home places. From the 1990s, when historians started advocating the case for 'putting migration into history', there has been a concerted challenge to the myth of the 'static' society – the tendency to see 'normal' community life as settled and movement away from the birthplace as deviant. The 'putting migration into history' project has resulted in works with titles such as *Migration in World History*, *Migration in European History* and *Migration in Irish History*.[1] Much remains to be done, not least at the level of towns and cities.[2]

Our aim here is to advocate putting migration into Belfast history by describing a framework for doing so, giving an overview of four centuries of migration, and indicating the potential of a new set of resources that awaits further exploration. We are especially keen to demonstrate the value of considering together different types of evidence that are usually treated apart. To that end we offer a range of short case studies, all based on extracts selected from a recently developed online resource, Documenting Ireland: Parliament, People and Migration (DIPPAM). This brings together three sets of evidence: the Enhanced Parliamentary Papers on Ireland database (EPPI); the Irish Emigration Database (IED); and the Voices of Migration and Return database (VMR).[3] The case studies are grouped in three sections: the first, 'Trajectories' (Lambkin), is about tracing the routes of migrant stories, using extracts from all three databases (EPPI, IED, VMR); the second, 'Letters' (Fitzgerald), is about exploring the relationship between Belfast, its hinterland and its overseas diaspora, using extracts from IED; and the third, 'Voices' (Devlin Trew), is about reflecting on migrant memory and sense of belonging, especially in relation to the experience of return, using oral history extracts from VMR. By attending to the tones of actual voices of migrants (as captured by VMR), we may hear more clearly the migrant voices that lie dormant in our written records, and be more mindful of the many more migrant voices that lie forever out of reach. In this way we hope to indicate the value of putting migration into Belfast history and encourage others to join in the project.

We begin by considering the interconnectedness of all the different aspects of migration – immigration, internal migration, emigration, return migration, the formation of diasporas and the relationship between diasporas and home places – and the difficulty of getting a grip on such a slippery or fluid phenomenon, on what has been called the 'throughotherness' of migration.[4] All these aspects can be found either expressed or implied in John Luke's mural *Belfast 1613* (see Plate 30) on the tympanum inside of the dome of Belfast's City Hall, completed for the Festival of Britain in 1951.[5]

The central figure in the picture is Sir Arthur Chichester, Lord Deputy (1605–15). He reads the Town Charter of Belfast awarded in 1613. The bell on which he stands and nearby anchor function as punning symbols of 'Bel[l]-fast', anglicized form of the Gaelic place-name *Béal Feirste*, 'mouth of the sand-bank ford'.[6] He is framed by signs, some of them anachronistic, of the town's linen and shipbuilding industries: to the left, bundles of flax, a woman at a spinning wheel, a handloom weaver, lengths of linen on a bleach green, the market house and court house, and a bolt of finished linen being inspected; to the right, blacksmiths, rope-makers and shipwrights; and to the rear, the arched bridge across the Lagan, with the forest of ship masts behind, the glass-works chimney, and the two church towers, the larger Anglican and the other Presbyterian. The hourglass on the loom suggests the importance of the industrious use of time and the Protestant work ethic.

Grouped around Chichester is a family of three generations: the father, holding the hand of the younger son who is turned to face the viewer; the older son with stick and dog; the wife with child in arms; the marriageable sister or daughter; and the white-bearded grandfather leaning on his stick. The sticks of the boy and the old man echo the pikes of the guards flanking Chichester. The strong presence of children, including the young girl seated happily on the bleach green with cat and kitten, also indicates that these immigrants are anchored fast in their new home and determined to remain as permanent settlers. Thus we have the process of immigration represented. The 'new world' of

Belfast implies the 'old world' of Britain. This pioneering generation of immigrants – now part of the British diaspora in Ireland – implies the 'family' type of relationship they and their descendants, reinforced by succeeding generations of immigrants and their descendants, will have with their sending society or home place of origin, eventually to be described as 'the Union', with the underlying agenda of 'Making Ireland British'.

Absent from Luke's picture is any obvious representation of the native inhabitants. Beyond the town in the middle distance is a road winding through the ordered countryside, past whitewashed cottages to the limestone quarry. Beyond it again is the forbidding, wooded height of the Cave Hill (translated from the Irish *Binn Uamha* 'peak/cliff of the cave', also known as *Beann Mhadagáin*: 'peak of Madagán', which suggests the natives still living in the uplands and the danger that they pose to the new settlers.[7] In this way is implied the process of internal migration – displacement of natives from the fertile river valley site of Belfast. Less obviously implied is the possibility of accommodation between 'Planter' and 'Gael' and internal migration by natives from the countryside into the town.

The industrial growth of Belfast, as represented by Luke, implies not only the process of internal migration but also that of emigration – particularly the displacement of natives from the island to become part of the Irish diaspora in Britain, Europe, North America in a relationship with its sending society or home place of origin focused on the project of 'Re-making Ireland Irish'.

Finally, notwithstanding the determined faces of the immigrants anchored fast in Luke's picture, the continuing threat to the success of their project implies the possibility of return migration or retreat by the immigrants and their descendants to the home place of Britain and conversely return migration by the emigrants and their descendants to the home place of Ireland. So what we have cleverly represented by Luke is the dynamic process of migration, with the large ship under construction as a powerful reminder that it may be used for carrying people, as well as goods, both into and out of Belfast.

But working within the limitations of what can be expressed and implied in the two dimensions of a 'portrait' and only within terms of the two competing projects, 'Making Belfast British' and 'Re-making Belfast Irish', we will fall well short of comprehending its complexity. That complexity becomes apparent as soon as we try interpreting a snapshot of Belfast migration on one day alone, say Census Day 1901, Sunday 31 March.

A way of trying to visualize Belfast migration on that Census Sunday in 1901 is to imagine the state of the property market, as represented by all the 'For Sale', 'To Let' and 'Sold' signs then on display. This thought experiment is a version of that proposed by Robert Scally in *The End of Hidden Ireland*:

> If one could have scanned the earth from an orbiting satellite for the movement of its peoples, its surface would have appeared fitfully dormant until the sudden buzzing and swarming which followed the Napoleonic wars. Liverpool would immediately attract the eye as a center of the boiling activity.[8]

If one could have scanned Belfast as it were from 'Scally's Satellite' and picked out all the 'For Sale', 'To Let' and 'Sold' signs, what kind of patterns would have emerged? How many properties were undergoing a change of occupier? Where exactly were they? How many properties were newly built and available for first-time occupation? How long had they been on the market? On a Sunday there would not have been much sign of removal vans and people actually moving in and out, but on a weekday would not Belfast have been buzzing with such activity? To what extent was the changing of places of residence fertility- and mortality-related, in the sense of being influenced by the birth or death of a family member? In many cases no doubt, the appearance of 'For Sale', 'To Let' and 'Sold' signs across the city was connected with announcements of Births and Deaths in its newspapers.

Focusing on one particular day in Belfast's history highlights the difficulty of capturing such a dynamic and ever-changing picture, which would have been different the week before and after, let alone the year before and after. Going forward to Census Sunday a decade later, 2 April 1911, would provide yet another fascinating and complex picture of the extent of movement into, within, and out of the city. There are the residents who have not moved house, and then immigrants (including both Belfast residents born outside Ireland and Belfast-born returned emigrants); internal migrants (including Belfast residents who have changed place of residence within Belfast; Belfast residents born elsewhere in Ireland; and also former residents of Belfast now resident elsewhere in Ireland); and emigrants absent from the Irish data, who perhaps turn up in the census records of other countries (former Belfast residents now resident outside of Ireland).[9] The difficulty of getting to grips with this 'throughotherness' of migration is of course part of the general problem of 'uncertainty' that faces the historian, much like it does the particle physicist:

> … the more detailed the research of an historian into one aspect of phenomenon (such as immigration, or internal migration, or emigration in the case of migration) the more difficult it becomes to know in equivalent detail about its other aspects, let alone about how they interrelate.

> Foregrounding and highlighting one aspect comes at the price of backgrounding and hiding others. So far as migration in Irish history is concerned, we find that historians have tended to treat immigration and emigration as separate phenomena rather than as aspects of the same phenomenon. We also find that by comparison with emigration, immigration and internal migration have been little studied, especially the latter.[10]

To get a better handle on this slipperiness or 'throughotherness', a new framework or model for analysing migration has been proposed, according to which migration is seen as a three-way process of three stages (leaving, crossing, arriving); three directions (inward, internal and outward); and three outcomes (segregation, integration, modulation).[11] This 'three-way' or 'SDO' model (3 **S**tages; 3 **D**irections; 3 **O**utcomes) can be applied to Belfast history at both macro- and micro-levels. We shall return later to the application of this model in tracing individual migrant trajectories within the city, between Belfast and its rural migration hinterland, and outwards to the diaspora; whilst acknowledging the significance of migrant memory and belonging in all of these contexts. But first we offer a brief outline of migration in Belfast history over the last four hundred years.

MIGRATION IN BELFAST HISTORY 1613–2013: A PROFILE

To 1700

The somewhat unpromising site of modern Belfast was first touched by human contact during the Mesolithic period (8000–4500BC) and archaeological remains chart the activities of these hunter-gatherers in the Lagan estuary. Modest but continuous permanent settlement at the site of the ford of the river is traceable in the centuries up to 1600.[12] In

1611 the commissioners appointed to review the progress of Plantation acknowledged the expanding urban form and the recent settlement of migrants drawn from England, Scotland and the Isle of Man. In the decades that followed the issuing of a charter in 1613, British migrants continued to arrive into Belfast and by 1640 the settlement's population is estimated to have been between four and five hundred inhabitants. Most of this growth was down to migrants who came in roughly equal proportion from England and Scotland. Demographic recovery from the warfare of the 1640s was both rapid and strong and recent estimates suggest a population of 2,000 may already have been reached by the 1660s and that this, by the close of the century, was approaching the impressive total of about 5,000. By 1706 it was reckoned that fully 60 per cent of the town's inhabitants were Presbyterian, probably reflecting the strong inward migration from Scotland in the last two decades of the century.[13]

1700–1800

In the first half of the eighteenth century, Irish demographic performance, in general, slackened as immigration sharply reduced and subsistence crises and famine (particularly in the later 1720s and early 1740s) checked 'natural' population expansion. Against this less than propitious backdrop, urban as well as rural dwellers struggled. One recent historian of early modern Belfast has described the early eighteenth century as a period of 'difficulties' for the town, pointing to a reduction in housing stock during the second quarter of the century and the competitive mercantile disadvantage in a growing Atlantic economy that the port endured in comparison to Derry.[14] Nonetheless, Belfast attracted rural-urban migrants and continued to grow, if slowly and fitfully, so that by 1750 the population is thought to have been around 8,000.[15] An increasingly dynamic and largely textile driven rural economy in Ulster after mid-century was matched by impressive demographic growth, and it is clear that by the final quarter of the century the pace of migration from the increasingly populous countryside into the town was showing signs of quickening. George Benn, Belfast's first real historian, charted the expansion in his *History of the Town of Belfast* published in 1823. Benn was himself part of this population inflow as he had arrived in Belfast from Tandragee, County Armagh, in the early nineteenth century, and his own father had been an immigrant from Cumberland, England.[16] He noted the growth from a settlement of 8,549 inhabitants in 1757 to one of 18,320 inhabitants by 1791 and also described how new housing along the main arterial routes had served to transform small rural satellite clusters of cabins to the north and west of Belfast into virtual suburbs. Benn recounted how 'many old people can distinctly tell the small number of houses that once existed upon roads which are now nearly populous streets'.[17] By 1800 Belfast's population had likely reached or surpassed 20,000 souls but it very much retained the feel and status of a town rather than a city and continued to lag far behind the capital. Dublin, which in 1700 had been a city of around 60,000 inhabitants, had by 1800 expanded to accommodate a population of just over 180,000.[18] Throughout the eighteenth century Dublin had attracted Ulster migrants south and consequently taken some of the flow of rural-urban migration that might otherwise have been directed towards Belfast.

1800–1900

Against a backdrop of exceptionally dynamic population growth in early-nineteenth-century Ulster, the increasingly industrial Belfast attracted ever greater numbers of rural migrants and gradually climbed the ranks of the demographic league table of Irish cities. On the eve of the Great Famine (1845) Belfast vied with Cork (both with populations around the 80,000 mark) for the position immediately behind Dublin as Ireland's second most populous city.[19] Whilst Belfast roughly quadrupled in size between the Union and the Famine, its denominational complexion also began to alter as increasing numbers of rural (very predominantly Ulster) Catholics made their way towards the city. As the cotton mills in particular offered rural dwellers employment in the city, the religious geography of Belfast changed quite rapidly. Whilst Catholics had never comprised more than one in ten of the eighteenth-century town's population, they had already come to make up a third of the population by the 1830s.[20] Geographically specific data relating to the origins of pre-Famine migrants to the city has remained elusive. Whilst we might assume that most Protestant rural-urban migrants were drawn from the proportionately more Protestant Ulster counties of Antrim and Down, and Catholic migrants from the more Catholic south and west, this cannot be definitively demonstrated. One traveller's account of 1835 which referred to a recent influx of 'uneducated Catholic labourers from the south and west' pouring into the city encouraged an earlier generation of scholars to identify this pattern, which becomes more evident after 1845.[21] We need to be conscious of the uncomfortable census statistic that shows that a smaller proportion of Belfast's population (10.5 per cent) were born within the seven other Ulster counties in 1841 than at any point up to the First World War.[22]

The transition in the decades after 1815 to what might be properly labelled mass emigration from Ulster to Britain and to overseas destinations inevitably siphoned off some of those rural dwellers who might otherwise have made their way to Belfast, and of course also saw people migrating from the city itself. Belfast, akin to the hotel lobby revolving door, saw new arrivals enter as longer-standing residents departed. However, even increased emigration and the excess mortality due to the crisis of the Great Famine failed to reverse the upward trajectory of Belfast's population statistics. Between 1841 and 1851, the decade that encompassed the worst years of hunger and disease, the city was clearly subject to net inward migration and added more than 20,000 souls to its total population.[23] The Famine's impact in Ulster was most keenly felt in the more Catholic southern and western counties and from here significant numbers travelled along the Lagan corridor towards Belfast. The Famine decade thus witnessed a marked acceleration of Catholic settlement in the southern and western approaches to the city.[24] Belfast in these years was also subject to an ongoing flux of pauper migrants passing through the city port to Britain and being returned to Ireland by the Poor Law Unions there. The General Relief Fund established in the city had by January 1849 disbursed no less than £45,000 to provide for the removal of over 11,000 'strange paupers' to their 'home unions'.[25] Whilst almost two-thirds of these were repatriated within the county of Antrim, in which Belfast sat, hundreds of others were dispatched to more distant counties such as Cork, Kerry, Limerick, Galway, Mayo or Roscommon.[26] The recent expansion of the railway network served to facilitate this assisted migration out of Belfast and would continue to ease access to the city from its rural hinterland in the following generation.[27]

In the second half of the nineteenth century Belfast's growth outstripped that of any other city in Ireland or Britain. Indeed, just as late-twentieth-century Dublin has been paralleled with metropolitan areas in the US, one might suggest that Belfast a century before bore resemblance in many ways to an American city.[28] In this half-century rapidly industrializing America urbanized as fast as any society in global history and the particular atmosphere associated with this frenzied pace of expansion was arguably also detectable in Belfast by the close of the nineteenth century. We shall return to this theme later. The census of 1861 was a significant marker in the city's demographic history in two interrelated ways. Firstly, that year served to mark a peak in the proportion of Belfast's population that was Roman Catholic in background (34.1 per cent). Secondly, the proportion of the urban population recording a birthplace within Ireland but beyond the bounds of the city or the two surrounding counties of Antrim and Down also peaked at 19 per cent (about 80 per cent of whom were born in one of the other seven Ulster counties).[29] From 1861 on it would appear that the area from which migrants into the city were drawn was contracting whilst the flow of migrants was simultaneously increasing in volume. In short, more rural migrants were being attracted to Belfast but from a more restricted geographical hinterland, and, as Antrim and Down were more disproportionately Protestant in terms of their population makeup, inward migration served to make Belfast an increasingly Protestant city.[30] In the two final decades of the century, when Belfast increased in population (bearing in mind a municipal boundary extension in 1896) by just short of 60 per cent (from 208,122 in 1881 to 349,180 in 1901) the proportion of Catholics within the population declined by a full 4.5 per cent, dropping below a quarter for the first time since the early nineteenth century.[31] The central reason behind this trend relates to employment opportunities in the city. As Clarkson observes of late Victorian Belfast's labour market, it proved 'less able, or less willing, to absorb Catholics than Protestants.[32] When the 1901 Census confirmed that Belfast had outstripped Dublin to become the largest city on the island, the powerful symbolism was not lost on Unionists who celebrated their ascendancy over their old southern rival. The rise in population was portrayed as being closely connected to industrialization and contrasted with the Catholic, pre-industrial south and west as Belfast sought metaphorically to 'snuggle up' ever more closely to the motherland across the Irish Sea.[33] Despite this outward projection as a commercial, industrial urban hub we should remain conscious of the regular reminders Edwardian citizens would have had of the surrounding countryside. With only one in five of the city's population having been born in the city around 1900 there were close connections through family ties that linked urban workers back to the land and farming communities, particularly of counties Antrim and Down.

1900–2010

Whilst Belfast's population continued to rise after 1900, the pace of expansion and of inward migration slackened quite sharply as economic growth and employment opportunities slowed during the opening decade of the new century. In the decade up to the First World War the rate of demographic growth was less than a third of that which had prevailed during the 1890s. Indeed, it was in the early years of the century, as emigration continued, that Belfast made the transition from positive to negative net migration and the city during the twentieth century lost more inhabitants than it gained.[34] From the post-war period the core city consistently lost population, and the highest outflow from the city since partition occurred during the 1970s and 80s when on average the loss amounted per year to 10,700 (from 1971 to 1991).[35] Even in the most recent decade to 2010, the core city population continued to show a small decline in spite of increased immigration in the years 2004 to 2008.[36] Out-migration from Belfast has formed two principal streams. A significant outflow has been part of the suburban expansion to the neighbouring counties of Antrim and Down, to the extent that in 2001 the Belfast urban area had a population of almost 500,000 while the greater Belfast metropolitan area reached a population of over 700,000.[37] A second stream has consisted of emigrants who have left Belfast to emigrate out of Northern Ireland, forming at least one half to two thirds of the Northern Ireland emigrant cohort overall.[38]

While it is not possible to entirely disaggregate outflows from Belfast into suburban and external (from Northern Ireland) streams, part of the movement outward was in the form of step-migration, i.e. migrants from other parts of Northern Ireland residing for a period in Belfast before emigrating away from Northern Ireland altogether.

The inter-war decades and particularly the Great Depression of the 1930s hit Belfast's traditional industrial base hard, dependent as it was on export markets. Compensatory growth in the service sector provided jobs for some but inward migration to Belfast from the rural hinterland became even more sluggish than it had been in the Edwardian era.[39] In the post-war era, demographic stagnation leading on to actual population decline reflected particularly outward migration to the developing suburban fringe of Greater Belfast and ultimately increasing movement of commuters to the Regional City, which encompassed a zone stretching to a radius of twenty-five miles from the city centre. Stormont resisted Belfast Corporation's desire to extend the city boundary (eventually extended in 1973), which, allied to strategic development for new industries and residential housing on 'greenfield' sites well beyond the inner city, meant that the trend of the late nineteenth century was effectively reversed.[40] Young adults of the post-war generations raised in the city could now be found moving out to addresses in housing developments occupying spaces in the former farmland from which grandparents and great-grandparents had flocked into the city. Although the trends towards de-industrialization and the loss of inner-city population were shared with many other British cities, the evolving troubles exacerbated the problems faced by Belfast after 1969. In the 1970s the trend towards inner-city redevelopment and resettlement on the suburban fringe was accelerated by communal violence. That the out-migration was disproportionately amongst the city's Protestant population reinforced the perception that the trend was a neat reversal of what had occurred in the late Victorian period.[41]

Besides those leaving the city for the outer suburbs or to become commuters from the hinterland, there were significant numbers emigrating from Northern Ireland altogether. In the era of *Titanic* the vast majority of Belfast emigrants crossed the Atlantic, but from 1930 (following the general all-Ireland pattern) most opted for migration to Britain, while Canada and the USA were the preferred overseas destinations for Northern Ireland emigrants generally. The significant proportion of children in the external emigrant flow (and here we may recall Luke's mural) indicates the importance of family groups in the outflow until the 1970s, and whilst Protestants were more prominent in the movement out to the suburban fringe, Catholics were disproportionately more likely to leave the city and state altogether.[42] Although labourers and domestic workers characterized the emigration flow in the interwar period and skilled trades people that of the post-war years, by the 1980s university students and young professionals comprised a large part of the emigrant cohort.[43]

The spaces vacated by those moving away were never wholly filled by immigrants, though by the early twenty-first century the city had attracted a slightly more diverse population. While the proportion of those born in Great Britain steadily declined during the twentieth century (from 7.2 per cent in 1911 to 3.4 per cent in 2001) and those born in independent Ireland also decreased (from a high point in 1926 of 5.5 per cent to 2.3 per cent in 2001),[44] the proportion of international immigrants had increased to between 2-3 per cent of the city's population in the first decade of the twenty-first century.[45] At this juncture Belfast has edged towards the position in which close to one in ten of its population have been born outside Northern Ireland, yet as the more volatile global economic environment of recent years illustrates, predictions about what the future holds remain risky in the extreme.

TRACING MIGRANT TRAJECTORIES

In this section we turn from the macro-level of outlining migration in Belfast history to the challenge of the micro-level in tracing the trajectories of individual migrants, and here we offer three brief case studies from the DIPPAM online resource mentioned above. The first, of the 'Sandy Row' district, was prompted by the way Belfast migration is represented in the outdoor museum of the Ulster Folk and Transport Museum, Cultra, particularly in its 'Town Area' by a terrace of six reconstructed houses. This originally stood, from the 1820s until the 1970s, in Tea Lane (later re-named Rowland Street and now Rowland Way), in the mainly Protestant working-class district of Sandy Row.[46] The museum visitor may be encouraged to consider stories of individual migrants whose trajectories took them from cottages in the 'Rural Area' of the museum, such as the Drumnahunshin house, to terraced houses, such as those in Tea Lane, and possibly on from there to a more salubrious street elsewhere within Belfast (more internal migration), or out of Belfast to Britain, America or elsewhere in the Irish diaspora (emigration).

Take the following IED, a missing relatives notice extract from the *Belfast Weekly Telegraph*, 5 December 1931:[47]

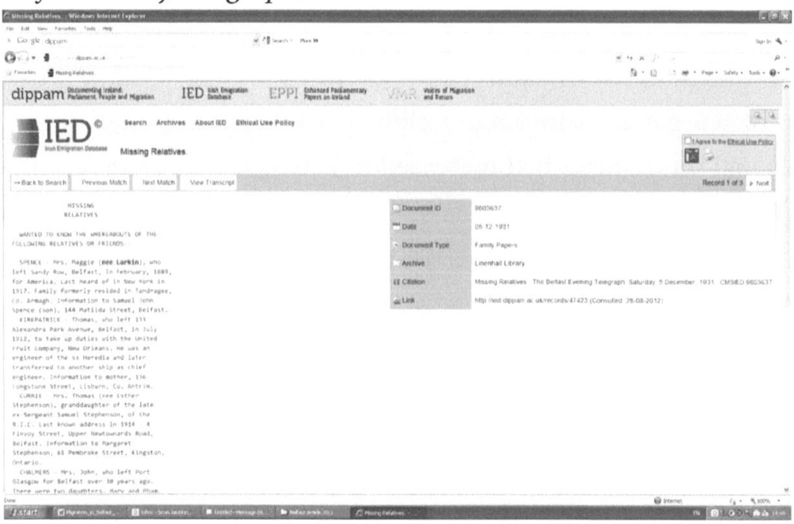

Maggie Larkin, we infer, was born into a family resident in the market town of Tandragee, County Armagh; she moved to Sandy Row, Belfast (rural-urban, internal migration); and then moved on in 1889 from Belfast to New York (emigration). Her son, Samuel John Spence was presumably born in Sandy Row and he was still in the Sandy Row area (Matilda Street – but not in Sandy Row proper) in 1931 when he placed this notice in the newspaper. We are given no indication here of the original in-migration or immigration of the Larkin family to Tandragee (taken at face value, the English origin of the family name Larkin suggests that it may have arrived in Ulster with the large-scale immigration from Britain of the seventeenth century that followed the Plantation of Ulster). We do have a hint, in that the son is trying to trace his mother, of the possibility of further in-migration in the form of her return or re-immigration to Belfast, back from New York. Thus we have exemplified the three directions of migration – inward (including return), internal, and outward. What is revealed here is part at least of the 3-**S**tages (leaving, crossing, arriving) and 3-**D**irections (inward, internal, outward) aspects, if not the more elusive 3-**O**utcomes (segregation, integration, modulation) aspect, of the migration trajectories of two members of the Larkin and Spence families.

Migration may result, broadly speaking, in three different types of outcome, according to the three main coping strategies that are open to migrants, and these can be summarized as 'segregation', 'integration' and 'modulation'. New arrivals make key choices about how to establish themselves in their 'new world' or have these made for them by default: whether to begin new and separate settlements for themselves (segregation) or settle into established communities (integration). In practice the outcome is rarely clear-cut: many migrants continue throughout their lives to 'switch' or 'modulate', like a change of mood, between seeing their new world as 'the land of the stranger' or the 'land of plenty and sweet liberty'. Such ambivalence about the new world may persist in the descendants of the migrant generation, making it difficult to determine when exactly the process of migration may be considered complete. Amongst many descendants of the British immigrants of the seventeenth century in Ulster, as amongst many descendants of Irish emigrants around the world, there continues to be a strong sense of being 'in diaspora', of being connected with their original British or Irish homeland.[48] The 'Missing Relatives' extract referred to above raises these issues of segregation, integration and modulation: how did Maggie Spence regard her moves from Tandragee to Belfast to New York? How did her new neighbours regard her? Did she feel 'at home' in all three places, or not? How did her son feel about his move from Sandy Row to Matilda Street? What kind of relationship did Maggie in New York have with her family in Belfast (there had evidently been some contact over the twenty-eight years since her departure but when her son actively seeks her in 1931 she has not been heard of for fourteen years). Thus, this brief and ostensibly inconsequential newspaper announcement yields evidence about the migration history of the Sandy Row district of Belfast.

The following EPPI extract, relating to specifically to 'Tea Lane' in Sandy Row, illustrates in rather more detail the possible outcomes of migration, in a context that is part of the deep history of the Northern Ireland conflict:[49]

Missing Relatives - Windows Internet Explorer

File Edit View Favorites Tools Help

dippam Documenting Ireland: Parliament, People and Migration

IED© Irish Emigration Database

Search Archives

Missing Relatives.

Back to Search | Previous Match | Next Match

MISSING RELATIVES

WANTED TO KNOW THE WHEREABOUTS OF THE FOLLOWING RELATIVES OR FRIENDS:-

SPENCE - Mrs. Maggie (**nee Larkin**), who left Sandy Row, Belfast, in February, 1889, for America. Last heard of in New York in 1917. Family formerly resided in Tandragee, Co. Armagh. Information to Samuel John Spence (son), 144 Matilda Street, Belfast.

This is the testimony of Bridget Kane to the Commissioners conducting the parliamentary inquiry into the riots that took place in Belfast in July 1857. Specifically, she is being asked about the circumstances that forced her to migrate from her home in Tea Lane, Sandy Row, Belfast to English Street, Belfast. It is worth quoting her story as re-told by Andrew Boyd in *Holy War in Belfast* [emphases added]:

> That same evening [12 July 1857], *Brigid Kane*, an inoffensive Catholic who lived in *Tea Lane* in the heart of *Sandy Row*, heard prolonged cheering outside her house and, on looking out, saw a crowd of people waving flags and bunches of orange flowers and dancing around an immense effigy that was supposed to represent Dan O'Connell, the Catholic leader, who was dead since 1847. She saw them carry the effigy up and down *Tea Lane*, then set it alight outside her front door and dance while it blazed.
> *Brigid Kane* accepted the burning of the effigy as a warning. *Next day*, when a friendly neighbour advised her to leave, she packed her belongings and found herself another house in *English Street*, within the safety of *the Pound*.[50]

In this short extract, five discrepancies are evident between Boyd's re-telling and the original account. The important one for our migration purpose here is whereas Boyd says 'next day … she found herself another house in English Street', her actual testimony was that she moved 'on the 9th of September', about six weeks after the event. We have here an insight into the circumstances of forced internal migration, caused by sectarian violence, which is distorted in Boyd's re-telling by the dramatic liberties that he takes with his primary source.[51]

Various questions about migration outcomes (segregation, integration, modulation) are raised by this extract. How long had Bridget Kane, a Catholic, been living in the heart of the predominantly Protestant Sandy Row area? Was she born there or had she moved in from somewhere outside Belfast? How many other Catholics were living in the area? Did she feel safe and 'at home' (integrated) there before the riot? That she was warned by neighbours and did not move out immediately suggests that she might have done. How did she feel about moving to the relatively 'segregated' safety of English Street in the Pound area of the predominantly Catholic Lower Falls Road? If she felt relieved, did she, as it were, turn her back on her old neighbours in Tea Lane, Sandy Row; did she continue to keep in touch; or did she move out of Belfast altogether? The evidence to answer these questions in this specific case is lacking but here we may benefit from attending to the actual voices of other migrants who articulate their feelings on these matters, as for example in this third extract from VMR, transcribed from an audio interview with 'Gary' who grew up in Sandy Row in the 1960s and 70s in which he describes the impact of internal migration (this time urban-suburban rather than rural-urban, or intra-urban) in relation to the most recent 'Troubles':

> I think that the biggest aid to peace in Sandy Row and the Shankill and probably Lower Falls and everywhere else was when they built the ring road 'cause they *knocked* all those wee houses *down* to put the ring road in, right? Okay, and all those people *were taken* and the redevelopment as they called it. So they *flattened* all those wee houses so we all had to *go somewhere.* So they *shuffled* us all *off* to Lisburn, and Bangor, and Carrick, and all these places, right? So you got all these people *moved from* the Shankill, the Falls, Sandy

> Row, Newtownards Road, blah, blah, blah, all the way out, and that's the first wee *diaspora* thing, twelve miles away. (Author's emphasis.)[52]

Listening to the full interview it is possible to determine much more about how well Gary felt 'integrated' or otherwise in Sandy Row, how he adjusted to his migration out into part of the Sandy Row 'diaspora', and how he felt about his old home afterwards, issues not often so openly discussed in surviving written evidence such as migrant letters.

Having considered this sequence of extracts from DIPPAM, which is intended to illustrate the potential of applying the SDO (stages, directions, outcomes) model of migration to primary sources, we finally refer briefly in this section to the potential of new electronic resources for the mapping of individual migration trajectories. The difficulty of mapping is well illustrated by the case of Bridget Kane.[53] In order to locate her places of residence in Tea Lane and English Street and gain some sense of the quality of her life there we need to go to large scale historic mapping such as the Royal Irish Academy's *Irish Historic Towns Atlas*. Here we encounter the limitations of mapping on paper that were highlighted at a seminar in the Royal Irish Academy in June 2010 marking the launch of the latest volumes in the *Irish Historic Towns Atlas* series, when Tadhg O'Keefe suggested that in future the series should 'seek to capture experiences of 'town-dwelling' or 'being-in-the-town'. This may be more readily achieved with a move to digital mapping and the use of GIS (geographical information systems) technology, which enables both the 'layering' and 'mirroring' and 'stitching' of digital maps and the linkage of all kinds of digital files (text, image, audio, and video) to any point on a map. This should make it easier, for example, not only to pinpoint the location of Bridget Kane's house in Tea Lane and the one to which she moved in English Street but also to access all types of surviving evidence that might help us towards an understanding of what living in these properties must have been like for her and her neighbours, not least the six terrace houses from Tea Lane that are preserved in the Ulster Folk and Transport Museum.

LISTENING TO THE VOICES OF MIGRANT LETTERS

Perhaps the most valuable type of evidence for migration stories, especially before voice recording, is migrant letters. Through them we can 'hear' individual voices more clearly and fully than we can through the types of written record such as those of the extracts above that hint at or capture those of Maggie Spence and Bridget Kane. The contemporary correspondence of trans-Atlantic emigrants from Ulster can supplement social statistics in measuring the parallel in more qualitative terms. As early as the immediate post-Famine years, one emigrant, William Montgomery, on a return visit to his home district of Portadown, County Armagh, gave expression to his view that Belfast, in appearance and environment could be set against the cities he had encountered in the New World. Furthermore he plainly set out the stark contrast to be drawn, in his own mind, between that city and the small market town he had departed years before. Writing fairly regularly to his cousin, Joseph Searight, in Philadelphia, William confided his strong desire to resist pressure from the family at home to return permanently to Portadown in order to be closer to his ageing father. Whilst on a return visit in the summer of 1850 to what he clearly considered the stifling environment of Portadown, he wrote to his cousin in the following terms:

> The country people all say they hope I will remain at home [but] I cannot see a change in the appearance of things here from the time I left … I must confess the signs of decay

> are much more abundant than those of recovery or vitality. Belfast is much improved not only in appearance but in commerce, and it is the only place that looks like a city of the United States and where I feel at home.[54]

Clearly this migrant could see in Belfast as early as 1850 some of the advantages of city living he had experienced in US centres like Cincinnati and New Orleans. Relenting to family pressure he ultimately returned home to endure the dreaded 'quietness' of north Armagh until the mid-1850s when he relocated to Manchester in England.[55] Comparisons with North America have also been drawn by historians of the turn of the century city. In the course of a 2006 BBC NI documentary on the Belfast Dock strike of 1907, John Gray, formerly Librarian at the Linenhall Library, likened the atmosphere in 1890's Belfast to a gold rush town in the American west, because of the constant stream of new migrants flooding into the city.[56]

Another Irish migrant writing from the American west in 1885 illustrated how those overseas sought to adjust and update their picture of home from afar. In March 1885 James Stewart in San Francisco wrote a letter in reply to an old friend back home in Belfast, referred to only as Mr Coulter. Admiring the previously enclosed likeness (portrait photograph) sent out by Coulter, James politely noted the familiarity of the image and its power to allow him to imagine himself back in Belfast once more. A few lines on in his letter he developed the idea of being back on the banks of the Lagan and mused about the city's past and future growth:

> I expect there are some portions of Belfast that would now seem strange to me if I were suddenly landed there. There have been a great many changes in different localities –

> all no doubt improving the appearance and adding to the prosperity of the town. Your description of the alterations, and of the different new streets that have been laid out, was to me very interesting. It would seem to be a question only of a little time when Belfast will outstrip Dublin in size & population as it is now ahead in commercial importance. Its reputation in this part of the world is that of a wide-awake, progressive town, excelled in this respect by none other in the United Kingdom, although it falls short of the rapid progress of some of the American cities & towns.[57]

One can imagine James Stewart reading Coulter's letter in San Francisco and perhaps with eyes closed trying to imagine how those newly laid out streets would have altered the picture of Belfast he had taken away with him upon his departure. Coming through Stewart's reply, just under a year away from the introduction of the First Home Rule Bill (April 1886), was the sense of competition with Dublin and the pride the author took in the contrast; the dynamic, progressive northern city cast with its old southern rival. Stewart though, confirming his status now as an American citizen, reminded Coulter that ultimately everything was bigger and better in the United States.

The final letter to which we wish to refer is not, in fact, an emigrant letter at all but it nicely illustrates that in practice there could be limited enough difference between the experience of a rural-urban internal migrant from that of a trans-oceanic migrant. Not unlike many an emigrant letter this document was penned on St Patrick's Day, in this instance that of 1879. Then Ellen Breeze, residing at 144 Donegall Pass, Belfast wrote a short letter home to her mother, apparently in the area between Killinchy and Killyleagh on the west shore of Strangford Lough.[58] Although only some twenty miles away her letter reveals that both herself and her sister Martha, who may have been lodging with an aunt in Donegall Pass, wrote home regularly but, as emigrants often did, complained about the lack of return letters. The letter also mentions that their aunt had recently had a letter from an uncle, very probably the C.K. Breeze who had been in San Francisco for at least four years, mapping out for the modern reader the triangular correspondence that served to describe the outline shape of the Breeze family diaspora.[59] What Clarkson has described as an 'intricate web of kinship' connected town with countryside but also stretched overseas.[60] Just as farther-flung emigrants often did, Ellen reported to those at home about 'bumping into' a mutual acquaintance, Mr Stevenson, in Belfast's leading department store, Anderson & McAuley's. Visits home from Belfast were referred to in Ellen's letters and this might seem to stress the contrast with emigration.[61] Those leaving Ulster who crossed the Irish Sea could return home fairly frequently and, as steam passages came to dominate the trans-oceanic routes from the early 1860s, return trips became a more viable proposition for overseas emigrants.

While letters are usually much richer sources for the stories of individual migrants and their families than such as newspaper advertisements or parliamentary inquiries, there are limitations to the evidence they provide. Oral history has the advantage of not only recording actual voices but also enabling researchers to put questions on details or issues about which letters may be more or less silent. So for our final section of case studies from DIPPAM we turn to extracts from VMR.

BELFAST VOICES OF MIGRATION AND RETURN

The city's link with the wider world has, over the past few centuries, largely been through its emigrants; those like William Montgomery and James Stewart above, who formed what we might call the Belfast diaspora. Montgomery's migration trajectory in particular stands as a reminder that transnationalism is not only a recent phenomenon and demonstrates the importance of individual migrant testimonies in uncovering the ever-present ideology of return.[62] Commercial and cultural links fostered by Belfast natives, most especially in the United States and throughout the British Empire and Commonwealth, have been of enormous benefit to the city over the last four hundred years. In the twentieth century as in the nineteenth, emigration continued to have a profound effect on Belfast; not only its commercial development but also the contribution made by the diaspora to the peace process.[63] This has not only occurred at the highest level of peace negotiations, but includes the efforts of ordinary emigrants who themselves grew up in interface neighbourhoods that witnessed the worst of the violence, and here we may be reminded of the Sandy Row experiences of Maggie Spence, Bridget Kane and 'Gary'.

'I try to direct business to Belfast': The Benefits of Diaspora

How many previous Belfast migrants, for whom we have no comparable record, had experiences similar to that of Craig from the Oldpark neighbourhood in North Belfast, who left Belfast in 1966 to attend his brother's wedding in Toronto? He stayed there for a year before returning to Belfast and, although he found employment at home, Craig decided to return to Toronto in 1968. Having started out in the credit business, Craig got into banking and worked his way into prominent positions in the banking industry in Canada and later started his own consultancy. Craig is one of a group of Irish-Canadian business people who have been involved in the promotion of peace in Northern Ireland through business development. Though optimistic about the peace process, Craig is fully aware that social deprivation in his old neighbourhood is a part of the problem and that business development that would create more employment opportunities has to be part of the solution.

> I certainly have tried to promote business back and forth to the North. I have spent time over there trying to direct business into Belfast, two bids in the last couple of years. Tried to sell a call centre that was going out of business, going under. Tried to sell it to a Canadian client here. [I'm] direct at saying, 'Yeah, the war is over, it's open for business'. I have a certain influence in my circle and *I try to direct business to Belfast*. I could have taken it to Dublin, I could have taken it to New Brunswick, I tried to direct it to Belfast. And would I be doing that if I was a Canadian who had forgotten about Ireland, cutting off the Irish ties? No, I wouldn't have done that.[64]

In addition, Craig is involved with an Irish business association in Toronto formed about twenty years ago by two businessmen from Belfast, one Protestant, one Catholic; the goal of which has been to provide the opportunity for the public discussion of Irish issues. Their guest speakers have included leading academics, British, Irish and Northern Irish cabinet ministers, and many of the main actors in the peace process (e.g. Gerry Adams, former Taoiseach Bertie Ahern, General John de Chastelain and Judge Peter Cory). Craig feels that his own participation at these events has moderated the staunchly Unionist views he held previously.

> We provide a forum for people to come and talk and for both sides to hear a different view. I mean I wouldn't be going along to hear Gerry Adams. If I had my druthers,

> would I go and hear him? No, but I think having someone like that come and talk to a forum then that changes my view of what goes on, or may do, or gives me a different perspective on what's going on. We're all ex-pats and we all have some influence over there in business or otherwise.[65]

Thus, the contribution of Belfast emigrants abroad may be seen positively in material terms such as business investment but their influence may also be experienced in less tangible but nonetheless influential 'socio-political' means. However, emigration from Belfast has also certainly had negative effects felt in the absence of those who have left. What skills, talents and attitudes did these emigrants take with them? What might their voices have added to the discourse of peaceful accommodation, to our conception of Belfast's past? What nuances, counter narratives or hidden histories might they reveal?

'The people with hair left': Emigrant Ambivalence

The specific motives of individual migrants often cannot be gleaned from the surviving written records, but can from oral interviews. Thomas was born in Scotland in 1952 and grew up in a working-class housing estate in Dunmurry, south Belfast, where he had Protestant and Catholic friends. He recalled that as his generation reached adulthood in the late 1960s, his Protestant friends immediately took up apprenticeships after finishing school and it never occurred to him to question why there were no obvious job training prospects for young Catholics like himself. With few options open to him, Thomas worked on and off at labouring jobs around Belfast. Though vaguely aware of the emerging civil rights movement, he was more interested in the counter-cultural scene that was alive in the city during the mid-1960s, linked to larger counter-cultural movements in cities like London, New York and San Francisco. As with many other young people, Thomas grew his hair long and spent his free time drinking, smoking dope and socializing with other like-minded individuals who frequented the vibrant music clubs of the scene. In the following excerpt he describes what happened to the emerging liberalization in Belfast with the outbreak of full conflict in 1969:

> It was quite obvious to me for about a year Belfast was humming. There was a lot going on in Belfast, it was a very good place to be. And then really from August '69, it just vanished over night and it became a very, very hairy place to be, if you had hair. And there'd been one or two pubs, clubs in Belfast where people like that would meet from all different areas and all different sorts of outlooks but basically their goal was to have fun and there was never any mention of all that [political] stuff and people got along really well. So I would say perhaps two generations, maybe three, just vanished, you know, and went to England and wherever. You know, the best way to express it really, *the people with hair left*. Long-haired people got out then because they were frowned upon by all sides.[66]

As Thomas described, with the outbreak of the conflict the emerging counter-culture of 1960s Belfast was shut down almost overnight. This and the lack of employment drove Thomas, like many of his young cohort, to leave Belfast for London in 1970 where the counter-culture was in full swing. He set up in the Ealing neighbourhood and was amazed to find the area was the locus for young Belfast people like him. Thomas's narrative is a reminder of the 'safety-valve' function of emigration as suggested by Hirschman's exit-voice polarity theory: that it is the younger and least conservative element in society that is most likely to depart and who, had they stayed at home, would have been most likely to demand change.[67] Thus, it is by their departure that their impact on the home society is most strongly felt.

Though Thomas returned to live in Belfast for a couple years in the late 1970s, he moved to London permanently in 1981. His life there since has not been easy, and at the time of his interview he was living with his wife and two children in a poor housing estate in a high crime area in south-east London where, as he described, 'there is no relief from the concrete at all'. Sitting in his flat with iron bars on the door and windows, Thomas spoke powerfully of the extent and often the subtlety of discrimination still regularly experienced by working-class Irish people living in England. Nevertheless, when asked if he'd consider returning to Belfast, he was not in favour and related his impression of the city garnered on a visit back home a few months previously:

> I definitely wouldn't go back to Belfast if I was going back to Ireland, but Tyrone, everywhere else, yeah, I could live *here*, I feel at *home here* now. But I didn't feel at home in Belfast. I didn't like this place maybe because I was disappointed in it. … Well the propaganda here [in Britain] is that everything is hunky dory and there's all these dramatic changes going on in Belfast but when I got *there* I didn't think there was anything particularly dramatic that had changed. Still seemed a pretty depressing place actually … grey, dull, windswept. … But you know, having said that probably living in Belfast again, like what we used to do, the countryside is not far away, the hills are not far away, the sea is not far away.[68]

Thomas' narrative reveals his continuing ambivalence towards his native city. *Home Here* is Ireland – the rural Tyrone of Thomas' grandparents – a reminder that the dream of return for so many Irish people living in British cities is the rural Irish idyll of the imagination. Belfast is *there,* not home, though its position is somewhat mitigated by the proximity of the countryside that surrounds the city.

'People who've left have been completely abandoned': Emotional Geographies of Home and Away

What individuals remember of home, as with Thomas above, and how they narrate these memories reconstructs home over and over again. Homes are thus created and sustained by narratives, which are more likely to be found in the intimate personal domain of letters, memoir and oral interviews.[69] For emigrants from Belfast, especially those who left because of the conflict, the traditional link between home and safety was ruptured, thus attitudes towards the city may be ambivalent. This is the case of Orla from a working-class Catholic background who grew up in North Belfast during the 1960s and '70s in a neighbourhood she described as 'under siege'. As a teenager, she vividly recalled her home being ransacked by British soldiers looking for guns while she and her younger brother were held at gunpoint in the upstairs bedrooms. The guns never materialized but her father, who had himself served in the British Army in World War Two, was nevertheless taken away as a suspect and Orla told how she would never forget 'the look of absolute shock and disbelief' on his face as he was led away. Not long after, she 'took off' for England, living in several cities before eventually enrolling in a college course in Liverpool. In 1981, Orla returned to Belfast, having accepted a job as a social worker in the Divis Flats in the Lower Falls area, but was unprepared for the anguish and brutality of the Hunger Strikes. When one of her colleagues was murdered later that year, a terrified Orla decided to move back to Liverpool where she has remained ever since. In spite of her need to get away from the violence and her abhorrence of sectarianism, the wrench of emigration ('leaving') was nonetheless difficult for Orla and she continued to travel 'home' ('crossing') to Belfast four or five times per year ('arriving') to see her family and friends. She described her feelings on the journey 'home':

> I used to always be very excited going to Belfast and as the plane was coming into land, I was always sitting in my seat crying and relieved to be home and to be back in my home and my country where I felt I absolutely belonged. And then when I'd get picked up, the drive down from the airport, the drive down the M2 into Belfast and I'd see the Cave Hill which is the hill I used to play on when I was a kid come into view. I would see the docks and the Harland and Wolff shipyard and I would feel I was home.[70]

However, Orla's ritualistic keen or lament for Belfast has dissipated with the progress of the peace process in recent years:

> What started to happen is I would get off the plane and do that same journey and notice I wasn't crying. … And I think I felt sad initially when I noticed that and then I think I felt relieved because it couldn't pull at me anymore. … There was no more guilt that I had to go home and help rebuild it. … Some of us have always felt that we ought to go home and rebuild it because we've had time out.[71]

Orla's strong sense of belonging to her native city was tinged with the guilt that some emigrants feel about having left Belfast in its time of trouble, especially those like Orla who would see themselves as political or social activists. However, Orla has instead channelled her activism into improving the welfare of Irish people in Britain. As the first ever chair of Irish Community Care (ICC) in her region to hail from Northern Ireland, for example, she took steps to make sure that the ICC served all Irish people regardless of religious, political or North/South affiliation. On one level, this meant ensuring a balanced display of symbols such as flags and emblems and the use of prayers and anthems at public events. More critically, it also required the commitment to assist those on both sides who had been 'put out' of Northern Ireland with accommodation and other forms of aid 'on the quiet'. However, Orla felt that home and diaspora relations were a two-way street:

> We get no funding to Irish Community Care whatsoever from Northern Ireland sources and yet we support Northern Irish people … I think *people who've left have been completely abandoned*. That's what I think. Nobody noticed us going, nobody's ever tried to look at us, why we might have gone, you know, both Catholics and Protestants.[72]

Significantly, as emigrants with a 'failed return' in the course of their migration trajectories, Craig, Orla and Thomas all experienced 'leaving', 'crossing' and 'arriving' in various directions that encouraged multiple notions of belonging and 'home'.[73] Yet none of them felt that their identity as individuals 'from Belfast' was in any way lessened as a result. However, even as Craig actively continues to seek out opportunities to 'give back' to his native city, Orla's narrative begs the question, does the home place have a duty of care towards its emigrants? Thomas' and

Orla's stories are a reminder that many emigrants from Belfast retain traumatic memories and ambivalent feelings about their native city; for them post-conflict public relations needs to be more than propaganda.

CONCLUSION

Our three sets of case studies, 'Trajectories', 'Letters' and 'Voices', based on extracts from DIPPAM, demonstrate that 'listening' to the voices of individual migrants to be found in this range of sources is potentially of great value. If we are concerned, as O'Keefe urges, to 'capture experiences of town-dwelling or being-in-the-town', we need to further the project of 'putting migration into Belfast history', not least to explore how Belfast has been regarded as 'home' by both its residents and its diaspora. Within reach is a more nuanced understanding of the migration process, particularly when evidence is examined in terms of the SDO model of three stages (leaving; crossing; arriving) three directions (immigration, including return; internal migration; emigration) and three outcomes (segregation; integration; modulation).

In addition, bringing diverse source materials together provides a vantage point from where we can view not only multidirectional migrant trajectories through space, but multidirectional perspectives through time. The direction and scale of the 'fitfully dormant', 'swarming', 'buzzing' and 'boiling' activity of migration in Belfast history, observable as it were from the vantage point of 'Scally's satellite', needs to be located and quantified as accurately as possible.

At the same time, what may emerge from further study of the qualitative evidence of individual migrant stories is a better understanding of the migration history of Belfast's many constituent communities. How typical or representative a district such as Sandy Row may be of Belfast's migration history as a whole is of course not possible to say without reference to equivalent case studies across the city. In pursing such comparative studies we may find the idea that communities may vary in the extent to which they are 'open' or 'closed' to migration.[74] The 'closed' image of a 'walled' community under siege is a dominant one in Irish history, particularly in the history of Belfast, but this 'static' image returns us to the limitation of 'portraits', such as that provided by Luke, and 'snapshots,' such as those provided on Census Sundays, in representing dynamic processes such as migration. We need to remember that the usual condition for 'walled' communities is for their gates to be open, permitting migration in and out, and be prepared to wrestle with the resulting 'throughotherness'. Our case studies remind us that Belfast society in the past as in the present was never static. Every hour that passed brought births and deaths as well as new inhabitants moving in or around the city as well as those departing or perhaps returning, the constant flux of migrant traffic.

Notes

Chapter 1

1. Phillip J. Waller, *Town, City and Nation: England 1850–1914* (Oxford: Oxford University Press, 1983), p.283.
2. Emrys Jones, 'The Social Geography of Belfast', *Journal of the Statistical and Social Inquiry Society of Ireland*, 29, 2 (1954), pp.1–18, p.3.
3. George Benn, *History of the Town of Belfast* (Belfast, 1823).
4. Stephen A. Royle, *Belfast Part II, 1840–1900, Irish Historic Towns Atlas*, 17, (Dublin: Royal Irish Academy, 2007).
5. Belfast, PRONI D2088/11/2: Annual Reports of the Linen Merchants' Association (hereafter abbreviated to 'Annual Report') [1899], pp.26, 27.
6. J. Bardon, 'Belfast at its Zenith', *History Ireland*, 1, 4 (1993), pp.48–51.
7. Belfast, PRONI D2088/22/9: List of Mills Closed in Ireland Since 1873.
8. Belfast, PRONI D3134/1: Memoirs of the Working Life of William Topping, 1903–1956.
9. Cited in Bardon, 'Belfast at its Zenith'.
10. Belfast, PRONI D2088/11/1: Annual Reports [1894], p.11.
11. Andrew G. Malcolm, 'The influence of factory life on the health of the operative as founded upon the medical statistics of this class at Belfast', *Journal of the Statistical Society of London*, 19, 2 (1856), pp.1–31, p. 170.
12. M.D. Thomas, 'Manufacturing Industry in Belfast, Northern Ireland', *Annals of the Association of American Geographers*, 46, 2 (1956), pp.175–196.
13. D.L. Armstrong, 'Social and Economic Conditions in the Belfast Linen Industry, 1850–1900', *Irish Historical Studies*, 7, 28 (1951), pp.235–269.
14. Stephen A. Royle, *Portrait of an Industrial City: 'Clanging Belfast', 1750-1914* (Belfast: Ulster Historical Foundation, 2011), Chapter 2.
15. Thomas, 'Manufacturing Industry'
16. Ibid.
17. Belfast, PRONI D2088/11: Annual Reports; Belfast, PRONI D2088/2/1: Belfast Linen Trade Circular: Central Council of Irish Linen Industry.

18. Belfast, PRONI D2088/11/1: Annual Reports [1891], p.17; Belfast, PRONI D2088/11/1: Annual Reports [1888], p.15; Belfast, PRONI D2088/11/1: Annual Reports [1895], p.26; Belfast, PRONI D2088/11/1: Annual Reports [1902], p.15.
19. Belfast, PRONI D2088/11/2: Annual Reports [1875], p.6.
20. Belfast, PRONI D2088/11/2: Annual Reports [1880], p.10.
21. Belfast, PRONI D2088/11/2: Annual Reports [1880], p.13.
22. Belfast, PRONI D2088/11/2: Annual Reports [1888], p.11.
23. Belfast, PRONI D2088/11/1: Annual Reports [1894], p.21.
24. Belfast, PRONI D2088/11/3: Annual Reports [1905], p.15.
25. Belfast, PRONI D2088/11/3: Annual Reports [1910], p.11.
26. Belfast, PRONI D2088/11/3: Annual Reports [1911], p.16.
27. Belfast, PRONI D2088/11/1: Annual Reports [1890], p.13; Belfast, PRONI D2088/11/3: Annual Reports [1897], p.15; Belfast, PRONI D2088/11/1: Annual Reports [1891], p.16.; Belfast, PRONI D2088/11/1: Annual Reports [1894], p.21.; Belfast, PRONI D2088/11/3: Annual Reports [1902], p.15; Belfast, PRONI D2088/11/3: Annual Reports [1907], p.18; Belfast, PRONI D2088/11/1: Annual Reports [1892], p.10; Belfast, PRONI D2088/11/3: Annual Reports [1896], p.16.
28. Belfast, PRONI D2088/11/3: Annual Reports [1902], pp.15, 16.
29. Belfast, PRONI D2088/11/3: Annual Reports [1898], p.20.
30. Belfast, PRONI D2088/11/3: Annual Reports [1902], p.12.
31. Belfast, PRONI D2088/11/2: Annual Reports [1881], p. 6.
32. Belfast, PRONI D2088/11/2: Annual Reports [1881], pp.6, 7.
33. Belfast, PRONI D2088/11/2: Annual Reports [1882], p.6.
34. Belfast, PRONI D2088/11/2: Annual Reports [1883], p.8.
35. Belfast, PRONI D2088/11/2: Annual Reports [1883], p.14.
36. Belfast, PRONI D2088/11/2: Annual Reports [1884], p.6.
37. Belfast, PRONI D2088/11/2: Annual Reports [1884], p.8.
38. Belfast, PRONI D2088/11/2: Annual Reports [1886], p.11.
39. Belfast, PRONI D2088/11/2: Annual Reports [1894], p.8.
40. Belfast, PRONI D2088/11/1: Annual Reports [1895], pp.9, 10.
41. Belfast, PRONI D2088/11/3: Annual Reports [1896], p.11.
42. Belfast, PRONI D2088/11/3: Annual Reports [1896], p.18.
43. Belfast, PRONI D2088/11/2: Annual Reports [1880], p.9.
44. Belfast, PRONI D2088/11/2: Annual Reports [1880], p.12.
45. Belfast, PRONI D2088/11/2: Annual Reports [1881], p.9.
46. Belfast, PRONI D2088/11/2: Annual Reports [1885], p.9.
47. Belfast, PRONI D2088/11/2: Annual Reports [1886], p.11.

48. Belfast, PRONI D2088/11/1: Annual Reports [1891], p.12.
49. Belfast, PRONI D2088/11/1: Annual Reports [1891], pp.12, 13.
50. Belfast, PRONI D2088/11/1: Annual Reports [1892], p.14.
51. Belfast, PRONI D2088/11/1: Annual Reports [1894], p.18.
52. Belfast, PRONI D2088/11/1: Annual Reports [1894].
53. Belfast, PRONI D2088/11/3: Annual Reports [1896], p.10.
54. Belfast, PRONI D2088/11/3: Annual Reports [1896], p.11.
55. Belfast, PRONI D2088/11/3: Annual Reports [1898], p.11.
56. Belfast, PRONI D2088/11/3: Annual Reports [1899], p.11.
57. Ibid.
58. Belfast, PRONI D2088/11/3: Annual Reports [1900], p.9.
59. Belfast, PRONI D2088/2/1: Belfast Linen Trade Circular: Central Council of Irish Linen Industry.
60. Belfast, PRONI D2088/11/2/17: Annual Reports [1901], p.8.
61. Belfast, PRONI D2088/11/2: Annual Reports [1876], p.7.
62. L.P. Gross and T.R. Snyder, *Philadelphia's 1876 Centennial Exhibition* (Charleston, SC: Arcadia Publishing, 2005).
63. Belfast, PRONI D2088/11/2: Annual Reports [1879], p.10.
64. Belfast, PRONI D2088/11/1: Annual Reports [1887], p.10.
65. Belfast, PRONI D2088/11/1: Annual Reports [1888], p.7.
66. Belfast, PRONI D2088/11/1: Annual Reports [1890], p.9.
67. Belfast, PRONI D2088/11/1: Annual Reports [1892], p.8.
68. Belfast, PRONI D2088/11/1: Annual Reports [1893], p.9.
69. Belfast, PRONI D2088/11/1: Annual Reports [1894], p.18.
70. Belfast, PRONI D2088/11/1: Annual Reports [1895], p.22.
71. Belfast, PRONI D2088/11/3: Annual Reports [1904], p.13.
72. Belfast, PRONI D2088/11/3: Annual Reports [1911], p.14.
73. Belfast, PRONI D2088/11/3: Annual Reports [1904], pp.18, 19.
74. Belfast, PRONI D2088/11/3: Annual Reports [1905], p.16.
75. Belfast, PRONI D2088/11/36: Annual Reports [1917], p.16.
76. Belfast, PRONI D2088/11/34: Annual Reports [1914], p.16.
77. Armstrong, 'Social and Economic Conditions', p.239.

Chapter 2

1. The research for this chapter was completed while holding grants from the Economic and Social Research Council (RES-148-25-0054) and the Leverhulme Trust. The support of both is gratefully acknowledged.
2. See, in particular, Simon Gunn, *The Public Culture of the Victorian Middle Class: Ritual and Authority in the English Industrial City 1840–1914* (Manchester: Manchester University Press, 2000); Tristram Hunt, *Building Jerusalem: The Rise and Fall of the Victorian City* (London: Weidenfeld and Nicholson, 2004). The metaphor of a civic religion is developed by David Cannadine, 'The Transformation of Civic Ritual in Modern Britain: The Colchester Oyster Feast', *Past & Present*, 94 (1982), pp.128–9. For a comprehensive overview of recent work, see Martin Daunton (ed.), *The Cambridge Urban History of Britain*, vol. 3: *1840–1950* (Cambridge: Cambridge University Press, 2000).
3. Mary Daly, *Dublin: The Deposed Capital 1860–1914* (Cork: Cork University Press, 1984); Jacinta Prunty, *Dublin Slums 1800-1925: A Study in Urban Geography* (Dublin: Irish Academic Press, 1998). Matthew Potter, *The Municipal Revolution in Ireland: A Handbook of Urban Government in Ireland since 1800* (Dublin: Irish Academic Press, 2011) is an ambitious attempt to present a more positive account of Irish civic life in the mid and late nineteenth century, but the difference in the scale of operations described there and in the works cited in note 2 remains striking.
4. Frank Wright, *Two Lands on One Soil: Ulster Politics before Home Rule* (Dublin: Gill & MacMillan, 1996); Sean Farrell, *Rituals and Riots: Sectarian Violence and Political Culture in Ulster, 1784–1886* (Lexington, Ky: University Press of Kentucky, 2000); Catherine Hirst, *Religion, Politics and Violence in Nineteenth-Century Belfast* (Dublin: Four Courts, 2002); Mark Doyle, *Fighting like the Devil for the Sake of God: Protestants, Catholics and the Origins of Violence in Victorian Belfast* (Manchester: Manchester University Press, 2009).
5. A.T.Q. Stewart, 'The Transformation of Presbyterian Radicalism in the North of Ireland 1792–1825' (MA thesis, Queen's University, Belfast, 1956). For later work, see G.J. Slater, 'Belfast Politics 1798–1868' (D.Phil. thesis, University of Ulster, 1982); B.M. Walker, *Ulster Politics: The Formative Years 1898–86* (Belfast: Ulster Historical Foundation, 1989); Wright, *Two Lands on One Soil.*
6. John Bew, *The Glory of Being Britons: Civic Unionism in Nineteenth-Century Belfast* (Dublin: Irish Academic Press, 2009).
7. The best antidote here is Henry Patterson, *Class Conflict and Sectarianism: The Protestant Working Class and the Belfast Labour Movement 1868–1920* (Belfast: Blackstaff, 1980); ibid, 'Independent Orangeism and Class Conflict in Edwardian

Belfast: A Reinterpretation', *Proceedings of the Royal Irish Academy*, 80C (1980).

8. Claire Allen, 'Urban Elites, Civil Society and Governance in Early Nineteenth-Century Belfast c.1800–32' (Ph.D. thesis, Queen's University, Belfast, 2010).
9. *First Report of the Commissioners Appointed to Enquire into the Municipal Corporations in Ireland* (Parliamentary Papers 1835, vol. 28), pp.701, 701, 728–31.
10. See, for example, British Library, Add Ms 35,739, ff 19, 113, 180; Add Ms 35734, ff 309, 326; Add Ms 35740, f. 120 (papers of the earl of Hardwicke, lord lieutenant, 1801-5); BL, Add Ms 40191, 89-91, 133-7, 142, 150; Add Ms 40,290, 29, 133-5 (papers of Robert Peel, chief secretary 1812–18).
11. These points are discussed in more detail in S.J. Connolly and Dominic Bryan, *Civic Identity and Public Space: Belfast 1780-2010* (Manchester: Manchester University Press, forthcoming). For Stewart, see *Belfast News Letter* [hereafter *BNL*], 24 November 1812.
12. BNL, 10 February 1818.
13. BNL, 15 February 1820. The Parade was Castle Place, frequently used for military displays. For the role of processions in representing social hierarchy, see Robert Darnton, 'A Bourgeois Puts his World in Order' in *The Great Cat Massacre and Other Episodes in French Cultural History* (London: Allen Lane, 1984).
14. *Northern Whig*, 24 December 1832.
15. *BNL*, 19 January, 23 December 1836; *The Times*, 27 December 1836.
16. *Report of the Commissioners Appointed to Enquire into the State of the Municipal Affairs of the Borough of Belfast* [hereafter *Municipal Affairs*] (Parliamentary Papers, 1859, volume 10), pp.161, 187, 215; George Dawson to Sir William Freemantle, 10 May 1850 (Public Record Office of Northern Ireland [hereafter PRONI], T2603/10).
17. *Municipal Affairs*, pp.63-4; *BNL*, 17 December 1847.
18. *Municipal Affairs*, p.169. The must recent account of the chancery suit is G.R. Hall, *Ulster Liberalism 1778–1876* (Dublin: Four Courts, 2011), pp.199-205.
19. *BNL*, 2 December 1857.
20. Sally Sheard, 'Nineteenth-Century Public Health: A Study of Liverpool, Belfast and Glasgow' (Ph.D. thesis, Liverpool, 1993), pp.185-200. For the baths issue, see H.G. Calwell, *Andrew Malcolm of Belfast 1818–1856, Physician and Historian* (Belfast: Brough, Cox and Dunn, 1977), pp.79–91.
21. Emrys Jones, *A Social Geography of Belfast* (London: Oxford University Press, 1960), p.52. The socially progressive legislation of the early Belfast council was first emphasized in Ian Budge and Cornelius O'Leary, *Belfast: Approach to Crisis: A Study of Belfast Politics 1613–1970* (London: Macmillan, 1973), pp.56-7, and discussed at more length in O'Leary, 'Belfast Urban Government in the Age of Reform', in David Harkness and Mary O'Dowd (eds), *The Town in Ireland* (Belfast: Appletree Press, 1981), pp.187–202.

22. Charles Abbot, Journal of a Tour in Ireland and North Wales, September–October 1792 (PRONI T3488/1, from an original in the National Archives, the Public Record Office); J.A. Pilson, *History of the Rise and Progress of Belfast and Annals of the County Antrim* (London: Longman, 1846), p.25.
23. H.D. Inglis, *A Journey Throughout Ireland during the Spring, Summer and Autumn of 1834* (5th ed., London: Whittaker & Co., 1838), p.343.
24. BNL, 6 August 1847, 5 March 1847, 1 October 1847.
25. S.J. Connolly, 'Like an Old Cathedral City: Belfast welcomes Queen Victoria, August 1849', *Urban History* (forthcoming).
26. Gillian McIntosh, 'Symbolizing the Civic Ideal: The Civic Portraits in Belfast Town Hall', *Urban History*, 35, 3 (2008), pp.363–81.
27. Gunn, *Public Culture*, Chapter 6.
28. Pilson, *History*; George Benn, *A History of the Town of Belfast* (London and Belfast: Marcus Ward, 1877). For the idea of Belfast as a town without a history, see S.J. Connolly and Gillian McIntosh, 'Imagining Belfast', in S.J. Connolly (ed.), *Belfast 400: An Urban History* (Liverpool, 2012).
29. David Patterson, *The Provincialisms of Belfast and the Surrounding Districts Pointed out and Corrected* (Belfast: Alex Mayne, 1860).
30. See note 18 above.
31. For Clarke, Budge and O'Leary, *Belfast*, p.65; *Report of the Commission of Enquiry into the Origin and Character of the Riots in Belfast in July and September 1857* (Parliamentary Papers, 1857–8, vol. 26), p.243; for Hughes, ibid., p.242.
32. Robert D. Storch, 'The Policeman as Domestic Missionary: Urban Discipline and Popular Culture in Northern England, 1850-1880', *Journal of Social History*, 9, 4 (1976), 481–509; Robert D. Storch, 'The Plague of the Blue Locusts: Police Reform and Popular Resistance in Northern England, 1840–57', *International Review of Social History*, 20 (1975), pp.61–90.
33. Michael Adcock, 'Remaking Urban Space: Baron Hausmann and the Rebuilding of Paris 1851–1870', *University of Melbourne Library Journal*, 2, 2 (1996), pp.25–35.
34. O'Leary, 'Belfast Urban Government', p.197.
35. BNL, 28 January 1891.
36. D.J. Owen, *History of Belfast* (Belfast: Baird, 1921), pp.399–400.
37. Gillian McIntosh, *Belfast City Hall: One Hundred Years* (Belfast: Blackstaff Press, 2006).
38. For example, John Gray, *City in Revolt: James Larkin and the Belfast Dock Strike of 1907* (Belfast: Blackstaff, 1985), pp.4–14.
39. Sybil Gribbon, *Edwardian Belfast: A Social Profile* (Belfast: Appletree Press, 1982); Budge and O'Leary, *Belfast*, pp.109–14; W.A. Maguire, *Belfast* (Keele: Keele University

Press, 1993), pp.74–8; Gillian McIntosh, 'Ireland's First Jewish Lord Mayor: Sir Otto Jaffe and Edwardian Belfast's Civic Sphere', *Jewish Culture and History*, 11, 3 (2009), 1–20.

40. Third report of Her Majesty's commissioners for Enquiring into the Housing of the Working Classes: Ireland (Parliamentary Papers, 1884–5, vol. 31), pp.58–60.
41. A. Mayne, 'Indeterminacy: The Birmingham Improvement Scheme, 1875-1914', in ibid, *The Imagined Slum: Newspaper Representations in an English Speaking World, 1800-1914* (Leicester: Leicester University Press, 1993), pp.57–97.
42. Robin Milward, 'The Political Economy of Urban Utilities', in Daunton (ed.), *Cambridge Urban History*, iii.329, 333.
43. Robert Scott, *A Breath of Fresh Air: The Story of Belfast's Parks* (Belfast: Blackstaff, 2000).
44. Don McCloy, *Creating Belfast: Technical Education and the Formation of a Great Industrial City, 1801–1921* (Dubin: Nonsuch, 2009).
45. John Burnett, *A Social History of Housing 1815–1985* (London: Methuen, 1986), p.184.
46. John Lynch, *A Tale of Three Cities: Comparative Studies in Working Class Life* (Basingstoke: Macmillan, 1998), pp.112–13.
47. *British Medical Journal*, 3 October 1896.
48. Sheard, 'Public Health', pp.220–5; Roger Blaney, *Belfast: 100 Years of Health* (Belfast, 1988), Chapter 4.
49. *Municipal Affairs*, pp.18, 387; *Belfast Health Commission. Report to the Local Government Board for Ireland* (Parliamentary Papers, 1908, vol. 31), pp.98–99.
50. James Montgomery, borough engineer, Report on River Blackstaff, 17 July 1873 (PRONI LA/7/3DF/1).
51. Obituary of Montgomery from *Minutes of Proceedings of the Institute of Civil Engineers*, 78 (1883-4), preserved in PRONI LA/7/3DF/2, no. 141; Sheard, 'Public Health', 155–8.
52. *Belfast Health Commission*, pp.13, 97–8.
53. Christopher Hamlin, 'Mumbling in Bumbledom: On the Enormity of Large Sanitary Improvements in Four British Towns, 1855–1885', *Victorian Studies*, 32 (1988), pp.60–9.
54. Report by Thomas Ross Salmond, engineer to the Belfast Harbour Commissioners, 31 October 1871 (PRONI LA/7/3DF/1, no. 86).

Chapter 3

1. The work of the practice has been documented by the author in his unpublished Ph.D. thesis 'The work of Young & Mackenzie, architectural practice and dynasty, and its significance to Ulster's built environment, c.1850-1950' (Q.U.B., 2011). An account of Robert Young's career has been published by Paul Larmour in 'Robert Young: founder of a dynasty' in *Perspective*, Vol. 4 (4), 19.
2. *Irish Builder*, Jubilee Number, 1909, p.184.
3. *Belfast News Letter*, 17 December 1847.
4. There have been many good accounts of Belfast's history; concerning its architectural appearance, chief among accounts are: Paul Larmour, *Belfast: An Illustrated Architectural Guide* (Belfast: Friar's Bush Press, 1987); C.E.B. Brett, *Buildings of Belfast, 1700–1914* (Belfast: Friar's Bush Press, 1985); Marcus Patton, *Central Belfast a Historical Gazetteer* (Belfast: Ulster Architectural Heritage Society, 1993) and Emrys Jones's chapter 'Late Victorian Belfast: 1850-1900', in J.C. Beckett and R.E. Glasscock (eds), *Belfast: The Origin and Growth of an Industrial City* (London: BBC Books, 1967). The development of the Edwardian and modern city is well documented in Frederick W. Boal and Stephen A. Royle (eds), *Enduring City: Belfast in the Twentieth Century* (Belfast: Blackstaff, 2006), in which Paul Larmour's comprehensive essay 'Bricks, stone, concrete and steel: the built fabric of twentieth-century Belfast' can be found. There are, of course, many good general accounts of Victorian architecture; one of the most comprehensive, which includes a strong selection of Belfast buildings, is James Stevens Curl's *Victorian Architecture: Diversity & Invention* (Reading: Spire Books, 2007).
5. For a description of Lanyon as county surveyor, see Brendan O'Donoghue, *The Irish County Surveyors 1834–1944: A Biographical Dictionary* (Dublin: Four Courts Press, 2007), pp.232–4; Paul Larmour provides a good overview of his career in 'Sir Charles Lanyon', *Irish Arts Review Yearbook 1989–90*, pp.200–206.
6. Robert Young, 'Recollections: a session at Glasgow College' held at the Public Records Office of Northern Ireland (PRONI D.2930/1/21). Young also wrote more extended memoirs of 1906, 'Recollections of a nonagenerian (PRONI D.2930/1/20) which were partially published by Aiken McClelland as 'Reminiscences of Robert Young', in Jim Gracey and Aiken McClelland (eds), *Irish Booklore*, Vol. 1 (2), Jan. 1971 and Aug. 1971.
7. 'Recollections of a nonagenarian' (PRONI D.2930/1/20). The panoptican design was a significant development in prison architecture, described as the 'symbol of the collapse of society and the triumph of utility' in Tristram Hunt, *Building Jerusalem: The Rise and Fall of the Victorian City* (London: Phoenix, 2004), p.101.
8. *Irish Builder*, 1 November 1859.

9. Young & Mackenzie file papers (PRONI D.2194/17/3; 41/3; 92/3) and *Belfast News Letter*, 17 March 1860.
10. The 1868 entries for architects were: James Anderson; Bell & Marsh; Boyd & Batt; James Ewart; R. & H. Fulton; W. Gray; Daniel Hanna; Wm Hastings; Anthony Thos. Jackson; Thos. Jackson; Archibald Kent; Lanyon, Lynn & Lanyon; Wm Matier; W. Milling; J.J. Montgomery; Wm Moore; A. McAlister; H. McClarnon; H. McCracken; James McNea; J. O'Neill; Sherry & Hughes; F. Stirratt; Mortimer Thompson; Thos. Turner; Wm R. Waters; J.S. Whittiston and Robert Young.
11. *Northern Whig*, 3 January 1888, also noted in C.E.B. Brett, *Buildings of Belfast*, pp.53–4.
12. Patton provides a good description of the building in: Marcus Patton, *Central Belfast*, pp.121–2.
13. *Irish Builder*, 1 September 1882.
14. Mark Girouard, *Cities and People* (New Haven and London: Yale University Press, 1985), p.265.
15. Among R.M. Young's many contributions to Belfast's cultural, artistic and antiquarian life, in 1892 he edited *The Town Book of the Corporation of Belfast (1613–1816)*, followed by *Ulster in '98* in 1893, and in 1896 he wrote *Historical Collections Relative to Old Belfast*.
16. *The Architect*, 8 March 1879 – the drawing was signed by Thomas Duff who trained and worked for the firm at the time.
17. *Irish Builder*, 15 April 1880 – William Ewart, M.P. laid the stone.
18. The cost of Belfast Academy was £10,000: *Irish Builder*, 22 April 1880.
19. *Irish Builder*, 15 July 1882.
20. Bill of quantities for shops and offices for R. J. McConnell, November 1882 (PRONI D/2194/18/6); plans (81/10); *Belfast News Letter*, 7 October 1882.
21. Specification (PRONI D/2194/25/7); *Belfast News Letter*, 8 September 1889.
22. *Belfast News Letter*, 7 October 1882.
23. Larmour, *Belfast: An Illustrated Architectural Guide*, p.48.
24. *Irish Builder*, 15 March 1888.
25. From a printed account produced for the visit of Mechanical Engineers to Belfast, 3 August 1888 included in one the firm's scrapbooks (in private ownership).
26. Marcus Patton, *Central Belfast*, p.107.
27. *Belfast News Letter*, 6 August 1894: 'Library Association of the United Kingdom. Visit to Messrs. Robinson & Cleaver's.
28. *Northern Whig*, 12 March 1888.
29. Ibid.
30. Ibid.

31. *Northern Whig*, 12 March 1888. The staircase was removed from the building during its subdivision into separate smaller shop units in the 1990s and is now in Ballyedmond, Co. Down.
32. Printed account produced for the visit of Mechanical Engineers to Belfast, 3 August 1888, in one the firm's scrapbooks (in private ownership).
33. Ibid.
34. *Belfast News Letter*, 6 August 1894.
35. *Northern Whig*, 20 June 1889.
36. Ibid.
37. A drawing of 1895 was lodged with the Corporation, which is still on the Building Control files, showing a hexagonal tower; the parapet on the Donegall Place elevation also had a Dutch style central gable, which was not followed through to the final design either.
38. Baird & Stevenson's Quarry, Glasgow, reported in the *Northern Whig*, 5 May 1899.
39. The extension was indicative of the continuing success of the company. The *Northern Whig* in remarking on the extension described it as 'strengthening its stakes' in 'these times of keen competition', the shop offering 'everything necessary for the adornment of the person or the furnishing of a mansion', 8 June 1912. Also, *Irish Builder*, 31 August 1912.
40. *Northern Whig*, 5 May 1899; *Belfast News Letter*, 16 December 1897 and 5 May 1899.
41. *Northern Whig*, 5 May 1899.
42. Ibid.
43. Asa Briggs, *Victorian Cities* (Harmondsworth: Penguin, 1968), pp.45–6.
44. *Northern Whig*, 5 May 1899.
45. *Northern Whig*, 20 December 1890: 'New Buildings in Queen Street'. This building at the time of writing (2012) is still standing, within the Linen Conservation Area of the city; however, it is under threat of demolition and replacement and has been the focus of considerable public and media attention with many concerned that another good example of industrial period architecture, encapsulating the character and grain of the city, could potentially be lost.
46. Bill of quantities (PRONI D.2194/23/10), *Northern Whig*, 20 December 1890 and *Belfast News Letter*, 22 December 1890.
47. *Belfast News Letter*, 22 December 1890.
48. Estimate and plans (PRONI D/2194/63/3).
49. Specifications (PRONI D.2194/91/5); estimate (3/1); working papers (48/7, 55/2 and 91/5); *Belfast News Letter* and *Northern Whig*, 11 July 1891.
50. Specifications (PRONI D.2194/86/7); *Belfast News Letter*, 4 June 1901.

51. Specifications and bill of quantities (PRONI D.2194/71/1), working papers (107/10); *Northern Whig*, 17 May 1902; *Irish Builder*, 1900, p.390.
52. C.E.B. Brett, *Buildings of Belfast*, p.70.
53. Patton records that Charles Lanyon, George Smith, and W.G. Gilliland had had offices on the site, while in the Scottish Provident Building itself, firms included Young & Mackenzie, Berkeley D. Wise, John Seeds, Henry Lynn and John MacGeagh, and Hobart & Heron in *Central Belfast*, p.121; the *Belfast News Letter* also recorded that John Lanyon's practice had moved into the building in August 1899, a year before John Lanyon's death – 15 February 1900.
54. *Irish Builder*, 1901, p.599.
55. For an account of this dominance, see Sean Connolly, *Religion and Society in Nineteenth-Century Ireland* (Dundalk: Economic & Social History Society of Ireland, 1985), pp.3-4.
56. The positioning of Church House so close to the railway terminus is a good example of the impact of the railways in the development of Belfast in a similar fashion to other Victorian cities in Britain; J.R. Kellett's work on this aspect of urban development is illuminating. He described the Victorian railway as 'the most important single agency in the transformation of the central area of many of Britain's major cities': J.R. Kellett, 'The railway as an agent of internal change in Victorian cities' from J.R. Kellett, *The Impact of Railways on Victorian Cities* (London: Routledge & Kegan Paul, 1969) in R.J. Morris & Richard Rodger, *The Victorian City: A Reader in British Urban History 1820–1914* (London & New York: Longman, 1993), p.184.
57. *Church Extension Bazaar* leaflet of 1905, p.21, held at the Library of the Presbyterian Historical Society.
58. D.A. Taylor, *Reproductions of the Plans of Proposed Assembly Buildings for the Presbyterian Church in Ireland, Belfast*, 1901, pp.4–5.
59. Andrew Saint, 'The cult of Wren', in David Crellin, David and Ian Dungavell (eds), *Architecture and Englishness 1880–1914* (Oxford: Society of Architectural Historians of Great Britain, 2006), p.53.
60. J.S. Curl, *Victorian Architecture: Diversity & Invention*, p.439.

Chapter 4

1. J.R.R. Adams, 'Reading Societies in Ulster', *Ulster Folklife* 26 (1980), p.63.
2. PRONI D777/1. Notebook relating to the meetings of the Belfast Reading Club 1889–1901.
3. PRONI D777/1. The information in this chapter is based on the handwritten minute book except where indicated otherwise.
4. Further information on Godfrey William Ferguson and his career can be found on the Irish Architectural Archive at http://www.dia.ie/architects/view/1877 (accessed 14/09/2010).
5. 1901 census was used to calculate age.
6. *Belfast Directory for 1887, Volume XII* (Belfast: Belfast News Letter, 1887) pp.274, 465; *The Belfast and Province of Ulster Directory for 1890, Vol. XIII* (Belfast: Belfast News Letter, 1890) p.273. The Minute Book records the attendance of R. Parker LLD on 3 February 1891. Based on the qualification that was appended to the name, the only Parker living in Belfast in 1887 and 1890 with a law degree, from Trinity College, Dublin, was Henry R. Parker, the headmaster of Methodist College.
7. Trevor Montague, *A to Z of Almost Everything. A Compendium of General Knowledge* (London: Little, Brown, 2007) p.1225. This source was used to find out the genres of the plays.
8. Catherine Morris, 'Becoming Irish? Alice Milligan and the Revival', in *Irish University Review*, Vol. 33, No. 1 (Spring–Summer, 2003) p.80; *Shan Van Vocht*, 7 February 1896. A home reading circle under this scheme was started by Mrs. B. Hobson, Antrim Road. *Shan Van Vocht*, 6 March 1896.
9. Angelique Day and Patrick McWilliams, *Ordnance Survey Memoirs of Ireland Volume 8, Parishes of Co. Antrim* (Belfast: Institute of Irish Studies, 1991) pp.131–2; National Library of Ireland Pamphlets 369 (15) *Rules of Tandragee Reading Society* (Newry, 1817).
10. *Catalogue of the Belfast Medical Library* (Belfast: Joseph Smyth, 1826) p.1. A transcript of this document is provided online by the Ulster Medical Society at http://www.ums.ac.uk/bms/cat_1826.pdf (accessed 24/5/2010).
11. Minutes record this as Miss Clark's address. The 1901 census confirms that Miss Florence Clark and her sister Miss Edith Clark lived at 13 Kinnaird Terrace. The 1901 and 1911 census were accessed at http://www.census.nationalarchives.ie (accessed 27/10/2011).
12. *The Belfast and Province of Ulster Directory for 1897* Vol. XVIII (Belfast: *Belfast News Letter*, 1897), p.122.
13. *Belfast News Letter*, 20 December 1899.

14. *Belfast News Letter*, 29 August 1890; the peerage notes relating to Sir Thomas Sinclair http://www.thepeerage.com/p36554.htm (accessed 03/10/2011).
15. *Belfast News Letter*, 19 May 1898.
16. *The Belfast and Province of Ulster Directory for 1897*, p.122 and *The Belfast and Province of Ulster Directory for 1895*, p.16. Both directories give the name of Bigger's house as 'Airdrie' rather than the Gaelic 'Ard Righ'. Information about his interests was obtained from the Ulster History Circle – http://www.ulsterhistory.co.uk/bigger.html (accessed 19/10/2011).
17. *Belfast News Letter*, 17 December 1886.
18. *Belfast News Letter*, 20 December 1899.
19. Book of Witnesses entries for St Anne's Parish Church – http://www.belfastcathedral.org/heritage/book-of-witnesses (accessed 30/09/2011).
20. Book of Witnesses entries for St Anne's Parish Church; *The Belfast and Province of Ulster Directory for 1895*. Vol. XVI (Belfast: Belfast News Letter, 1895), p.572; *The Belfast and Province of Ulster Directory for 1897*, p.736; *Belfast News Letter*, 30 July 1889, 31 July 1895.
21. Caoimhghin S. Breathnach, 'The Medical Sciences in twentieth-century Ireland', in *Irish Journal of Medical Science Vol. 169, No. 3.*, p.221; 1911 census; *The Belfast and Province of Ulster Directory for 1897*, p.646.
22. 1901 census; *The Belfast and Province of Ulster Directory for 1897*, p.735.
23. *Belfast News Letter*, 31 January 1894.
24. *Belfast News Letter*, 23 October 1897.
25. PRONI D2052/12. Minute Book Of Ballygan Book Club, May 1828.
26. Angelique Day and Patrick McWilliams, *Ordnance Survey Memoirs of Ireland Vol. 27 Parishes of Co. Londonderry* (Belfast: Institute of Irish Studies, 1994), pp.11–12.
27. PRONI D777/1, 23 November 1896.
28. Information on Thomas J. Andrews was found at Royal Society online at http://www.aim25.ac.uk/cats/18/11937.htm (accessed 19/10/2011). Dr Andrews was a member of Belfast Literary Society and read papers for this club. His manuscripts are held at the library of Queen's University, Belfast. (Andrews M.S.2) Although the name Thomas Andrews is associated with the Titanic, the Mrs Andrews of the Belfast Reading Club has been identified as the wife of the chemist, inventor and educationalist as the Thomas Andrews of Titanic fame did not marry until 1908.
29. Information about the Campbell family was obtained at http://thepeerage.com/p36278.htm (accessed 14/09/2010); 1911 census.
30. *Belfast News Letter*, 29 July 1898.

31. PRONI will calendar for Sir Charles Lanyon; http://applications.proni.gov.uk/DCAL_ PRONI-willscalendar/willssearch.asp (accessed 30/09/2011).
32. *The Belfast and Province of Ulster Directory for 1895.* p.572 and *The Belfast and Province of Ulster Directory for 1897* p.736. Also http://www.igp-web.com/IGPArchives/ire/down/photos/tombstones/1headstones/knockbreda-parish-cem.txt (accessed 21/09/2010). No Lanyons are included in the 1901 or the 1911 census.
33. *Belfast News Letter*, 1 November 1890.
34. *The Belfast and Province of Ulster Directory for 1895*, p.512 provided information about Godfrey Ferguson. Robert Graeme-Watt's occupation taken from 1901 census.
35. A brief, unreferenced, biography of Thomas Sinclair is included in Linder, Seth *The Famous Faces of North Belfast* (Octagon Design, not dated), p.10; *Belfast News Letter*, 26 June 1899, 6 March 1900, 17 April 1900.
36. *The Belfast and Province of Ulster Directory for 1897*, pp.121–2.
37. Ibid., pp.274–5.
38. *The Belfast and Province of Ulster Directory for 1895.* p.lxxxvii.
39. 1901 census.
40. *Belfast and the Province of Ulster Directory for 1900 Volume XXI* (Belfast; *Belfast News Letter*, 1900) p.1079.
41. 1911 census.
42. PRONI will calendar for Miss Macpherson; see Note 31 (accessed 30/09/2011).
43. *Belfast News Letter*, 27 June 1887.
44. The census of 1901 details four female servants; a children's maid, housemaid, parlour maid and cook and in 1911 they had three servants as a children's maid was no longer required.
45. Fraulein Berger attended meetings on 9 April 1895, 6 January 1896 and 13 April 1896. Fraulein Helmkampf attended the meeting on 29 November 1894.
46. Gillian McClelland and Diana Hadden, *Pioneering Women: Riddell Hall and Queen's University Belfast* (Belfast: Ulster Historical Foundation, 2005), p.38.
47. Minutes dated 26 October 1891 and November 1896.
48. *The Belfast and Province of Ulster Directory for 1895*, p.505.
49. *Belfast News Letter*, 1 February 1869.
50. *The Belfast Literary Society 1801–1901* (Belfast: McCaw, Stevenson & Orr, 1902), p.163.
51. *The Belfast Directory for 1887* (Belfast: Belfast News Letter, 1887), p.77.
52. Northern Ireland Senate, 1921–72 – http://www.ark.ac.uk/elections/hnisen.htm (accessed 22/09/2010); PRONI will calendar for Adam Duffin – see Note 31 proni.gov.uk (accessed 30/09/2011).
53. *Belfast News Letter*, 17 February 1893; John Anderson, *History of the Belfast Library*

and Society for Promoting Knowledge (Belfast, 1888), pp.94, 96; McClelland and Hadden *Pioneering Women,* p.38; Seamus Deane, Andrew Carpenter and Jonathan Williams (eds), *The Field Day Anthology of Irish Writing: Irish Women's Writing and Traditions* (New York: New York University Press, 2002), p.372.

54. *Belfast News Letter*, 3 October 1889.
55. *Belfast News Letter*, 18 May 1899.
56. *Belfast News Letter*, 9 January 1899.
57. James Winder Good, 'Two Irish Patriots' in *Studies: An Irish Quarterly Review,* Vol. 10, No. 38 (June, 1921) p.240; Details of the manuscript document and the auction were found online at http://www.icollector.com/Drennan-Letters-1775-1793-A-transcription-by-Maria-Ruth-and-Dorothy-Duffin-Unpublished_i10466965 (accessed 28/07/2011).
58. Information about Maria Duffin obtained from Belfast City Council [http://belfastcity.gov.uk/burialrecords/search.asp] (accessed 14/05/2011); R.W.M. Strain, *Belfast and its Charitable Society: A Story of Urban Social Development* (London: Oxford University Press, 1961), p.122.
59. 1911 census stated that they were married 34 years and they had nine children born and still living.
60. McClelland and Hadden, *Pioneering Women*, pp.37–38. Chapter 5 is called 'Miss Ruth Duffin' and relates her educational experiences and her work at Riddell Hall.
61. McClelland and Hadden, *Pioneering Women*, p.39; Ruth Duffin, *Escape* (London: Dent, 1929); Ruth and Celia Duffin, *The Secret Hill* (Dublin: Maunsel, 1913). Copies of *Escape* and *The Secret Hill* can be found at POETRY 81.2/DUFF in the Linen Hall Library.
62. Dunowen, Cliftonville, Belfast, Antrim, Northern Ireland', *Mapping the Practice and Profession of Sculpture in Britain and Ireland 1851–1951*, University of Glasgow History of Art and HATII, online database 2011 [http://sculpture.gla.ac.uk/view/place.php?id=msib3_1257767369 (accessed 25/06/2011).
63. 1901 and 1911 census information. He was listed as a stockbroker in his brother's will, see footnote 67.
64. 1911 census; PRONI will calendar for Charles Terence Duffin; see Note 31 (accessed 30/09/2011).
65. Emma S. Duffin, *The Magic Glasses* (Belfast: Quota, 1935). A copy of this book is available at the Linen Hall Library at POETRY 53.1/DUFF.
66. Deane *et al* (eds), *The Field Day Anthology of Irish Writing: Irish Women's Writing and Traditions*, pp.365–7.
67. The Duffin family correspondence and diaries can be found at PRONI D2109.
68. *Belfast News Letter*, 3 October 1890.

69. Helen Duffin, *Over Here* (London: Methuen, 1918). A copy can be found at the Linen Hall Library FICTION 83.1/DUFF.
70. 1901 census.
71. Occupations derived from 1901 and 1911 census and *The Belfast and Province of Ulster Directories* from 1895 and 1897.

Chapter 5

1. C. Withers, 'Towards a history of Geography in the public sphere', *History of Science*, 37, 1999, pp.45–78; C. Withers and D. Finnegan, 'Natural History Societies, fieldwork and local knowledge in nineteenth-century Scotland: towards a historical geography of civic knowledge', *Cultural Geographies*, 10, 2003, pp.334–353: P. Elliot; 'The birth of public science in the English provinces; natural philosophy in Derby, c.1690–1760', *Annals of Science*, 57, 2000, pp.61–100; S. Naylor, 'The field, the museum and the lecture hall: the spaces of natural history in Victorian Cornwall', Paper from the annual conference of the Society for the History of Natural History, May 2002.
2. Arnold Thackray, 'Natural Knowledge in the Cultural Context: The Manchester Model', *American Historical Review*, 1974, 79, pp.672–709.
3. Sam Alberti, 'Amateurs and Professionals in One County: Biology and Natural History in Late Victorian Yorkshire', *Journal of the History of Natural History* 34, 2001, pp.115–147.
4. Simon Naylor, 'Introduction; historical geographies of science - places, contexts, cartographies', *British Journal for the History of Science*, 38, March 2005, pp.1–12.
5. A. Deane, The Belfast Natural History and Philosophical Society Centenary Volume, 1821–1921, p.89.
6. See, for example, E. Estyn Evans, *The Personality of Ireland* (Cambridge: Cambridge University Press, 2005); Robert Lloyd Praeger, *The Way that I Went* (Dublin: Collins, 1998) and *Populous Solitude* (Dublin: Hodges, Figgis & Co, 1941) especially Chapters 6 and 7.
7. John Wilson Foster (ed.), *Nature in Ireland: a Scientific and Cultural History* (Dublin: The Lilliput Press, 1997).
8. David N. Livingstone, *Putting Science in its Place: Geographies of Knowledge* (Chicago: Chicago University Press, 2002), pp.87–88.
9. Helena C.G. Chesney, 'Enlightenment and Education', in Foster (ed.), *Nature in Ireland*, pp.367–408.
10. Lynn Merrill, *The Romance of Victorian Natural History* (Oxford: Oxford University Press, 1989), p.ix.

11. Sir Henry George Lyons, *The Royal Society 1660–1940, a history of its administration under its charter* (Cambridge: Cambridge University Press, 1944); M. Stimson, *Scientists and Amateurs: A History of the Royal Society* (New York: Greenwood Press, 1948); Margery Purver, *The Royal Society: Concept and Creation* (Massachusetts: Routledge & Kegan Paul, 1967); Marie Boas Hall, *All Scientists Now: The Royal Society in the Nineteenth Century* (Cambridge: Cambridge University Press, 1984); Michael Hunter, *The Royal Society and its Fellows* (London: British Society for the History of Science, 1982); Morris Berman, *Social Change and Scientific Organisation: The Royal Institution, 1799–1844* (London: Heinemann, 1978).
12. Ralph S. Bates, *Scientific Societies in the United States*, 3rd edition (London: M.I.T. Press 1965); James McClellan III, *Science Reorganised: Scientific Societies in the Eighteenth Century* (New York: Johns Hopkins University Press, 2006); Roy Porter and Mikulas Teich (eds), *The Scientific Revolution in National Context* (Cambridge: Cambridge University Press, 1992); Lewis Pyenson and Susan Sheets-Pyenson, *Servants of Nature: A History of Scientific Institutions, Enterprises and Sensibilities* (London: HarperCollins, 1999).
13. Robert Schofield, 'Histories of Scientific Societies: Needs and Opportunities for Research', *History of Science*, 2 (1963), pp.70–83. See, for example, Samuel Alberti, 'Field, Lab and Museum: The Practice and Place of Life Science in Yorkshire' (unpublished Ph.D. thesis, Sheffield and Leeds, 2000); Simon Naylor, 'The field, the museum and the lecture hall: the spaces of natural history in Victorian Cornwall', Paper given at the annual conference of the Society for the History of Natural History (2002); Ian Inkster and Jack Morrell (eds), *Metropolis and Province; Science in British Culture 1780–1850* (London: HarperCollins, 1983).
14. Steven Shapin and Arnold Thackray, 'Prosopography as a Research Tool in the History of Science: The British Scientific Community', in *History of Science*, 12 (1974), pp.8–9; Michael Neve, 'Science in a Commercial City: Bristol 1820-1860', in Inkster and Morrell (eds), *Metropolis and Province*, pp.179–204.
15. Ian Inkster, 'Science and the Mechanics' Institutes, 1820–1850: the Case of Sheffield', in *Annals of Science*, 32 (1983), pp.451–474.
16. David E. Allen, 'The natural history society in Britain throughout the years', *Archives of Natural History*, 14, 3 (1987), pp.242–259; Philip Lowe, *Locals and Provincials: A Model for the Social Organisation Provincial Science in the Nineteenth Century* (M Phil, Sussex, 1978).
17. W.A. Maguire, *Belfast: Site and City* (Keele: Ulster Museum, 1991), pp.59–61.
18. Bayles, 'Science in its local context', pp.79–112.
19. Edmund Getty, 'Introduction, a Popular Guide to the Royal Botanic Garden of Belfast', p.vii.

20. Eileen McCracken, The Palm House and Botanical Garden, p.20.
21. Royal Belfast Botanical Garden Minute Book, 27 March 1864.
22. *Belfast News Letter*, 22 May 1842.
23. Edmund Getty, 'A Popular Guide to the Royal Botanic Garden of Belfast', p.19.
24. L. Proudfoot, 'Cultures, power and the manufacture of place in Ireland', in Dominique Vanneste (ed.), *Space and place: mirrors of social and cultural identity?: Studies in historical geography*, Series, Acta geographia lovaniensia, (Leeuven: Geografisch Instituut, Katholieke Universiteit Leuven, 1996), pp.53–63.'
25. Helena Chesney, 'Enlightenment and Education' in John Wilson Foster, *Nature in Ireland*, pp.367–386.
26. BNHS Council Minutes 5 June 1831, 15 November 1831, 16 May 1832, 3 September 1832.
27. A Deane, The Belfast Natural History and Philosophical Society Centenary Volume, 1821–1921, (Belfast: The Society, 1924), pp.4–12.
28. BNHS Public Night 6 January 1840, reported in the *Belfast Chronicle*, 12 January 1840.
29. Unidentified newspaper clipping form The Belfast Natural History Scrapbook, p.41.
30. BNHS Council Minutes, 7 January 1834.
31. A. Deane, *The Belfast Natural History and Philosophical Society Centenary Volume, 1821–1921* (Belfast, 1824), p.16.
32. Ibid., title page.
33. A. Deane, Belfast Natural History and Philosophical Society Centenary Volume, 1821–1921, p.71.
34. Ibid., p.2.
35. BNHS List of Rules 1821, (PRONI D/3263/C/8).
36. Kate Newmann, *Dictionary of Ulster Biography* (Belfast: The Institute of Irish Studies, 1993), p.69.
37. Ibid., p.5.
38. William Hutton was elected a corresponding member of the society in 1826. He exchanged geological specimens (minerals), shells and insects from 1826 to at least 1829. Professor B. Silliman, University of Yale, communicated and exchanged specimens from 1826.
39. Letters from William Hutton, Newcastle-upon-Tyne to James McAdam, Secretary of BNHS, 29 March 1826, 27 September 1828, 14 October 1829 (Public Records Office of Northern Ireland, PRONI D/3263/BB/1/13).
40. Ibid., pp.95–6.
41. Newmann, *Dictionary of Ulster Biography*, p.216.
42. Ibid., p.110.
43. Bayles, 'Science in its local context', p.174.

Chapter 7

1. *The Guardian*, http://www.guardian.co.uk/travel/2006/nov/15/travelnews.belfast.uk (accessed 21/07/2011).
2. Anon, *Belfast and its Environs; or The Stranger's Guide* (Belfast: John Henderson Booksellers, 1855) p.21.
3. Adam and Charles Black, *Black's Guide to Belfast, the Giant's Causeway, and the North of Ireland, etc.* (Edinburgh: Adam and Charles Black Publishers, 1854), p.300.
4. Glenn Hooper, *The Tourist's Gaze: Travellers to Ireland 1800–2000* (Cork: Cork University Press, 2001), p.xviii.
5. William Williams, *Creating Irish Tourism: The First Century 1750–1850* (London: Anthem Press, 2010), p.xi.
6. Richard Colt Hoare, *Journal of a Tour in Ireland ad 1806* (London: W. Miller, 1807).
7. 'Travelling in Ireland', *Metropolitan Magazine*, 41:162 (October 1844), p.221.
8. Thomas Richards, *The Imperial Archive* (London: Verson, 1993), p.3.
9. *Guide to Killarney and Glengarrif* (Dublin: William Curry, 1835), p.136.
10. Henry Inglis *Ireland in 1834: A Journey throughout Ireland in the Spring, Summer and Autumn of 1834* (London, 1835) p.50.
11. Melissa Fegan, '"Isn't it Your Own Country?": The Stranger in Nineteenth-Century Irish Literature' *The Yearbook of English Studies*, 34 (2004) 31–45, p.33.
12. Frederick Temple Hamilton Temple, Marquis of Dufferin and Ava and George Boyle, *Narrative of a Journey from Oxford to Skibbereen during the Irish Famine* (Oxford: J.H. Parker, 1847), p.5.
13. Queen Victoria, *Leaves from the Journal of our Life in the Highlands from 1849 to 1861* (London: Smith, Elder and Co. 1860), p.244.
14. Queen Victoria, *Leaves from the Journal of our Life in the Highlands from 1849 to 1861*, p.245.
15. Ibid., p.246.
16. John Hervey Ashworth, *The Saxon in Ireland, Rambles of an Englishman in Search of a Settlement in the West of Ireland* (London: John Murray, 1851), p.v.
17. Harriet Martineau, *Letters from Ireland* (London: John Chapman, 1852), p.5.
18. Black, *Black's Guide to Belfast*, p.306.
19. Horace Greely, Letter to *Freeman's Journal* (Dublin, 1851).
20. William McComb, *McComb's Guide to Belfast, The Giant's Causeway and the Adjoining Districts* (Belfast: William McComb, 1861), p.vi.
21. *Belfast News Letter*, Wednesday, April 7, 1852; Issue 11713.
22. *Belfast and its Environs*, p.4.
23. John Murray, *Handbook for Travellers in Ireland* (London: John Murray, 1864), p.23.

24. McComb, *McComb's Guide to Belfast,* p.v.
25. Ibid., p.v.
26. Revd Richard Harcourt, *Rambles through the British Isles* (New York: Carlton and Lanahan, 1870), p.51.
27. Murray, *Handbook for Travellers*, p.47.
28. *Belfast and its Environs*, p.19.
29. *Belfast and its Environs*, p.19.
30. William Makepeace Thackeray, *The Irish Sketch Book* (1843) (Belfast: Blackstaff Press, 1985), p.136.
31. Washington, *Echoes of Europe*, p.225.
32. Thackeray, *The Irish Sketch Book*, p.280.
33. Murray, *Handbook for Travellers*, p.54.
34. Harcourt, *Rambles through the British Isles*, p.52.
35. Murray, *Handbook for Travellers*, p.56.
36. *Belfast and its Environs*, p.55
37. Murray, *Handbook for Travellers*, p.63.
38. Washington, *Echoes of Europe*, p.224.
39. Murray, *Handbook for Travellers*, p.57.
40. David Spurr, *The Rhetoric of Empire: Colonial Discourse in Journalism, Travel Writing and Imperial Administration* (London: Duke University Press, 1993), p.17
41. Murray, *Handbook for Travellers*, p.50.
42. McComb, *McComb's Guide to Belfast*, p.2.
43. Ibid., p.v.
44. Ibid., p.1.
45. Murray, *Handbook for Travellers*, p.49.
46. William Pembroke Fetridge, *The American Travellers' Handbook for Travellers in Europe and the East vol 18* (New York: Fetridge and Co., 1879), p.56.
47. Thackeray, *The Irish Sketch Book*, p.282.
48. McComb, *McComb's Guide to Belfast*, p.5.
49. E.K. Washington, *Echoes of Europe: or, Word Pictures of Travel* (Philadelphia: James Challen and Sons, 1860), p.264.
50. Thackeray, *The Irish Sketch Book*, p.281.
51. Ibid., p.283.
52. Hooper, *Travel in Ireland*, p.3.
53. Thackeray, *The Irish Sketch Book*, p.136.

Chapter 8

1. This essay grew out of research for *Reconstructions of the Gothic Past*, a multi-strand thematic research project carried out in the Department of History of Art and Architecture, Trinity College Dublin from 2008–2011. The project examined Gothic buildings in Ireland not just as monuments of one particular period, but as historical 'documents'. It was funded by the Irish Research Council for the Humanities and Social Sciences (IRCHSS). A key deliverable of the project is the website Gothic Past: A Visual Archive of Gothic Architecture and Sculpture in Ireland – www.gothicpast.com. Particular thanks go to my colleagues Roger Stalley, Rachel Moss, Niamh NicGhabhann, Danielle O'Donovan, Éimear O'Connor and Katy Milligan as well as Fr. Michael Murtagh (C.Ss.R), Fr. Brendan G. McConvery (C. Ss. R.) and Fr. Thomas McGlynn for assistance and support while researching and writing about the Church of the Most Holy Redeemer, Clonard.
2. 'Men's Mission'. Pearse Hutchinson, *Collected Poems* (Oldcastle, Co. Meath: Gallery Books, 2002). pp.52–3. Reproduced by kind permission of the author and The Gallery Press.
3. The author's doctoral thesis, 'Building Catholic Ireland', examines the relationship between money and ecclesiastical building activity and the impact of church-building projects on the Irish art industry sector between 1850 and 1932.
4. Emmet Larkin, 'The Devotional Revolution in Ireland', *The American Historical Review*, vol. 77, no. 3 (1972), pp.625–52. For a recent discussion about this topic in the context of Belfast, see S.J. Connolly, 'Cardinal Cullen's other capital: Belfast and the "devotional revolution"', in Dáire Keogh and Albert McDonnell (eds), *Cardinal Paul Cullen and his World*, (Dublin: Four Courts Press, 2011) pp.289–307.
5. Following the 1850 Synod of Thurles, Cullen left no stone unturned in encouraging religious orders to establish communities in Ireland, although the first official parish mission in Ireland was actually given at Athy, Co. Kildare in 1842 by the Irish Vincentian fathers. Emmet Larkin, 'Paul Cullen: the great ultramontane', in Dáire Keogh and Albert McDonnell (eds), *Cardinal Paul Cullen and his World*, (Dublin: Four Courts Press, 2011) pp.15–33.
6. The Passionist order's first 'mission' in Ireland was in 1849; they were officially founded in 1856 at Mount Argus in Dublin. By 1869 they had established a house in the Ardoyne area of Belfast. They erected a temporary church there to a design by John O'Neill, brother of the community's superior, Reverend Alphonsus O'Neill. In 1900, a permanent building, the Church of the Holy Cross, was constructed to plans commissioned from Dublin-based architect, Walter G. Doolin. J.J. Tracey, 'A dissertation on the buildings of John O'Neill and O'Neill and Byrne, architects, 1862–

1883', unpublished thesis presented as part of Master of Architecture degree course, Queen's University, Belfast, 1987, p.208, (ill.) p.30 (copy in the Irish Architectural Archive (IAA), Dublin); Gearoid Crookes, 'The Career and Architectural Works of Walter G. Doolin (1850–1902)', unpublished M.A. thesis, University College Dublin, 1987; pp.79–98, Fig. 6:6-15,8:6ab (copy in IAA).

7. The history of the Belfast Redemptorist community is covered in James Grant, *One Hundred Years with the Clonard Redemptorists* (Blackrock, Co. Dublin: Columba Press, 2003). Appendix 5 (pp.260–269) is devoted to the history of the fabric of the church. Grant's research builds on earlier work by the congregation's archivist Revd Patrick O'Donnell (C.Ss.R), [*Clonard Church and Monastery* (Belfast: n.d.)] The text also includes a number of archive photographs of the area, some of which are reproduced in this essay courtesy of the Redemptorist Community, Clonard Monastery. Publications on the congregation's history in Ireland include: Joseph Prost, Emmet Larkin, and Herman Freudenberger, *A Redemptorist Missionary in Ireland, 1851–1854: Memoirs by Joseph Prost* (Cork: Cork University Press, 1998). John Sharp, *Reapers of the Harvest: The Redemptorists in Great Britain and Ireland, 1843–1898* (Dublin: Veritas, 1989). The congregation's Irish provincial archivist has also published on Redemptorist history: Brendan McConvery, 'Hell-Fire & Poitín Redemptorist Missions in the Irish Free State (1922–1936)', *History Ireland*, vol. 8, no. 3, The Catholic Church through the Ages (Autumn 2000), pp.18–22. Clonard Church is temporarily closed for refurbishment. 'Temporary church to host Novena in Clonard', Marie Louise McCrory, *Irish News*, 16 June 2011; Clonard's own 'Men's Mission' was organized by the Redemptorists in 1981 to replace the men's confraternity annual retreat, which had experienced declining numbers in the preceding years. Grant, *One Hundred Years with the Clonard Redemptorists*, p.141. The Church of the Most Holy Redeemer is known locally as Clonard Church and will be referred to forthwith in this chapter as such.

8. John Joseph McDonnell (1857–1924), trained as an architect in the offices of Timothy Hevey (1846–1878). Their careers are discussed in part three of this chapter.

9. David Hempton, *Religion and Identity: Religious and Political Cultures in Britain and Ireland since 1700* (Cambridge: Cambridge University Press, 1996), pp.72–92. Hempton explores the circumstances that saw Catholicism become an integral component of Irish national identity by the late nineteenth century.

10. Diarmaid Ferriter, *The Transformation of Ireland, 1900–2000* (London: Profile Books, 2004), pp.85, 369.

11. Francis McHenry (O.S.B.), *Architecture and the Liturgy*, Published for the Catholic Truth Society of Ireland. (Wexford: John English & Co., 1967), p.5. Francis McHenry

(O.S.B.), *Architecture and the Liturgy*, Published for the Catholic Truth Society of Ireland. (Wexford: John English & Co., 1967), p.5.

12. Richard Hurley and Wilfrid Cantwell, *Contemporary Irish Church Architecture* (Dublin: Gill and Macmillan, 1985), p.22.
13. Emmet Larkin, 'Economic Growth, Capital Investment and the Roman Catholic Church in Nineteenth-Century Ireland', *American Historical Review*, vol LXXII (1967), p.852.
14. A. C. Hepburn, *A Past Apart: Studies in the History of Catholic Belfast, 1850–1950* (Belfast: Ulster Historical Foundation, 1996), pp.68–82, 113–136. Marianne Elliott, *The Catholics of Ulster: A History* (London: Allen Lane, 2000).
15. A list of new churches constructed in the 1870s is given in Ambrose Macaulay, *Patrick Dorrian, Bishop of Down and Connor, 1865–85* (Dublin: Irish Academic Press, 1987), pp.122–23. Those built during the office of Dorrian's successor, Patrick McAlister are discussed in Macaulay's biographical study: *Patrick McAlister: Bishop of Down and Connor, 1886–95* (Dublin: Four Courts Press, 2006), pp.145–157.
16. Grant, *One Hundred Years with the Clonard Redemptorists*. Illustrations to the text include an image showing the large crowds who attended the Silver Jubilee celebrations of Our Lady's Confraternity in 1922. Another shows crowds pouring down Clonard Gardens in the 1940s to attend the weekly Thursday night novenas, known as 'Clonard Thursday'.
17. Cunningham, 'Church Reorganization'; Emmet Larkin, 'The Devotional Revolution in Ireland', *The American Historical Review*, vol. 77, no. 3 (1972), pp.625–52; Donnchadh Ó Corráin and Tomas O'Riordan, *Ireland, 1815–70: Emancipation, Famine and Religion* (Dublin: Four Courts, 2010). Cullen's influence on Irish society has recently been examined in a collection of essays edited by Dáire Keogh and Albert McDonnell, *Cardinal Paul Cullen and His World* (Dublin: Four Courts Press, 2011).
18. Sharp, *Reapers of the Harvest: The Redemptorists in Great Britain and Ireland, 1843–1898*, p.124.
19. The Redemptorist Church of St Alphonsus in Limerick was built in 1858 to plans drawn up by P.C. Hardwick. George Coppinger Ashlin, Goldie and Child and others carried out subsequent work on the building. Further information on the careers of these architects is available via the Dictionary of Irish Architects (DIA). This online resource is available through the website of the Irish Architectural Archive: http://www.dia.ie. The site contains information about architects, builders, and craftsmen who were active in Ireland between 1720 and 1940. A full description of the Church of St Alphonsus may be accessed here: http://www.buildingsofireland.ie/niah/search.jsp?type=record&county=LI&regno=21521011 (accessed 08/11/2011).

20. The Church of St Joseph, St Alphonsus Road, Dundalk was built by James McAdorey of Dundalk at a cost of £11,351. Christine Casey & Alistair Rowan, The Buildings of Ireland: North Leinster (1993), pp.265–6, Pl. 135.
21. By 1880, it is estimated that some two thousand 'mission' retreats had taken place in Ireland; they were given by the following orders: Augustinians, Capuchins, Carmelites (calced and discalced), Dominicans, Franciscans, Jesuits, Oblates, Passionists, Redemptorists, Rosminians and Vincentians. Larkin, *Paul Cullen: The Great Ultramontane*, pp.15–33.
22. The first appearances of confraternities in nineteenth-century Belfast are mentioned in the 1845 *relatio status* of Cornelius Denvir, Bishop of Down and Connor. Connolly, 'Cardinal Cullen's other capital', p.299.
23. The first listing for Clonard Street in the Belfast Corporation Minute books is 1 October 1855. Stephen Royle et al., *Irish Historic Towns Atlas. No. 17, Belfast Part I, 1840–1900* (Dublin: Royal Irish Academy in association with Belfast City Council, 2007).
24. Clonard House was a Regency-style villa previously occupied by the Kennedy family, also prominent flax mill owners. When McConnells bought the site they retained Clonard House while developing the terraces of houses on Clonard Street and Gardens, Cupar, Odessa and O'Neill Streets. After the Redemptorists no longer needed Clonard House to accommodate their community they derived a rental income from it. The house was demolished to make way for modern housing in recent years. The history of the foundation of Clonard is dealt with in chapter two of Grant, *One Hundred Years with the Clonard Redemptorists*, pp.35-48.
25. McDonnell's career is discussed later in the chapter. A full list of his works is available on the DIA database.
26. In the case of Clonard the debate concerned the relative merits of two revived medieval styles. The original description alludes to British and French debates on the relative merits of Classical versus Gothic Revival architecture. See, for example, Bernard Porter, *Battle of the Styles: Society, Culture and the Design of the New Foreign Office, 1855–1861* (London: Continuum International Publishing Group, 2011). Remarks on the Redemptorists style preference for the new church, cited by Grant (p.59), were first recorded in the congregation's domestic records and quoted by the congregation's archivist Revd Patrick O'Donnell (C.Ss.R), in a booklet entitled *Clonard Church and Monastery* (Belfast: n.d.).
27. Kevin Whelan, 'The Catholic Parish, the Catholic Chapel and Village Development in Ireland', *Irish Geography* vol. 16, no. 1 (1983), pp.

28. James F. White, *The Cambridge Movement: The Ecclesiologists and the Gothic Revival* (Cambridge: Cambridge University Press, 1962).
29. Jeanne Sheehy and Ulster Architectural Heritage Society, *J.J. McCarthy and the Gothic Revival in Ireland* (Belfast: Ulster Architectural Heritage Society, 1977), p.7.
30. W.J. Smythe, *A Notice of St. Patrick's Church, Jordanstown* (Printed for private distribution, 1868). Cited in J. Sheehy, *The Rediscovery of Ireland's Past: The Celtic Revival, 1830–1930* (London: Thames and Hudson, 1980), pp.66–69.
31. Rosemary Hill, *God's Architect: Pugin and the Building of Romantic Britain* (London: Penguin, 2008).
32. A.W.N. Pugin, *Contrasts or a parallel between the noble edifices of the fourteenth and fifteenth centuries, and similar buildings of the present day: shewing the present decay of taste; Accompanied by appropriate Text,* (Salisbury, 1836); A.W.N. Pugin, *The True Principles of Pointed or Christian Architecture: set forth in two lectures delivered at St. Marie's Oscott* (London, 1841). In the same year as *Principles* was published, Pugin wrote the first of two articles for the *Dublin Review*, a Catholic intellectual journal edited, nominally at least, by Bishop Nicholas Wiseman. This piece and a second published in 1842 were combined into an 1850 publication entitled *The Present State of Ecclesiastical Architecture in England and some remarks relative to ecclesiastical architecture and decoration.* A 2004 edition of the text includes an introduction by Roderick O'Donnell giving the context for the initial articles.
33. J.J. McCarthy, *Suggestions on the Arrangement and Characteristics of Parish Churches* (Dublin: Irish Ecclesiological Society, 1851). McCarthy became known as the 'Irish Pugin' (a moniker he may have self-fashioned) and his *Suggestions* adopts a similar approach to Irish church design to that of Pugin's text *The Present State of Ecclesiastical Architecture in England.*
34. Ibid., pp.41–42.
35. McDonnell was probably right: one of the reasons given for the bankruptcy of the McNaughton brothers who built Clonard Church was that the Mountcharles limestone blocks were difficult to cut. Additionally they had to be transported from the quarry in Donegal. Using brick as an alternative (which McDonnell did for the monastery) would therefore have been wiser as it could have been provided from any one of the brick manufacturers close to Belfast. Grant, *One Hundred Years with the Clonard Redemptorists*, p.42.
36. Entries for Edward Welby Pugin and George Ashlin may be accessed on the DIA database. There is more detailed information on the partnership in the unpublished M.Litt thesis: Mildred Butler, *The Early Career of George Coppinger Ashlin (1859–1869): Gothic Revival architect* (Trinity College Dublin, 2001).

37. Paul Larmour, 'An Edwardian Stylist', *Perspective,* 4 (Jan/Feb 1996), pp.59-61. Hevey put his draughtmanship skills to good use by supplying the *Irish Builder* with significant numbers of illustrations. The full list may be viewed in his DIA entry.
38. Ross was one of three Catholics elected under the pre-1896 franchise and ward system. Another was John Hamill, whose daughters later made donations to Clonard Church. Hepburn, *A Past Apart: Studies in the History of Catholic Belfast, 1850–1950,* p.9.
39. A. C. Hepburn, *Catholic Belfast and Nationalist Ireland in the Era of Joe Devlin, 1871–1934* (Oxford: Oxford University Press, 2008), p.12.
40. Kennedy Fitzgerald Associates, 1995. Paul Larmour and Ulster Architectural Heritage Society, *The Architectural Heritage of Malone & Stranmillis* (Belfast: Ulster Architectural Heritage Society, 1991); Simon Walker, *Historic Ulster Churches* (Belfast: Institute of Irish Studies, Queen's University, 2000), p.174
41. Paul Larmour, *Belfast: An Illustrated Architectural Guide* (Belfast: Friar's Bush Press, 1987), p.91. St Paul's church was dedicated in 1888.
42. Grant, *One Hundred Years with the Clonard Redemptorists*, p.59. Grant's text is based mainly on material in the Domestic Archives at Clonard. Each house was required to keep a chronicle of daily life – the Clonard Domestic Chronicle. As noted by Grant, the reliability of this source is somewhat variable due to changes in personnel who recorded the entries.
43. St Anthony's Church, Willowfield drawings collection, Diocese of Down and Connor, Diocesan Archive, Belfast. The present-day Church of St Anthony, Woodstock Road was designed by Padraig Gregory in 1936 – his plans and other unexecuted designs form part of the collection housed in the Diocesan Archive. Gregory's biographical details may be found in the DIA database.
44. Larmour, *Belfast: An Illustrated Architectural Guide*, p.65. These sketch plans have not been located in the archives at Clonard or elsewhere.
45. A report on the inaugural meeting of Bishop Henry's Belfast Catholic Association notes 'Rev. H. Laverty Adm. read the minutes … Mr. J.J. McDonnell, J.P. then read the report of the Executive Committee' *The Nation*, 31 October 1896, p.6. McDonnell was a Justice of the Peace from 1893 and a member of the Corporation from 1899. R.M. Young, *Belfast and the Province of Ulster in the 20th Century*, edited by W.T. Pike (Brighton: W.T. Pike, 1909), p.600. In 1906, another McDonnell, a publican named James, is mentioned as being a member of the Catholic Association, a Councillor and also a supporter of Joe Devlin. See Hepburn, *Catholic Belfast and Nationalist Ireland in the Era of Joe Devlin, 1871-1934*, p.69.
46. Laverty was Henry's 'right-hand man … the most irascible of the CA leaders…' and was rewarded for his loyalty to the Bishop by being made President of St Malachy's

College and appointed to St Matthew's. Hepburn, *Catholic Belfast and Nationalist Ireland in the Era of Joe Devlin, 1871–1934*, pp.53, 68. A Catholic church for Willowfield was proposed at this time as the Woodstock Road area was home to large population of Catholics since 1884. Royle et al., *Irish Historic Towns Atlas. No. 17, Belfast Part II, 1840–1900*, pp.86–7 lists new streets in the area. McDonnell drew up a number of different plans for Willowfield church both Romanesque and Gothic Revival. A protracted building campaign, due to World War I and Irish partition, ensued and the church (St. Anthony's) was finally built in 1936 to Gregory's designs.

47. Larmour, *Belfast: An Illustrated Architectural Guide*, p.64.
48. McCarthy also designed the Infirmary building at Maynooth. Three sides of the College quadrangle were built to Pugin's plans in 1846-47. Hill, *God's Architect*, p.399.
49. The churches in question include St Patrick's (Roman Catholic), Monkstown, Co. Dublin and St Joseph's Glasthule, Co. Dublin.
50. Grant, *One Hundred Years with the Clonard Redemptorists*, pp.59–60.
51. The Public Records Office of Northern Ireland holds the plan for the executed design of Clonard Church (PRONI D.2403/A/1/10/14) as well as the earlier alternative design proposed by McDonnell and altered by Bishop Henry. (PRONI D.2403/A/1/10/12). PRONI, Belfast: D/2403/ Records of J.J. Brennan, architect, Belfast, and his predecessors in the firm, J.J. McDonnell and Hugh Lamont.
52. Grant, *One Hundred Years with the Clonard Redemptorists*, p.38 The site cost £2,360 with a further £100 per annum due in head rent to the Kennedy family. Rent of £50 per annum was payable on Clonard House to Bishop Henry.
53. Ibid., p.39.
54. Grant, *One Hundred Years with the Clonard Redemptorists*, pp.63–64. The principal reason for the excessive cost was that the builders who were successful in winning the tender, McNaughton brothers of Randalstown, went out of business. McDonnell subsequently had to manage the project using the more expensive option of sub-contractors. The reasons for the failure of McNaughton's company was undoubtedly complex, however the difficulties mentioned previously with regard to handling of building materials must have been a contributory factor. The final cost of building Clonard Church was £32,000.
55. Grant, *One Hundred Years with the Clonard Redemptorists*, pp.59, 71–72, 73, 120.
56. A list of the St Peter's administrators may be accessed at http://www.stpeterscathedralbelfast.com/tour-the-cathedral/history (accessed 08/11/2011).
57. St Peter's is one of the city churches that prompted Brewer et al. to describe Belfast as a 'Landscape of Spires'. St Peter's was only granted Cathedral status in 1986, one hundred years after spires were added to its west façade. Prior to this it was a Pro-

Cathedral – a parish church that is used as a cathedral, i.e. the episcopal seat. J.D. Brewer, M. Keane, and D.N. Livingstone, 'Landscape of Spires', in F.W. Boal and S. Royal (eds), *Enduring City: Belfast in the Twentieth Century* (Belfast: Blackstaff Press, 2006). A full list of McAuley's work may be found on the DIA database. See also: Larmour, *Belfast: An Illustrated Architectural Guide*, p.23.

58. Grant, *One Hundred Years,* p.51.
59. C.E.B Brett, *The Buildings of Belfast, 1700–1914* (2nd ed., Belfast: Friar's Bush Press, 1985), p.68.
60. Larmour, *Belfast,* p.64.
61. Thomas Rickman, *An Attempt to Discriminate the Styles of English Architecture from the Conquest to the Reformation,* 2nd ed. (London, 1819).
62. W.J.W. Roome, *A Brighter Belfast: Being the Story of the Shankill Road Mission* (Belfast: W.M. Strain & Sons, 1898), pp.49–54. These areas were plotted on a map entitled *Lightness vs Darkness* that was included as a fold out insert in the book. It was been reproduced in in Brewer et al., 'Landscape of Spires'.
63. Ibid. The final structure was a modified version of the plan included in Roome's text, which includes the elevation drawings (n.53). A full list of buildings by Roome may be found on the DIA database.
64. Paul Larmour, 'From building site to mission field', *Perspective,* May/June 1997, p.45.
65. William Whyte, 'How Do Buildings Mean? Some Issues of Interpretation in the History of Architecture', *History and Theory*, 45 (May 2006). Whyte concludes this having surveyed and assessed other methods of reading buildings as 'texts', including the Saussurian linguistic approach.
66. Claire Mitchell, *Religion, Identity and Politics in Northern Ireland: Boundaries of Belonging and Belief* (Aldershot: Ashgate, 2006), pp.69–81.
67. Colm Lennon, 'The Confraternities and Cultural Duality in Ireland 1450–1550', in Christopher F. Black and Pamela Gravestock, *Early Modern Confraternities in Europe and the Americas: International and Interdisciplinary Perspectives* (Aldershot: Ashgate, 2006), p.35.
68. See n.22.
69. For a full description of how the confraternities functioned and the benefits offered by membership, see Grant *One Hundred Years with the Clonard Redemptorists*, pp.113–128.
70. Connolly, 'Cardinal Cullen's other capital', pp.297–98.
71. For details of what constituted wrongdoings that the mission might seek to correct, see Grant, *One Hundred Years with the Clonard Redemptorists*, pp.80-84. McConvery, *History Ireland*, (2000), p.18-22.

72. Grant, *One Hundred Years with the Clonard Redemptorists*, pp.59–61.
73. 'The New Church Dedicated at Clonard', *Irish News and Belfast Morning News*, 2 October 1911. It should be noted here that the *Clonard Domestic Chronicle* records that few local people attended due to the entrance cost. The truth is probably somewhere in between.
74. Diocese of Down and Connor, Belfast Diocesan Archive, Somerton Road, Belfast. Letters file on Clonard Monastery.
75. 'Redemptorist Church Clonard', *Irish News and Belfast Morning News*, 5 May 1898.
76. Author interview with Fr. Michael Murtagh, (C.Ss.R.) Rector of Clonard (May 2011). Options included purchasing a seat or pew or contributing to replacement of the encaustic tiling in the nave with single or multiple tiles available to buy at a low individual cost. Within a month of the campaign being launched, a third of the total cost of replacing the tiles had been secured and over 700 families were contributing to the renovation programme via bank standing order: 'a different [and] exciting adventure' is how Fr. Murtagh described the journey that finally saw the newly renovated Church of the Most Holy Redeemer at Clonard reopened and dedicated for worship on 25 March 2012. Various sponsorship initiatives were successful in defraying costs associated with the renovations: they include the funding of 25,000 new floor tiles. See http://belfastmediagroup.com/clonard-beauty-unveiled/ (accessed 08/04/2012).
77. 'Temporary church to host Novena in Clonard', Marie Louise McCrory, *Irish News*, June 16 2011, p.7.

Chapter 9

1. *Census of Ireland, 1911. Province of Leinster*, British Parliamentary Papers (BPP), [Cd. 6049], 1912, p.14; *Census of Ireland, 1911. Province of Ulster*, BPP, [Cd. 6051], 1912, p.12.
2. For an introduction, see M. Haines, *Fertility and Occupation: Population Patterns in Industrialization* (London: Academic Press, 1979); M. Katz and M. Stern, 'Fertility, Class, and Industrial Capitalism: Erie County, New York, 1855–1915', *American Quarterly*, 33, 1 (Spring 1981), pp.63–92; E. M. Garrett *et al.*, *Changing Family Size in England and Wales: Place, Class and Demography 1891–1911* (Cambridge: Cambridge University Press, 2001); S. Sretzer, *Fertility, Class and Gender in Britain, 1860–1940* (Cambridge: Cambridge University Press, 1996).
3. The chapter is based heavily on L. Kennedy, L. Pozzi and M. Manfredini, 'Marriage, Fertility, Social Class and Religion in an Irish Industrial City: Belfast 1911', *Popolazione e Storia*, 2 (2010) pp.83-110.

4. J. Bardon, *A History of Ulster* (Belfast: Blackstaff Press, 1992).
5. T.W. Moody & J.C. Beckett (eds), *Ulster since 1800: A Political and Economic Survey* (London: British Broadcasting Corporation, 1954).
6. W.A. Maguire, *Belfast* (Keele: Ryburn Publishing, 1993), p.38.
7. A.C. Hepburn, *A Past Apart: Studies in the History of Catholic Belfast, 1850–1950* (Belfast: Ulster Historical Foundation, 1996).
8. *Hall's Ireland: Mr & Mrs Hall's Tour of 1840*, edited by M. Scott (London: Sphere, 1984), p.342.
9. L. Kennedy & P. Ollerenshaw (eds), *An Economic History of Ulster, 1820–1939* (Manchester: Manchester University Press, 1985).
10. *Census of Ireland, 1911. Province of Ulster: City (or County Borough) of Belfast*, BPP (1912). All references to the demographic and related structures of Belfast in 1911, unless otherwise stated, are based on calculations from this source.
11. B. Messenger, *Picking up the Linen Threads* (London: University of Texas Press, 1978); M. Cohen, *Linen, Family & Community in Tullylish, County Down, 1690–1914* (Dublin: Four Courts, 1997). For some autobiographical reflections, see William Topping, *A Life in Linenopolis: Memoir* (Belfast: Ulster Historical Foundation, 1992).
12. Calculated from W.E. Vaughan and A.J. Fitzpatrick, *Irish Historical Statistics: Population, 1821–1971* (Dublin: Royal Irish Academy, 1978), pp.81, 90.
13. BelFam (Belfast Family & Community History) database, compiled by Liam Kennedy. This contains digitised information on some 40,000 Belfast residents, as extracted from the household schedules of the census of Ireland, 1911. See http://www.belfastfamilyhistory.com (accessed 10/08/2010). These and later references to individual and household behaviour are taken from this source.
14. BelFam database: the Colquhoun household schedule, Wellington Park, Belfast.
15. BelFam database: the Burns household schedule, Dewey Street, Shankill, Belfast.
16. *Working Class Rents, Housing & Retail Prices*, BPP [Cd. 3864], 1908.
17. Mitchell's Court, Brown Square (Y2475 Hogg Collection, Ulster Museum, Belfast).
18. Among these counties, the largest source of internal migrants was County Armagh, followed by County Tyrone. It is clear that Belfast fits the kinds of generalizations found in the literature: that internal migrations usually involve short- rather than long-distance movements of people.
19. D. McRaild, 'Migration and Emigration, 1600–1945' in L. Kennedy and P. Ollerenshaw (eds), *Ulster since 1600* (Oxford: Oxford University Press, 2012).
20. On the Jewish community in Ireland, though the primary focus is on Dublin, see C. Ó Gráda, *Jewish Ireland in the Age of Joyce: A Socioeconomic History* (Princeton: Princeton University Press, 2006) and D. Keogh, *Jews in Twentieth-Century Ireland* (Cork: Cork University Press, 1998).

21. This becomes clear from an inspection of the more detailed census enumerators' returns.
22. On the role of family and kinship networks in recruiting factory labour, see M. Anderson, *Family Structure in Nineteenth Century Lancashire* (London: Cambridge University Press, 1971). For Belfast, see Messenger, *Linen Threads*, pp.33–34.
23. Our sample is described later and consists of information taken from the original manuscript forms filled in by households at or close to census night, 2 April 1911. The originals are held at the National Archives, Ireland, Bishop Street, Dublin.
24. D.H. Akenson, *Small Differences: Irish Catholics and Protestants, 1815–1922* (Montreal: McGill-Queen's, 1988).
25. For a longer time perspective, see F. De Brún, *Belfast and the Irish Language* (Dublin: Four Courts, 2006).
26. It is noteworthy, in terms of the religious composition of the force, that half of the policemen based in Belfast were from a Catholic background.
27. C. Ó Gráda, '"The Greatest Blessing of All": The Old Age Pension in Ireland', *Past and Present*, 175, 1 (2002), pp.124–61.
28. *Report of an Enquiry by the Board of Trade into the Earnings and Hours of Labour of Workpeople of the United Kingdom*, BPP, 88 (1911), pp.154, 176.
29. J. Lynch, *A Tale of Three Cities: Comparative Studies in Working Class Life* (Basingstoke: Macmillan, 1998).
30. S. Gribbon, *Edwardian Belfast: A Social Profile* (Belfast: Appletree, 1982), p.17.
31. Ibid., p.16.
32. Or to use other components of the cost of living, a shilling would have bought a pound of butter, one and a half lbs of pork, 20 lbs of potatoes, ten head of cabbage or a dozen herring. See, for example, the Belfast retail prices reported in the *Northern Whig*, 8 July 1911.
33. The earnings of male general labourers in the linen industry, for instance, averaged about seventeen shillings per week in 1906. Female spinners took home ten to eleven shillings per week. *Report of an Enquiry by the Board of Trade into the Earnings and Hours of Labour of Workpeople of the United Kingdom*, BPP, 80 (1909), p.49. The Report acknowledged (page 49 also): 'In Ireland the wages of labourers are noticeably low.'
34. Messenger, *Linen Threads*, p.30.
35. Ibid., pp.226–7.
36. Gribbon, *Edwardian Belfast*, pp.13–14.
37. H. Patterson, *Class Conflict and Sectarianism* (Belfast: Blackstaff Press, 1980); A.C. Hepburn, *A Past Apart*.
38. J. Gray, *City in Revolt: James Larkin and the Belfast Dock Strike of 1907* (Belfast: Blackstaff, 1985).

39. The Catholic share of the population of Belfast was 24 per cent in 1911. Catholics accounted for 18 per cent of positions in the legal profession and only 15 per cent of those in medicine. However, they made up 32 per cent of the general labouring class where wages were amongst the lowest and earnings intermittent. (These figures relate to male occupations only but the overall picture is little different.)
40. Hepburn, *A Past Apart*, p.64. These findings are derived from a sample of 4,050 household returns for Belfast 1901. The British data are for 1911.
41. Ibid., p.55.
42. J. W. Budd and T. Guinnane, 'Intentional Age Misreporting, Age-Heaping, and the 1908 Old Age Pensions Act in Ireland', *Population Studies*, 1992, 45 (3), 497-518.
43. BelFam database: the Rice household, Foxglove Street, Belfast.
44. Dataset of matched couples, Belfast, 1901 and 1911.
45. Budd and Guinnane, 'Intentional Age Misreporting', pp.497–99.
46. R.E. Kennedy, *The Irish: Emigration, Marriage and Fertility* (Berkeley: University of California Press, 1973), pp.139–72.
47. Ibid., p.144.
48. Ibid.
49. We have calculated the singulate mean age at marriage (SMAM) for men in Ireland in 1911 at 33 years and for women at 29 years. The SMAM is an indirect measure of age at marriage and the estimates will be affected by the problem of age reporting noted earlier, but only marginally, we suspect.
50. The generic term 'Protestant' in this table refers to the main churches only, that is, members of the Church of Ireland, Presbyterians, and Methodists.
51. This seems reasonable in view of the changed financial incentives facing older people. The picture is somewhat muddied though by the fact that age heaping – reporting an age ending in a five or a zero – was more pronounced in 1901 as compared to 1911. This is likely to be the lesser of the two effects.
52. Two points to bear in mind here: the 1901 ages are also subject to some error; the size of the sample is not large and could conceivably paint a misleading picture in relation to the population as a whole.
53. C. Ó Gráda and B. Walsh, 'Fertility and Population in Ireland, North and South', *Population Studies*, 49 (1995), p.266.
54. C. Ó Gráda, 'Economic Status, Religion and Demography in an Ulster Town in the early Twentieth Century', *History of the Family*, 13 (2008), 355.
55. E. Garrett, 'The Trials of Labour: Motherhood versus Employment in a Nineteenth-Century Textile Centre', *Continuity & Change*, 5, 1 (1990), pp.121–54. See also Sretzer, 'Fertility, Class and Gender in Britain passim.

56. M. R. Haines, 'Fertility, Nuptiality, and Occupation: A Study of Coal Mining Populations and Regions in England and Wales in the Mid-Nineteenth Century', *Journal of Interdisciplinary History*, 8, (Autumn, 1977), pp.245–280.
57. Garrett, 'Trials of Labour', p.148.
58. Even then, there are potential problems. Garrett *et al.*, warn of the possibility of selection bias: 'As they aged, the majority of women who continued to accumulate children would have moved into the home ... while those failing to add to the number of their surviving offspring would have been more likely to remain out at work, resulting in a concentration of women with low effective fertility among the older age groups reporting an occupation'. E. Garrett, A. Reid, K. Schürer & S. Sretzer, *Changing Family Size in England and Wales: Place, Class and Demography, 1891–1911* (Cambridge: Cambridge University Press, 2001), p.307.
59. Vaughan and Fitzpatrick, *Irish Historical Statistics*, pp.36, 38.
60. Calculated from the *Census of Ireland, 1911. Province of Ulster*.
61. M.E. Daly, *The Slow Failure: Population Decline and Independent Ireland, 1922–1973* (Madison: University of Wisconsin Press, 2006), p.94.

Chapter 10

1. I would like to acknowledge the help and advice I received from Dr Patrick Fitzgerald, Dr John Lynch and Dr Olwen Purdue in preparing this article; also my son Jeremy for providing me with the map.
2. L.E.E. Donaldson, 'The hidden history of industrial Belfast: a microstudy of immigration and internal migration in the industrial labour force, Belfast 1901', MSSc Dissertation, Queen's University Belfast, 2009, (unpublished).
3. Paul Guinness, *Migration* (London: Hodder and Stoughton, 2002), pp.2–5, 25–39.
4. Patrick Fitzgerald and Brian Lambkin, *Migration in Irish History 1607–2007,* (London: Macmillan, 2008), pp.297–9, 301–5 has a full explanation of Migration Theory.
5. See Donaldson, 'Hidden History', pp.92–100.
6. Jonathan Bardon, *A History of Ulster* (Belfast: Blackstaff Press, 1992), pp.271–2, 274; Kevin Kenny, *The American Irish, A History* (Harlow: Longman, an imprint of Pearson Education, 2000), pp.51–2; F.S.L. Lyons, *Ireland Since the Famine* (Glasgow: Collins/ Fontana, 1973), p.61; J.B. Doyle, *Tours in Ulster: A Hand-book to the Antiquities and Scenery of the North of Ireland* (Dublin: Hodges Figgis, 1855), pp.15–6.
7. Jonathan Bardon, *Belfast an Illustrated History* (Belfast: Blackstaff Press, 1982), pp.123-4.
8. John Butt, 'Belfast and Glasgow: Connections and Comparisons 1790–1850' in T. M. Devine and David Dickson (eds), *Ireland and Scotland 1600–1850: Parallels and*

Contrasts in Economic and Social Developments (Edinburg: John Donald Publishers, 1983), pp.200–1; W.A. Maguire, *Belfast* (Keele: Keele University Press, 1993), pp.59–61; Cormac O'Grada, *Ireland, A New Economic History* (Oxford: Oxford University Press, 1994) pp.295–6; W.E. Coe, *The Engineering Industry of the North of Ireland* (Newtown Abbot: David and Charles, 1969), p.11.

9. J.P. Lynch, *An Unlikely Success Story. The Belfast Shipbuilding Industry, 1880–1935*, (Belfast: Belfast Society, 2001) pp.2, 21–2; Raymond Gillespie, *The Transformation of the Irish Economy 1550–1700* (Dublin: Economic and Social History Society, 1998), pp.7–8.
10. D.M. McRaild, *Culture, Conflict and Migration. The Irish in Victorian Cumbria* (Liverpool: Liverpool University Press, 1998), pp.77–8; Paul O'Leary, Key Note Address at 'Belfast, The Urban Experience', Queen's University, 23–25 Sept. 2010; see Butt, 'Glasgow and Belfast', p.193; D.M. McRaild, 'Culture, Conflict and Labour Migration: Victorian Cumbria's Ulster Connection', *Saothar*, 21, (1996), pp.23–38.
11. Lynch, *Unlikely Success*, p.22.
12. J.P. Lynch, 'Technology, Labour and the growth of Belfast Shipbuilding', *Saothar*, 24 (1999), pp.33–43; see Lynch, *Unlikely Success*, p.26.
13. Lynch, *Unlikely Success*, p.26; see Lynch, 'Technology', p.41.
14. Donaldson, Hidden, pp.48–55.
15. Data extracted from Lynch, *Unlikely Success*, p.27 (Fig. 12).
16. Bardon, *Belfast*, pp.123–4
17. D.J. Owen, *History of Belfast*, (Belfast, W.G. Baird Ltd., 1921), pp.306–14; Maguire, *Belfast*, pp.102–12.
18. McRaild, *Irish in Cumbria*, pp.76–9.
19. Ian Adamson, 'The Ulster-Scottish Connection' in Ian S Wood (ed.), *Scotland and Ulster* (Edinburgh: The Mercat Press, 1994), pp.1–21; Foster, *Ireland*, pp.368–9.
20. Butt, 'Belfast and Glasgow', pp.193–201; Lynch, *Unlikely Success*, pp.23–4; Lynch, 'Technology', pp.38–42. The reasons suggested by Lynch apply to all shipbuilding areas and not just Clydeside.
21. McRaild, *Irish in Cumbria*, pp.46–7; K.A. Miller, *Emigrants and Exiles, Ireland and the Irish Exodus to North America* (Oxford and New York: Oxford University Press, 1985), pp.374–5. Miller suggests that these workers 'drifted back and forth across the Irish Sea' but it is more likely that they moved purposefully as McRaild has suggested.
22. These are on microfilm in The Public Record Office of Northern Ireland, the census returns for the 32 counties of Ireland, 1901 and 1911, are available online through the National Archive, Dublin.
23. Belfast and Ulster Street Directory, 1901 Directory, pp.468–70.

24. Bardon, *Belfast*, p.131; Photograph in Bardon, *Belfast*, p.173 shows a Shankill Road tram, and the frontispiece of Lynch, *Unlikely Success*. The latter appears to be a section of the former and forms part of the Welch Collection in the Ulster Museum.
25. Maguire, *Belfast*, p.64.
26. Emrys Jones, *A Social Geography of Belfast*, (London, 1960), pp.40–1.
27. Donaldson, 'Hidden', pp.66–82.
28. Jonathan Hamill, 'Childcare arrangements within the Belfast linen community 1890–1930' in Bernadette Whelan (ed.), *Women and Paid Work in Ireland 1500–1930* (Dublin: Four Courts Press, 2000), pp.120–32.
29. PRONI MIC/354/-/-.
30. BPP, Census of Ireland 1901. Part II General Report [Cd1190], p.138. The information for the Belfast figures was extracted from 'Table 24. Showing the Birthplaces of the Inhabitants of the Counties and County Boroughs of Ireland.
31. See Donaldson, 'Hidden', pp.87–91 further details of this study.
32. PRONI MIC/354/-/-.
33. Ibid.
34. PRONI MIC/354/3/9, Madrid Street, Return No. 130. The columns are left to right – return number, name, relationship to head of family, age, gender, occupation, marital status and place of birth.
35. PRONI MIC/354/3/22, Chadolly Street, Return No. 90, Joseph Cooper.
36. Belfast and Ulster Street Directory, 1900, p.416, Mr A. Dunlop, Sand Merchant, 9 Madrid Street.
37. PRONI MIC/354/3/19, Madrid Street, Return No. 11, Jane Dunlop.
38. PRONI MIC/354/-/-
39. Stephen Gwynn, *The Famous Cities of Ireland*, (Dublin, London, 1915), pp 335-6; see Bardon, *Belfast*, pp 123-4.
40. See Donaldson, Hidden, p. 68, Table 6.
41. PRONI MIC/354/3/22, Chadolly Street, Return No. 65.
42. The *Belfast News Letter*, 5 Jul. 1900.
43. PRONI MIC/354/1/78, Silvio Street, Return No. 141.
44. PRONI MIC/354/-/-.
45. PRONI VAL/7B/11/4, p.92.
46. Stephen Rosenblatt, *Belfast Irish Jewish Memorial Inscriptions Carnmoney 1912, City Cemetery 1873–1952, Millisle Farm Co Down, School Enrolments, Census 1901, 1911*, (Dublin, 2002), 48/61.
47. PRONI MIC/354/3/20, Beechfield Street, Return No. 3.
48. PRONI MIC/354/-/-.

49. Lynch, *Unlikely Success*, p.26; 'Technology', p.41.
50. Marilyn Cohen, *Linen, Family and Community in Tullylish County Down 1690–1914* (Dublin and Portland, OR: Four Courts Press, 1997), p.203.
51. Jeremy Black and D.M. McRaild, *Nineteenth-Century Britain* (Basingstoke: Palgrave Foundations, 2003), p.90. Black & McRaild suggest that these costs included higher food bills, extra washing, etc. and these costs fell upon the wife.
52. Sybil Gribben, *Edwardian Belfast. A Social Profile* (Belfast: Appletree Press and Ulster Historical Foundation, 1982), p.31.
53. PRONI MIC/354/3/22, Chadolly Street, Return No. 33.
54. J.P. Lynch, 'British or Irish? A Comparative Study of Working Class Life in Three Cities c1880-1925' (Ph.D. thesis, Queen's University Belfast, 1996), unpublished, ii, 210.
55. PRONI VAL/7B/13/6, p.52.
56. Belfast Directory, 1901, pp.468–70.
57. PRONI MIC/354/3/23, Island Street, Return No. 36.
58. J.P. Lynch, 'The Belfast Shipyards and the Industrial Working Class in F. Devine, F. Lane and N. Puirséil (eds), in association with the Irish labour History Society, *Essays in Irish History. A Festschrift for Elizabeth and John W. Boyle* (Dublin and Portland OR: Irish Academic Press, 2008), p.148.
59. PRONI VAL/7B/13/7, p.52.
60. Maria Luddy, 'Women and Work in nineteenth and early twentieth century Ireland', in Whelan, *Women and Paid*, pp.44–56; M.E. Daly, *Women and Work in Ireland* (Dublin: Economic and Social History Society, 1997), p.8.
61. Cohen, *Tullylish*, p.52; Black & McRaild, *Nineteenth Century*, p.245.
62. Lynch, 'British or Irish?', ii, 205.
63. PRONI MIC/354/3/20, Belvoir Street, Return No. 24.
64. Lynch, 'British or Irish', ii, 208.
65. PRONI VAL/7B/8/4, pp. 88-107.
66. PRONI MIC/345/3/20, Beechfield Street, Return No. 39.
67. Henry Patterson, 'Industrial labour and the Labour Movement 1820–1914' in Liam Kennedy and Philip Ollerenshaw (eds), *An Economic History of Ulster 1820–1939* (Manchester: Manchester University Press, 1985), p.165. Patterson's figures (Table 5.3) refer to 1906 and are from a Board of Trade Enquiry into earnings and hours of labour.
68. PRONI VAL/7B/8/8, pp.18–64.
69. http://www.ancestry.co.uk 1881 English Census (accessed 04/06/2008).
70. PRONI MIC/345/1/78, Snugville Street, Return No. 18.
71. PRONI VAL/7B/11/4, p.64.
72. Lynch, 'British or Irish?', ii, 212.

73. Ibid., ii, 209.
74. Ibid., ii, 205.
75. PRONI MIC/345/3/19, Madrid Street, Return No. 117.
76. PRONI VAL/7B/812, p.11.
77. Lynch, 'Belfast Shipyards', Table 3, p.142. The figure given is for Harland and Wolff in August, 1912.
78. Lynch, 'British or Irish?', ii 209.
79. It was impossible to tell from the records when or why she returned to Ireland.
80. Lynch, 'British or Irish?', ii 212. The figure given is for 1912 and it is possible that the 1901 pay rates were lower.
81. PRONI VAL/7B/8/12, pp.13–4.
82. PRONI MIC/354/3/19, Madrid Street, Return No. 167.
83. See Lynch 'Technology'; see Lynch, *Unlikely Success*, p.26.
84. McRaild & Martin, *Labour Migration*, p.64.

Chapter 11

1. Robin Cohen, *Global Diasporas: An Introduction* (London: Routledge, 1997); Jan Lucassen and Leo Lucassen (eds), *Migration, Migration History, History: Old Paradigms and New Perspectives* (Bern: Peter Lang, 1999); Dirk Hoerder, *Cultures in Contact: World Migrations in the Second Millennium* (Durham NC: Duke University Press, 2002); Patrick Manning, *Migration in World History* (New York: Routledge, 2005); Marc S. Rodriguez and Anthony T. Grafton, *Migration in History: Human Migration in Comparative Perspective* (Rochester NY: Rochester University Press, 2007); Klaus Bade, *Migration in European History* (Oxford: Wiley-Blackwell, 2003); Leslie Page Moch, *Moving Europeans: Migration in Western Europe since 1650* (Bloomington IN: Indiana University Press, 1992; 2003); Patrick Fitzgerald and Brian Lambkin, *Migration in Irish History, 1607–2007* (Basingstoke: Palgrave Macmillan, 2008).
2. This is not to say that the theme of migration has been completely neglected in previous histories of Belfast: L.A. Clarkson, for example, examines internal migration in 'The city and the country' in J.C. Beckett et al., *Belfast: The Making of the City* (Belfast: Appletree Press, 1983), pp.153–66; Stephen A. Royle and T.J. Campbell examine 'East Belfast and the suburbanisation of north-west County Down in the nineteenth century', in Lindsay Proudfoot (ed.), *Down History and Society* (Dublin: Geography Publication, 1997), pp.629–62; and most recently we have Stephen A. Royle's *Portrait of an Industrial City: 'Clanging Belfast', 1750–1914* (Belfast: Ulster Historical Foundation, 2011). Nevertheless, the kind of comprehensive examination of all aspects of migration being advocated here remains a *desideratum*.

3. All the primary resource materials referenced in this essay are included in the online resource *DIPPAM: Documenting Ireland: Parliament, People and Migration,* which is a suite of three databases: EPPI (Enhanced Parliamentary Papers on Ireland); IED (Irish Emigration Database) and VMR (Voices of Migration and Return), available at: www.dippam.ac.uk. Dippam was funded by the Arts & Humanities Research Council (AHRC) and developed through a partnership of Queen's University Belfast, the University of Ulster, the Centre for Migration Studies at the Ulster American Folk Park, and Libraries NI.
4. For discussion of 'throughotherness' in this context, see Fitzgerald and Lambkin, *Migration in Irish History*, pp.255–6, 262–3, 281, 284, 295.
5. Fitzgerald and Lambkin, *Migration in Irish History*, Plate 3. John Luke (1906–75) had worked both in Belfast's shipyards and in its York Street Flax-spinning Company before migrating to London to study at the Slade School of Art. He worked on the Northern Ireland government's pavilion at the Glasgow Empire Exhibition in 1938 and was commissioned to paint the large mural in the dome of the City Hall, Belfast, for the Festival of Britain.[5] His representation of industry, godliness and prosperity possibly tells us more about 1951 than 1613 and Unionist efforts to stress the apartness of British Ireland from Irish Ireland, imagined here to lie beyond the Cave Hill.
6. Patrick McKay, *A Dictionary of Ulster Place Names* (2nd edition, Belfast: Clo Ollscoil na Banriona, 2007), p.21.
7. McKay, *A Dictionary of Ulster Place Names,* p.39.
8. Robert Scally, *The End of Hidden Ireland: Rebellion, Famine, and Emigration* (Oxford: Oxford University Press, 1995), p.16.
9. The census records for Ireland in 1901 and 1911 are available online at: www.census.nationalarchives.ie/ (accessed 30/11/2011).
10. Fitzgerald and Lambkin, *Migration in Irish History*, p.37. The call for this kind of comprehensive and integrated approach to migration studies has recently been taken up by Russell King and Ronald Skeldon in their 'Mind the gap! Integrating approaches to internal and international migration', *Journal of Ethnic and Migration Studies*, vol. 36, no. 10 (2010), pp.1619-46.
11. Fitzgerald and Lambkin, *Migration in Irish History*, pp.16–68.
12. Ruairí Ó Baoill, *Hidden History Below our Feet: The Archaeological Story of Belfast* (Belfast: Tandem Design 2011), pp.10–93.
13. Raymond Gillespie, *Early Belfast: The Origins and Growth of an Ulster Town to 1750* (Belfast: Ulster Historical Foundation, 2007), pp.58, 73, 89, 159.
14. Ibid., pp.159–61.
15. Ibid., p.133.

16. C.J. Woods, 'George Benn', in *Dictionary of Irish Biography* (Cambridge: Cambridge University Press, 2009), vol.1, p.450.
17. George Benn, *History of the Town of Belfast* (Belfast: Marcus Ward, 1823), pp.86, 157, 186.
18. William Maguire, *Belfast: A History* (Lancaster: Carnegie Publishing, 2009), p.81; Joseph Brady and Anngret Simms (eds), *Dublin through Space and Time* (Dublin: Four Courts Press, 2001), p.68.
19. W.E. Vaughan and A.J. Fitzpatrick, *Irish Historical Statistics: Population, 1821–1971* (Dublin: Royal Irish Academy, 1978), pp.28, 32, 36.
20. Maguire, *Belfast*, pp.94–5.
21. Ian Budge and Cornelius O'Leary, *Belfast: Approach to Crisis: A Study of Belfast Politics, 1613–1970* (London: Macmillan, 1973), p.31; A.T.Q. Stewart, *The Narrow Ground: Aspects of Ulster, 1609–1969* (London: Blackstaff, 1997), p.144.
22. Budge and O'Leary, *Belfast*, p.30. Two more recent studies of Belfast sectarian violence in the nineteenth century make only fairly fleeting reference to this issue: Catherine Hirst, *Religion, Politics and Violence in Nineteenth-Century Belfast* (Dublin: Four Courts Press, 2001), pp.15, 22; Mark Doyle, *Fighting Like the Devil for the Sake of God: Protestants, Catholics and the Origins of Violence in Victorian Belfast* (Manchester: Manchester University Press, 2009), p.80.
23. Vaughan and Fitzpatrick, *Irish Historical Statistics*, p.36.
24. Fred Heatley, 'Community relations and the religious geography 1800–1886' in J.C. Beckett et al., *Belfast: The Making of the City*, p.137.
25. Christine Kinealy and Gerard MacAtasney, *The Hidden Famine: Hunger, Poverty and Sectarianism in Belfast* (London: Pluto Press, 2000), p.146.
26. Ibid., p.119.
27. Fergus Mulligan, *One hundred and Fifty Years of Irish Railways* (Belfast: Appletree Press, 1983), pp.105–19.
28. Clarkson, 'The city and the country' in Beckett et al., *Belfast*, p.159; Paul Clinch, Frank Convey and Brendan Walsh, *After the Celtic Tiger: Challenges Ahead* (Dublin: O'Brien Press, 2002), pp.68–71.
29. A.C. Hepburn, *Catholic Belfast and Nationalist Ireland in the Era of Joe Devlin, 1871–1934* (Oxford: Oxford University Press, 2008), pp.9–10.
30. Ibid., pp.9–10. It is interesting to note that this trend towards accelerated rural-urban migration in the final quarter of the nineteenth century runs counter to the trend in contemporary urban Britain where the rate of such migration was gradually reducing. See David Feldman, 'Migration', in Martin Daunton (ed.), *The Cambridge Urban History of Britain, Vol. III, 1840–1950* (Cambridge: Cambridge University Press, 2000), p.198.

31. Vaughan and Fitzpatrick, *Irish historical statistics*, p.37; Hepburn, *Catholic Belfast and Nationalist Ireland*, p.9.
32. L.A. Clarkson, 'Population change and urbanization, 1821–1911' in Liam Kennedy and Philip Ollerenshaw (eds), *An Economic History of Ulster*, 1820–1939 (Manchester: Manchester University Press, 1985), p.154.
33. James Loughlin, *Ulster Unionism and British National Identity Since 1885* (London: Frances Pinter Publishers, 1995), pp.26–7.
34. Frederick W. Boal, 'Big processes, little people: the population of metropolitan Belfast 1901–2001', in Frederick W. Boal and Stephen A. Royle (eds), *Enduring City: Belfast in the Twentieth Century* (Belfast: Blackstaff, 2006), p.77–9.
35. Boal, 'Big processes, little people', p.78.
36. See NISRA, 'Population and migration estimates Northern Ireland (2010) – statistical report, 30 June 2011' (Belfast, 2011), p.7. Available at: www.nisra.gov.uk/demography/default.asp3.htm (accessed 05/11/2011).
37. Boal, 'Big processes, little people', p.58. Note that these 2001 figures are based on Boal's definition of Belfast's core city = 232,319, Belfast Urban Area (city with outer suburbs) = 497,860, and Metropolitan Belfast (city, outer suburbs, plus outer metro area) = 723,447. His definition differs from official boundaries as measured in the 2001 census (where the population of the Belfast Urban Area = 276,459, Belfast Metropolitan Urban Area = 579,554, or Belfast as defined by four Westminster parliamentary constituencies = 395,102). Thus, it is important to note that while the official boundaries of Belfast have changed and will likely change again with urban development, scholars define the extent of the city differently: accordingly care is advised when examining the statistics. See also Stephen Roulston, *Growth of Belfast, Geography in Action* [website], available at: www.geographyinaction.co.uk/Urban_structure/Urban_growth.html (accessed 12/11/2011).
38. It is not possible to entirely disaggregate outflows from Belfast into internal and external (from Northern Ireland) streams as external emigration data is available at the Northern Ireland level only (e.g. Board of Trade emigration data).
39. Maguire, *Belfast*, p.191.
40. R.H. Matthew, *Belfast Regional Survey and Plan* (Belfast, 1964). Stormont Buildings, on the city's eastern fringe, housed Northern Ireland's devolved Parliament between 1932 and 1972.
41. Boal, 'Big processes, little people', pp.58–60, 77–9.
42. From the 1920s to the 1960s, approximately 25 per cent of emigrants from Northern Ireland were children and youth under twenty years of age with about 80 per cent of them under fifteen, thus indicating the significant number of family groups in the

emigrant flow (calculated from the Board of Trade emigration returns 1925–38, 1954–63). David Fitzpatrick, 'Emigration, 1871–1921' in W.E. Vaughan (ed.), *A New History of Ireland, Vol. 6: Ireland under the Union, II* (Oxford: Oxford University Press, 1996), p.616, has also noted the prevalence of family groups in nineteenth-century Ulster migration.

43. Analysis of migrant characteristics from the Board of Trade emigration returns (1925–38, 1954–63). For analysis of student and graduate emigration since the 1980s, see Robert Cormack, Anthony Gallagher, and R.D. Osborne, 'Higher education participation in Northern Ireland', in *Higher Education Quarterly*, 51, no.1 (1997), pp.68-85; and R.D. Osborne, 'Access to and participation in higher education in Northern Ireland', *Higher Education Quarterly*, 60, no. 4 (2006), pp.333–48; J. Devlin Trew, *Leaving the North: Migration and Conflict in Northern Ireland, 1921-2011* (Liverpool, forthcoming), chapters 2, 7. Even in the most recent data for the year to mid-2010, Northern Ireland has continued to lose primarily those in the 18–24 age group, largely students (Registrar General Northern Ireland, *Annual report 2010* (Belfast, 2011), p.11.
44. Boal, 'Big processes, little people', p.79.
45. Census 2001 Northern Ireland, Table KS05. One estimate of new immigration to Belfast (based on the four Westminster parliamentary constituencies) from May 2004–March 2006 of those born outside the UK and Ireland put the incoming figure as high as 7,506, with the majority incoming from new accession EU countries. This would have substantially added to the foreign-born contingent of the total population of Belfast already recorded at the time of the 2001 census (of 7,650). See Neil Jarman and Jonny Byrne, *New Migrants and Belfast: An Overview of the Demographic Context, Social Issues and Trends* (Belfast, 2007), pp.5–12. Belfast City Council estimated the number of international immigrants by 2006 as just over 2,500. See 'Population change in Belfast', *Belfast: The State of the City: Development Brief*, Issue 9 (October 2006), p.4.
46. For an illustration see the Ulster Folk and Transport Museum website: www.nmni.com/uftm/Collections/buildings/Town-Area-(1)/Tea-Lane (accessed 28/11/2011).
47. 'Missing relatives', *Belfast Evening Telegraph*, 5 December 1931, CMSIED 9803637.
48. Fitzgerald and Lambkin, *Migration in Irish History*, pp.63, 262, 283.
49. *Belfast Riots: Report of the Commissioners of Inquiry into the origin and character of the riots in Belfast in July and September, 1857* [C 2309], H.C. 1857-8, xxvi.
50. Andrew Boyd, *Holy War in Belfast* (Belfast: Grove Press, 1972), pp.15–16.
51. Four of the discrepancies are relatively minor: Boyd spells her name Brigid, whereas the Inquiry Report gives it as Bridget; he refers to 'orange flowers' whereas the Report specifies 'orange lilies'; he describes the effigy of O'Connell as 'immense' (suggesting something as large as the much-larger-than life-size effigy of 'Lundy' that is burned

annually in December in Londonderry) whereas Kane's testimony was that it was 'as large as Mr. Rea [one of the commissioners]'; and Boyd says that 'she saw them … set it alight outside her front door and dance while it blazed', whereas her testimony was 'I heard that it was burned'.

52. Gary, interview with J. Devlin Trew, Omagh, December 2004, sound recording, VMR-022.
53. Two major books that deal with the 1857 riots in Belfast, by Catherine Hirst, *Religion, Politics and Violence in Nineteenth-Century Belfast* and Mark Doyle, *Fighting Like the Devil for the Sake of God,* and both offer better quality maps of inner city Belfast than the centre-spread map in Boyd's paperback *Holy War in Belfast*. The Sandy Row and Pound districts are clearly marked. However, neither makes it easy to locate Tea Lane and English Street. The map in Doyle's book shows both but does not name them. Hirst's map names both but in a very small font size, with 'Tea Lane' being obscured by the 'Row' of 'Sandy Row'.
54. Letter from William Montgomery, Portadown, Co. Armagh to Joseph Searight, Philadelphia., dated July 24 1850. PRONI D.2794/1/2/56, CMSIED 9407005 (available at www.dippam.ac.uk).
55. Letter from William Montgomery, Manchester to Joseph Searight, Philadelphia, dated December 19 1857. PRONI D2794/1/2106, CMSIED 305016.
56. 'A Tale of Two Cities', episode 2, Hotshot films for BBC NI and broadcast on BBC 1 NI on 9 October 2006, 10.35 p.m.
57. Letter from James Stewart, San Francisco to Mr. Coulter, Belfast, dated September 22 1884. PRONI T3399/1, CMSIED 9403211.
58. Letter from Ellen Breeze, 144 Donegall Pass, Belfast to her mother, dated March 17 1879. PRONI T1381/3, CMSIED 8906022.
59. Letter from C.K. Breeze, San Francisco to William Breeze, Ireland, dated March 5 1875. PRONI T1381/1, CMSIED 8906007.
60. Clarkson, 'The city and the country', in Beckett et al., *Belfast*, p.156.
61. Letter from C.K. Breeze, San Francisco to William Breeze, Ireland, dated March 5 1875. PRONI T1381/1, CMSIED 8906007.
62. Eric Richards, 'Return migration and migrant strategies in colonial Australia', in David Fitzpatrick (ed.), *Home or Away? Immigrants in Colonial Australia* (Canberra, 1992), p.64; Angela McCarthy, *Irish Migrants in New Zealand, 1840–1937: The Desired Haven* (Woodbridge, 2005), p.196.
63. There is a growing literature on this topic. See especially, Joseph Ruane and Jennifer Todd, *The Dynamics of Conflict in Northern Ireland: Power, Conflict, and Emancipation*

(Cambridge: Cambridge University Press, 1996); Andrew J. Wilson, '"Doing the Business": Aspects of the Clinton Administration's Economic Support for the Northern Ireland Peace Process, 1994-2000' in *Journal of Conflict Studies,* 23, no. 1 (2003), pp.155–76, and several of his other publications; Paul Dixon, 'Performing the Northern Ireland peace process on the world stage' in *Political Science Quarterly,* 121, no. 1 (2006), pp.61–91; Feargal Cochrane, 'Irish-America, the end of the IRA's armed struggle and the utility of "soft power"' in *Journal of Peace Research,* 44, no. 2 (2007), pp.215–31; Niall Ó Dochartaigh, 'Reframing online: Ulster Loyalists imagine an American audience' in *Identities: Global Studies in Culture and Power,* 16, no. 1 (2009), pp.102–27.

64. Craig, interview with J. Devlin Trew, Toronto, September 2006, sound recording, VMR-064.
65. Craig, interview, VMR-064.
66. Thomas, interview with J. Devlin Trew, London, February 2007, sound recording, VMR-076.
67. Albert O. Hirschman, *Exit, Voice and Loyalty: Responses to Decline in Firms, Organizations and States* (Cambridge, MA: Harvard University Press, 1970); Enda Delaney, *Demography, State and Society: Irish Migration to Britain, 1921–1971* (Liverpool: Liverpool University Press, 2000), pp.18–19.
68. Thomas, interview, VMR-076.
69. Sara Ahmed, *Strange Encounters: Embodied Others in Post-Coloniality* (London: Routledge, 2000).
70. Orla, interview with J. Devlin Trew, Liverpool, July 2006, sound recording, VMR-056.
71. Orla, interview, VMR-056.
72. Orla, interview, VMR-056.
73. The 'return of failure' is defined according to the typology of return migration by Francesco P. Cerase, 'Migration and social change: expectation and reality: a case-study of breturn migration from the United States to Southern Italy' in *International Migration Review,* 8 (1974), p.249.
74. Fitzgerald and Lambkin, *Migration in Irish History,* pp.13–15.

Index

Note: Page references in bold refer to tables and illustrations.